BENEATH THE NEON

LIFE AND DEATH IN THE TUNNELS OF LAS VEGAS

BENEATH THE NEON

LIFE AND DEATH IN THE TUNNELS OF LAS VEGAS

BY MATTHEW O'BRIEN

PHOTOS BY DANNY MOLLOHAN

COVER PHOTO BY BILL HUGHES

HUNTINGTON PRESS · LAS VEGAS, NV

Published by Huntington Press

3665 South Procyon Avenue

Las Vegas, Nevada 89103

(702) 252-0655

(702) 252-0675 fax

books@huntingtonpress.com

Copyright © 2007, Matthew O'Brien

ISBN 978-0-929712-39-0

Design by Katherine Topaz, Topaz Design

Photos by Danny Mollohan, Bill Hughes

To the poets, artists, and madmen of the Las Vegas storm drains

ACKNOWLEDGMENTS

The people in the storm drains who shared their stories; Deke Castleman, Joshua Ellis, and my dad Matt; my mom Liz, my sisters Leslie and Cathy, my brother Eric, my sister-in-law Emily, my brother-in-law Pete, and David Dennis; Bill Hughes, Danny Mollohan, Joe Preston, and Kat Topaz; the *Las Vegas CityLife* staff and contributors, old and new; G.W. Fraser and Betty Hollister of the Clark County Regional Flood Control District; Lt. Tom Monahan of Metro Police; H. Lee Barnes, Bill Branon, Angela Brommel, Russ Cannon, Mark Danner, Adam Goldman, Michael Green, Kurt Harris, Jarret Keene, Chip Mosher, Brian Rouff, Cathy Scott, John L. Smith, Hunter S. Thompson, and Ingrid Truman; and Anthony Curtis, Bethany Coffey, Len Cipkins, and the rest of the Huntington Press staff.

AUTHOR'S NOTE

It all started in the summer of 2002, when I explored five storm drains with freelance writer Joshua Ellis. It culminated in the summer of 2004, when I took a sabbatical from *Las Vegas CityLife*, a weekly newspaper, and explored the flood-control system in full. It continued through 2006, as I returned to the drains for follow-up notes and to explore virgin tunnels. *Beneath the Neon: Life and Death in the Tunnels of Las Vegas*—which is set in the long, hot, and lonely summer of '04—chronicles my adventures in this uncharted underworld.

Matthew O'Brien
December 31, 2006

Standing in front of the storm drain, a stream of runoff pressing against my boots, I felt as if a double-barreled shotgun was pointed at my head. My chest was tight. My heart beat violently. As I stared into the darkness, which seemed as deep as a midnight sky, chills shot down my spine and shook my soul. The drain's two tunnels were each 12 feet wide and eight feet high, decorated with cobwebs and drooling algae. They exhaled mildewy air, which washed over me like bad breath.

I was at the bottom of a drainage ditch in downtown Las Vegas, just north of the Fremont Street Experience. The ditch was 20 feet deep, lined with concrete and surrounded by a barbwire fence ("No Trespassing!"). Ladder rungs jutted from the banks and flycatchers glided above the stream—and the half-sunken plastic bags, Styrofoam cups, and aluminum cans—swooping in and out of the tunnels. The sun, too, had spread its wings and was high in the sky. Late morning, it was already 90 degrees.

Exhaling, I slipped out of my backpack and unzipped the secondary pouch. It contained a tape recorder, four or five cassette tapes, a wire microphone, and fresh AA batteries. Removing the recorder, I placed it in a holster that hung from my hip and clipped the mike to the collar of my long-sleeve shirt. Then I ran the wire underneath the shirt, plugged it into the recorder, and pressed "Play" and "Record."

"Test one, test one," I said in a monotone voice. "Weber Drain, Weber Drain."

I rewound the tape and pressed "Play."

"Test one, test one. Weber Drain, Weber Drain."

Next, I unzipped the backpack's main pouch. It contained a four-cell Mag-Lite flashlight, a Mini Mag-Lite, an expandable baton, a knit cap, and fresh D and AA batteries. I removed the Mini Mag-Lite and placed it in a pocket of my cargo pants. I stuffed the baton into a sheath in the small of my back and put on the cap. Finally, I clutched the Mag-Lite in my left hand—its hard steel cooling my palm and fingers.

In the late morning of April 14, 2002, Timmy "T.J." Weber found himself in this same drainage ditch. A week and a half earlier, in a house on nearby First Street, Weber raped his girlfriend's 14-year-old daughter and killed his girlfriend and one of her sons. Police discovered the girlfriend's nude and bludgeoned body stuffed upside down in a storage container in a bedroom closet. A plastic bag secured with duct tape covered her head. Her 15-year-old son was found facedown on a mattress, his arms taped behind his back and a T-shirt stuffed in his mouth. He died of asphyxiation.

Following his carnival of crime, Weber left Las Vegas—but he soon returned.

A morbid curiosity drew me to the ditch. I wondered what what he heard, what he *smelled*. How, apparently without Did clues of his escape route remain? Could he hear

He ambushed his girlfriend's surviving son and an adult companion when they ventured to the family home on First Street to retrieve mementos for the funerals. A riotous melee ensued, in which all three men sustained injuries. Weber fled on foot, bleeding from the forehead. He weaved around crumbling bungalows. He dashed across dirt yards, dogs barking in chorus. He then climbed the barbwire fence surrounding the drainage ditch and disappeared into the storm drain.

A morbid curiosity drew me to the ditch. I wondered what Weber experienced in the storm-drain system. What he saw, what he heard, what he *smelled*. How, apparently without a light source, he'd splashed more than three miles upstream. Did clues of his escape route remain? Could he hear the police dogs barking overhead? The sirens screaming?

I also wondered what lurked beneath Las Vegas. Roman law forced Jews and Christians into a maze of catacombs. When surveyed by Pierre-Emmanuel Bruneseau and his staff in the early 1800s, the sewers of Paris yielded gold, jewels, and relics of the revolution. In the late 19th and early 20th centuries, a slave trade thrived in underground chambers along Portland, Oregon's, waterfront. And thousands of people lived in the subway and train tunnels of New York City in the 1980s and '90s.

What secrets did the storm drains of Las Vegas keep? What discoveries waited in the dark? What was behind the black curtains?

Shuffling toward the north tunnel of the drain, I imagined Weber slamming into the fence and climbing it frantically. He balanced on the edge of the ditch, feeling for the rungs with a foot. A splash broke the silence. Kicking through

Weber experienced in the storm-drain system. What he saw,
a light source, he'd splashed more than three miles upstream.
the police dogs barking overhead? The sirens screaming?

the stream—and the plastic bags, Styrofoam cups, and aluminum cans—he disappeared into the darkness. I pressed "Play" and "Record," snapped on the flashlight, and followed him.

The temperature dropped at least 25 degrees and the beam of the flashlight died in the semidarkness. I began up a corrugated slope, which was designed to slow the flow of the water, eyes adjusting and goosebumps rising on my neck. The fear was justified, I thought. Crack addicts assault each other on the streets. Armed bandits storm bars, casinos, and convenience stores. Gang members stomp rivals to death in the malls, right in front of the Gap. If such crimes occur in plain sight in Las Vegas, I wondered, what unspeakable atrocities—what unpardonable sins— take place in the city's storm drains? Are there any rules? Is there any hope?

The tunnel turned to the south. The cobwebs fluttered in the wind. And the stream, though only two inches deep, roared like the Colorado River. "I continue up the slope," I narrated nervously into the mike. "The footing is slick and visibility is low, about ten feet tops. I have no idea who or what lurks in the shadows. Another ex-con? A group of meth freaks? A pack of wild dogs? What in the *hell* am I doing in here?"

The tunnel trended to the north and the rectangle of light behind me began to close. The beam of the flashlight finally took form, unveiling graffiti scrawls and official markings on the walls: "12 x 8 x 6 2-17-00 HCC." (This section of the tunnel is 12 feet wide, eight feet high, and six feet long; its construction was completed on Feb. 17, 2000; and it was made by the Hydro Conduit Corporation.)

About 300 feet into the drain, the roar of the stream softened and I could hear the rush of aboveground traffic. I assumed I was under Bonanza Road, just north of U.S. Highway 95, but I was totally disoriented. (Without daylight, the horizon, and depth perception, that can happen.) A faint glow flickered behind me. Upstream, a drop inlet (commonly called a sewer) cast a rectangle of light on the floor, walls, and ceiling. I started toward the light, boots splashing rhythmically in the stream. The tunnel swung to the west, then straightened into perfect darkness.

In the depths of the drain, yarn-like cobwebs hung from the walls and ceiling. What size spider created *this* dreadful tableau, I wondered? I dramatically decided that it must've been the size of a compact car. Reaching behind my back, I unsheathed the baton and flicked the handle downward. The steel rod snapped into place. I inched upstream timidly, like a kid through a haunted house. A stray web tickled my face, causing me to flinch.

Regaining my composure and curious about what Weber experienced in the drain, I cut off the flashlight. A black curtain fell in front of me. I felt for the wall with my free hand, then continued upstream. The concrete gnawed at my hand. I imagined Weber—six-foot-three and 210 pounds—groping the walls, his bloody hands leaving perfect prints. He slammed into a lateral pipe. His breathing echoed in the tunnel. After slipping on algae, the back of his pants and shirt clung to his skin. He considered turning around—but realized that meant life in prison or the death sentence.

Aboveground, the police established a perimeter. They turned away vehicles attempting to enter it and searched the ones leaving. A helicopter clapped overhead. Patrolmen, police dogs, and SWAT personnel combed every property in the area. Eventually, they noticed the drainage ditch. Judging the barbwire fence secure—its gates locked, its posts sturdy, its chain links unbroken—they didn't immediately search it.

Finally captured after more than three weeks on the run, Weber—who was featured on *America's Most Wanted*—told investigators that his journey through the storm-drain system reminded him of the movie *The Fugitive*. He spent five hours underground, he said, emerging between Interstate 15 and Palace Station (a hotel-casino three miles outside of the police perimeter). He didn't indicate that he had a flashlight or that he'd previously explored the system.

Weber, however, neglected to note one obvious difference between his escape and the one portrayed in *The Fugitive*: Dr. Richard Kimble, played by Harrison Ford, was innocent. A Clark County jury found Weber guilty of several charges, including two counts of murder, and sentenced him to death.

Disoriented and out of breath—the darkness was suffocating—I cut on the flashlight. The tunnel snaked and tilted like a mineshaft, the north side of the floor cradling a six-inch-deep stream. Cockroaches covered the south side of the floor. The graffiti vanished. And I safely assumed that this was an area of Las Vegas left out of the guidebooks, only accessed in the most extreme situations.

A lateral pipe about four feet in diameter jutted into the tunnel. As I approached the pipe, my chest tightened and the goosebumps returned. I half-expected the poet Virgil, Dante's guide in *The Inferno*, to crawl from the outlet and offer to escort me through this dark and dank hell.

Beyond the pipe, which dead-ended into a drop inlet, the tunnel swung to the west. I steadied the beam of the flashlight on the near wall—hands shaking, arms and back tightening, eyes as big as slot coins. What lurks beyond the bend, I wondered? What bizarre scene will slowly take shape? What next?

As I rounded the bend, a faint light appeared in the distance. I sheathed the baton and surged upstream. The light grew brighter and brighter, like the coming of dawn.

Finally, I splashed out of the drain and into an open-air channel. Bulrush grass shot from the stream, reaching for the sun, and dragonflies levitated above the stalks like showroom magicians. Ducks drifted in and out of the brush. Mud and algae carpeted the floor. It was a muggy and marshy scene, slightly reminiscent of southern Louisiana—but it seemed a lot like heaven to me.

Anxious to figure out where I was, I climbed a column of rungs in the north wall of the channel. Main Street Station hotel-casino stared down at me and the Plaza squatted to the southeast, bordered by the Union Pacific railroad tracks. I'd walked about a half-mile—under the police perimeter, the highway, and the north end of Main Street Station.

On the other side of the wall, an open-air channel hooked northward. To the west, three 15-by-10 tunnels burrowed under a sand hill and disappeared into the darkness.

• • •

In the summer of 2002, while managing editor of the alternative weekly newspaper *Las Vegas CityLife*, I came up with the idea of exploring the storm-drain system. I was primarily inspired by Weber's escape route and a profile I'd read in Minneapolis-St. Paul's *City Pages* of a man who enjoyed exploring caves and sewers beneath the Twin Cities. But this assignment wasn't designed for a managing editor, I decided while shackled to my desk. Only the most daring and desperate mercenary would even *consider* accepting it. Realizing this, I pitched the story to *CityLife* contributor Joshua Ellis—who'd displayed brass balls in his weekly column and a flair for first-person narratives in his feature stories. To my mild surprise, he accepted it.

Two weeks after pitching the story, I called Josh to see how the assignment was coming along. It was around noon, but I got the impression that I woke him. (Ah, the life of a freelancer!) He groggily explained that, accompanied by freelance photographer Joel Lucas and armed with an 18-inch kukri knife, he'd explored a storm drain that began downtown and emptied into the Las Vegas Wash more than three miles away. He and Joel didn't encounter anyone, but they did see clothing and sleeping bags hanging in manhole shafts—storage spaces, he assumed, for street people living aboveground.

The drain was devastatingly dark, continued Josh in a morbid tone. He was now officially awake—and so was I. Scummy water that "stank like a corpse" covered the floor, and minnows spawned in the water by the thousands. Six-inch-long crawfish—the biggest he'd ever seen (and he's from Texas, where everything is big)—nested in the crevices.

"And that was all," said Josh. "No mutants, no fugitives, no mazelike catacombs. Just one tunnel, almost perfectly straight, leading on and on and on."

Intrigued, I asked Josh if he'd explored any other drains. He said that he hadn't, but he hoped to over the weekend. However, he added, "I may need a lift."

Anxious to place the story, I agreed to pick Josh up that Saturday morning. But before hanging up the phone, I explained that I would only serve as a chauffeur and that I had *no* intention of exploring the drains. The clothes I was wearing when I arrived at his house—a concert T-shirt, jeans, and casual work boots—further stressed my innocent-bystander role.

"You're not ready, man," said Josh, emerging from the house and looking me up and down.

"I'm not planning to go very far into the tunnels," I said, "if I go in at all. I'm just along for the ride, man."

In his right hand, Josh held the kukri knife and a Mag-Lite flashlight. A leather trench coat hung over his left arm. He was wearing a short-sleeve T-shirt, jeans, and black boots. Climbing back into my 1997 white-boy Camry, I pointed out that his outfit was no more elaborate than mine.

"I'll be fine," said Josh, flashing the kukri and a demented smile.

That Saturday, curious about what lurked beyond the shade line and not wanting to be labeled a punk-ass editor, I followed Josh into a pipe in the southeast valley and two storm drains in the southwest. Over the next few months, we explored three more drains. The research resulted in a two-part co-written series that was published in *CityLife* that summer and seemed to be well-received by our readers.

. . .

While tracking Weber's trail, Josh and I arrived at this same swampy fork in the flood-control system behind Main Street Station. Tired and intimidated, we turned around. I, again, was tempted to flip a bitch—*man*, was I tempted. But an obsessive curiosity about the 400-plus miles of the system that Josh and I didn't explore spurred me on.

Wishing that Josh were with me—or anyone, really—I waded into the southernmost 15-by-10 tunnel. The water was green-brown and shin-high. Glass crunched beneath my boots. I aimed the flashlight into the stream, which was composed mainly of urban runoff and escaped groundwater (even on a dry day, millions of gallons of water flow through the system), illuminating a 22-ounce beer can and an algae-covered loafer.

About a quarter-mile upstream, I splashed into another open-air channel. Bulrush shot from the north side of the floor—perfect cover for Weber—and hummingbirds hovered above the stalks. I waded through the mire, which I assumed hosted a variety of bacterial diseases, then continued upstream in the south tunnel. Rocks, sandbars, and cinderblocks cluttered the floor. A basketball floated by innocently, reminding me of my misspent youth. The moral, kids: If you neglect your schoolwork, you'll end up wandering around in the storm drains of Las Vegas when you're 33 years old. The stream was three inches deep in areas, knee-high in others. Beads of water jumped through the beam of the Mag-Lite. In an attempt to keep the flashlight dry, I held it higher (its butt resting against my shoulder).

Over the next mile or so, which followed the highway west, a pattern developed. I entered a dark tunnel, emerged in an open-air channel, then continued upstream in the tunnel; ducks shot from the stream and flapped away frantically; and the thunder of trains and the rush of fast-moving vehicles fell through ceiling grates.

Questions haunted me along this stretch. Why did Weber return to the scene of the crime? Did he want to kill the whole family? Was he obsessed with his girlfriend's daughter, whom he'd been sexually abusing since she was nine years old? As he groped the water-stained walls of the storm-drain system, did he feel any remorse?

Random images related to the crime flashed through my mind: Weber locking the front door of the house and forcing his girlfriend's daughter into a bedroom; the surviving son discovering his sister duct-taped to a bed, crying; two highway patrolmen arriving at the scene and stumbling on the 15-year-old son's body; one of the patrolmen, emerging from the home visibly shaken, struggling to explain the situation to the daughter and son; Metro police officers forcing their way into a bedroom and finding the girlfriend's body.

A car rattled a manhole cover, pulling me from my thoughts. Through the inlet of a tunnel, another open-air channel came into focus—a patch of bulrush, braided water, soaring walls. I imagined Weber approaching the channel, one hand tickling the tunnel wall. His feet rose slowly from the stream and landed softly. Ripples warped his reflection. At the edge of the shadows, he stopped and glanced over his shoulder. Then he squatted and surveyed the channel walls, which were bare, 30 feet tall, and topped with a chain-link fence. Five tunnels faced Weber, three straight ahead and two in a distant corner. He noticed an alley between the bulrush and the channel's south wall. Exhaling, he sprinted for it; the rush of the interstate drowned out the splashing. He emerged from the stalks, arms bleeding, and disappeared into the south tunnel.

Over the next mile or so, the pattern broke. The system trended from east-west to north-south, following I-15. The stream turned into wet gravel, then the gravel into sand. Instead of open-air channels, I emerged in dark and creepy chambers that were supported by concrete columns.

More questions accompanied me along these lonely corridors: Did Weber attempt to exit the system by climbing the walls of the open-air channels? How many manhole covers did he try to lift? Did he consider camping out in the drains? How long could he have survived unnoticed in the dark, exiting at night for food and drinking water? At any point during his escape, did he think that he wouldn't find a way out? Did he experience the same feelings that I was experiencing: anticipation, fear, exhilaration, fatigue, loneliness, and regret over ever setting foot in this concrete labyrinth?

As I entered another chamber, the questions bid me farewell. I slalomed through the columns, which were tangled with cobwebs, and was confronted by four seven-by-seven tunnels. Shaking out of the backpack, I removed a bottle of water from an exterior pouch. Then I reached into a pants pocket and retrieved my cell phone: "No Service." The clock read 3:35 p.m. I'd entered the system at 11:30 a.m., more than two miles downstream. Sweat rioted on my face. My arms and lower back were tight. My knees and ankles ached. I assumed I was under Charleston Boulevard at I-15, a notorious flood hazard that this channel was designed to drain, but the chamber provided few clues.

Lured by a bright light, I entered one of the middle tunnels. A gentle breeze greeted me, drying the sweat on my face. I breathed in the fresh air, crunched across a sandbar, and passed under a grate. The tunnel swung sharply to the west.

Beyond yet another open-air channel, I started up a straightaway. Exhaust fumes fouled the air; my breathing became labored and I felt nauseous. The tunnel—which seemed as long as a rural Nevada highway—allowed no fresh air, no sound, and no light. It was as still and dark as the inside of a coffin. The flashlight hung limply at my side, illuminating my scuffed and muddy boots. Will I ever reach the end of this storm drain, I wondered? Does it even *have* an end? Did I take a wrong turn? Did I miss a turn? Some drains in the flood-control system are more than five miles long. Had I accidentally entered one of these cruel and abusive beasts? Should I turn around? Should I keep going?

Again I thought of Weber. On April 14, 2002—regardless of what happened in the casinos—*he* was the luckiest person in Las Vegas. He stumbled on the perfect escape route: plenty of cover, just enough light, and no hope of tracking his scent. He couldn't have planned it any better.

But *this* straightaway must have challenged him. *This* straightaway must have brought the tough guy to his knees.

Suddenly, the tunnel snaked. I felt a soft breeze, heard the rush of the interstate, and saw a faint light in the distance. I surged up a straightaway, toward the light. The breeze stiffened. The rush of the interstate grew louder. And then the light began to fracture. I soon realized that a grate stretched across the inlet. Its bars were thick and tightly spaced. Between them, street signs and Palace Station billboards came into focus. My eyes bulged. My spirit sagged. I wanted to drop to my knees and cry a flood. What a cruel joke, I thought! What an evil, evil world! Strangely, I felt a twinge of sympathy for that bastard Weber. What did he feel at this moment, I wondered? Did he laugh? Did he cry? Did he consider this poetic justice?

As I approached the inlet, hinges took shape on the tunnel's west wall and a slice of light emerged between the east wall and the grate. Gradually, the light expanded … and I realized the grate was ajar. The sky, clouds, and palm trees— all more beautiful than I'd remembered—came into focus. Turning sideways, I slipped out of the drain. My feelings, as Hugo wrote of Jean Valjean's escape from the Paris sewers in *Les Misérables*, were "those of a damned soul seeing the way out of hell."

Nonetheless, as I staggered up an open-air channel and searched the walls for rungs, I was determined to further explore the storm-drain system. There was mystery and myth to be found, I was convinced, under "fabulous" Las Vegas. There were secrets to be discovered beneath the neon.

As the Spring Mountains swallowed the sun, the roadside sign flickered to life. Flashing light bulbs framed its diamond-shaped border. Its star, eight-pointed and 25 feet from the desert floor, pulsed in the sky. "Welcome," the lettering began in orange-red neon. "To Fabulous Las Vegas Nevada," it finished in block and cursive text.

Designed by Betty Willis and installed in 1959, the sign originally served as a beacon for tourists traveling from Southern California to Las Vegas on Highway 91 (also known as the Los Angeles Highway). Now, the sign itself is an attraction. Camera crews stake out its gravel median, souvenir shops hawk its likeness, and thousands of tourists a year pose between its steel supports, smiling drunkenly in the neon night.

The sign has stood through many changes. Highway 91, now known as the Strip, is no longer the main road into Las Vegas; the main road is Interstate 15, which was completed in 1963. The annual passenger count at McCarran International Airport, which sits east of the sign, shot from 1 million in 1960 to 46 million in 2006. The sign's backdrop has also blossomed—smaller spread-out hotel-casinos have been replaced by a seemingly never-ending row of megaresorts.

As I stepped onto the median, carrying my backpack by its top loop, two tourists huddled beneath the sign. One of them stood upright between the supports and swept her fingers through her hair. The other walked a short distance, adjusting a 35mm camera. In the Strip's northbound lanes, vehicles slowed in homage to the sign. The brake lights became lost in a kaleidoscope of colors: fire red, shock pink, sunshine yellow, Prince purple, and lounge-singer-suit blue. The tourist beneath the sign forced a smile. The camera flashed.

Slipping the backpack over my shoulders, I started across the median. Dry mud caked my boots. My thighs were tight, still not fully recovered from following T.J. Weber's trail. I'd spent the past three days in serious chill mode—transcribing the taped notes, writing a rough draft of the Intro, and watching three of the American Film Institute's 100 Greatest Movies. (I highly recommend *From Here to Eternity*, number 52 on the list; Ol' Blue Eyes really rocked it.) And while I felt mentally prepared to explore another drain—even anxious—my body gently protested.

Avoiding a pack of tourists, I crossed the southbound lanes of the Strip and angled into a wash. It ran parallel to the street, then transitioned into a rectangular channel. Cradling a shallow stream that flowed from the Bali Hai golf course, the channel went underground in two 10-feet-wide and six-feet-high tunnels. The sign flashed above the east wall: "Welcome to Fabulous Las Vegas."

Indeed, I'd found the appropriate place to begin my adventures underneath the Strip.

The stream disappeared into the storm drain's west tunnel. The east tunnel

I surveyed the walls, which were a dull orange in the candlelight.
addiction, desperation, and madness; of loneliness, love, and
Tales that the tourists posing prettily beneath the

was dark and dry. As I approached the drain and squinted into its depths, my chest tightened. I exhaled, then shook out of the backpack. After hooking up the recording equipment, I put on the knit cap. Then I removed the expandable baton from the pouch and stuck it in the sheath, wondering if anyone was watching me from inside the drain. If so, what were they thinking? Did they assume I was an undercover cop? A homeless person infringing on their territory? A wayward tourist? Were they sharpening their tongues—or their shanks?

I clutched the flashlight and entered the east tunnel with the uneasiness of walking into the barrel of a gun.

I was ambushed by darkness. It flowed along the floor, walls, and ceiling like floodwater. The beam of the flashlight fought through it, illuminating cockroaches and cracks between the concrete boxes, which were filled with the black tar used to seal them. The recording light glowed on my hip. Crickets chirped in chorus. Otherwise, it was remarkably quiet.

As I staggered into the darkness, crouching slightly (I'm six-foot-four in my boots), a muffled voice accompanied the crickets. I couldn't tell if it was coming from inside or outside the tunnel—but I certainly hoped the latter. I convinced myself it was just another frat boy frolicking around the famous sign, another Midwesterner turned mad by the betting and booze. The voice became louder and more distinct. Pausing and tilting my head, I finally distinguished: "You looking for something?"

"Excuse me?" I said, squinting into the darkness.

"You looking for something?"

If they could speak, I thought, they would tell startling tales: tales of regret; of triumph, disappointment, and—yeah—maybe even death. "Welcome to Fabulous Las Vegas" sign would never, ever, believe.

"I'm sorry," I said, continuing into the tunnel. "I'm having trouble hearing you. The crickets are chirping down here."

"Who are you?!"

Finally, about 300 feet into the drain, the beam of the flashlight found a low partition. Behind it, a man in a T-shirt and shorts sat on a chaise lounge. His right hand clutched a dirty sneaker.

"I'm a journalist," I quickly explained, not wanting to be attacked with a thrift-store Nike. "I'm exploring the storm drains for a book I'm working on. A few days ago, I walked a drain that started near the Las Vegas Library and opened up near Palace Station. It was about three and a half miles long. This is the first time I've been in this drain. Hope I'm not interrupting."

"I just got to save some money, so I can get out of here and get out of town," the man said drunkenly, perhaps assuming that I was a cop or county employee.

"Amen," I said. "I've been trying to escape this city for about seven years now."

"I've been here for six," he said, spraying deodorizer into the sneaker, "but not all of them in this tunnel." The man leaned forward and picked up another sneaker. The spray can hissed. I was surprised that someone hanging out in a storm drain would be this concerned about hygiene, but I didn't express it for fear of offending the man. We had a lot to talk about, I hoped.

A Navy-blue blanket draped from a crack in the ceiling, serving as the back wall of the campsite. Cigarette butts and adult-entertainment fliers littered the floor. Spray paint streaked across the tunnel's east side, "Aghast the Devil Stood … and Felt How Awful Goodness Is."

Intrigued by the graffiti, which I later learned was a variation of a line in Milton's *Paradise Lost*, I asked the man: "Did you write that?"

"Nah," said the man, who introduced himself as David. "This other guy that used to live here did that. I don't even pay attention to it. He got a job as a maintenance man. He moved out of here and into the apartments where he works."

"How long have you lived here?"

"A little over three months. I don't like it down here. The flash floods are really dangerous. It doesn't have to be raining here for it to kill you. It can be raining fifteen miles away in the mountains, and it'll come down in the wash."

"How'd you end up here?"

"It's just the way things worked out. I left my other camp at the same time he left this one. It was the easiest thing to do. I wasn't going to go back to the tunnels behind the Rio [hotel-casino], because I got mugged there. They got me good. I took an ass-beating. If I go back over there, I'll kill the motherfuckers. Basically, I don't want to kill nobody and get arrested. I'm not stupid. I'm just an alcoholic and a drug addict."

I trained the flashlight on the front partition, a door turned on its side and supported by 20-pound rocks. Just outside the camp, ants attacked a sheet of aluminum foil and an empty package of bologna.

"You got some ants over here," I said, slapping them off my boots.

"I know. That's why that garbage is out there: to keep the ants out of here. It's a weird thing. If I put stuff out there, they don't come in here."

"Is it tough to keep the camp clean?"

"Food is the problem," said David, rolling deodorant onto his armpits. What next, I wondered? A splash of French cologne? A pedicurist emerging from behind the blanket? "If you bring any type of food into the tunnels," he continued, "the ants try to get to it. And once you get ants you can't get rid of them. I used a whole can of Raid down here one day."

Still slapping my boots, I asked: "Do you mind if I come around to the far side of the camp?"

"I don't care, man. You don't threaten me. I got a good vibe about you."

I swung around the camp's west border, which was supported by two thin pieces of wood wedged between the floor and ceiling. "Do you get much traffic down here? You know, tourists wandering over from the 'Welcome to Fabulous Las Vegas' sign?"

"Traffic?" he repeated incredulously. "Hell no. You can't see anything in this son of a bitch. It's pitch black. Nobody comes down in here."

I laughed. After all, he had a point. "I thought it was interesting that as you walk into this tunnel you can see the sign, as if you're entering the real Las Vegas."

"It feels very strange walking out there and seeing people making movies and limousines parked. 'Welcome to Fabulous Las Vegas': Yeah, I guess that is kind of funny. Well, I can always tell my grandkids that I lived right next to that sign."

Rounding the camp, I stopped beneath a manhole behind the blanket. Rope wrapped around the rungs, supporting an improvised shelf that hung directly under the shaft. I swept the beam over the shelf, which was empty.

Noticing my curiosity, David rose from the chaise lounge and approached the shelf. "If there's a flash flood," he explained, "I put anything that I don't want to wash away up there. The rest of the stuff I don't care about. It's just trash."

David returned to the chaise lounge. I knelt at the back edge of the camp, between the blanket and the west border, and cut off the flashlight. A candle flickered atop a milk crate, unmasking David's dead eyes and red-brown hair. His skin was pale, freckled.

"It's very dank down here," he continued, "and it gets real dark. Two guys died

"

It feels very strange walking out there and seeing people making movies and limousines parked. 'Welcome to Fabulous Las Vegas': Yeah, I guess that is kind of funny. Well, I can always tell my grandkids that I lived right next to that sign. ~ David

in this tunnel, and sometimes I hear footsteps at two or three in the morning. I shine my flashlight down there, but nobody's coming."

"What happened?" I asked, peering over my shoulder. I heard exactly what David said, but I wanted more details. During my library research, which began in the summer of 2002, I hadn't come across any drownings in the south-central area of the storm-drain system—but, of course, these kinds of deaths often go unreported. Also, floodwater can carry bodies several miles before they're recovered.

"From what I heard, they got washed away. All I know is that the guy that used to live down here, I said to him, 'How come I hear footsteps at two or three in the morning? Then I look down the tunnel and nobody's coming?' He told me what happened, that two guys got washed away. Another friend of mine who used to live in the other [west] tunnel said he's seen them. It's weird."

"It is weird," I agreed. "These tunnels are creepy enough on their own." I surveyed the walls, which were a dull orange in the candlelight. If they could speak, I thought, they would tell startling tales: tales of addiction, desperation, and madness; of loneliness, love, and regret; of triumph, disappointment, and—yeah—maybe even death. Tales that the tourists posing prettily beneath the "Welcome to Fabulous Las Vegas" sign would never, ever, believe.

"What brought you to Las Vegas, David?"

"An inheritance from my mother, and I was a heavy-equipment operator. But I decided not to work and just drown my sorrows in booze. I knew how to hustle, claiming slot-machine credits and stuff like that, but now all that's about over."

"How long did the inheritance last?"

"Forty-three thousand dollars gone in less than forty days."

"What'd you spend it on?" I asked, knowing the answer.

"Video poker and table games."

"What've you been doing since the money ran out?"

"Just hustling. Usually I'd live on the streets for the first ten days of the month, while a friend of mine did his thing with his Vietnam check, his hookers, and his crack. Then he'd be broke, and I'd move in with him for the last twenty days of the month. But he moved back home and died with his family.

"I wanted to get out of town by May, but it's hard to keep plans when you drink and do drugs. Anyhow, I feel kind of lost. I want to go back to Missoula, Montana. I've lived there twice. I could go back there and work for a guy I used to work for and apply at the railroad. I could try there and with the county. I could start getting my life straightened out."

"What were your hopes when you moved to Vegas?"

"My mom had just hung herself. She committed suicide. What were my hopes? I don't know. I guess I didn't have any. I was lost. I didn't know how to deal with it other than to drink. I was divorced. My grandmother died. All the women in my family are gone. And all the prick-head men who put them in early graves are millionaires or multimillionaires."

When I came up with the idea of exploring the storm drains, I didn't it was simply too remote for a boy from the middle-class South. (a wallet or a wig—ha, ha, ha), graffiti, and maybe

"Do they ever help you out?" I asked, searching for clues that would set off my bullshit detector.

"My stepfather would, but I don't ask for anything."

"Do they know you live in this tunnel?"

"Nah, man. I'm forty-three years old. They don't care about me anymore."

"When was the last time you talked to your family?"

"Over six years ago, just before I came out here. They don't even know how to get a hold of me—and I don't really care to get in touch with them either. Why? I come out here with forty-three thousand dollars, and I'm going to call them up and ask for money? Jesus, that would be pretty fucking insulting."

I quietly agreed, then changed the subject. "You said you hustle. What do you mean?"

"Just walking into casinos and finding credits left in the slot machines." This is known as "claiming" or "silver-mining." Though illegal—according to state law, all abandoned money becomes possession of the house—it's popular among local street people.

"How much money can you make doing that?"

"The other night I walked into Mandalay Bay and then the Luxor, and there was three hundred quarters in a machine. I made seventy-five dollars in twenty minutes. This morning, I put twenty-two dollars in a video poker machine and ran it up to seventy dollars. But then I gave it all back."

"If you ever hit a jackpot, what would you do with the money?"

"First, I'd hire an attorney. I'm divorced. Then I'd make sure my kid was set for

consider that they might be inhabited. I couldn't make that connection;
I expected to find concrete, darkness, and water—miscellaneous items
a stray animal. But I did *not* expect to find people.

life. And then I'd move out of Las Vegas and live in Montana.

"See, I got one more shot at life," said David, dropping his head. "I talked to a street preacher today down by the Venetian. I asked him to pray for me. I did. I'm ready. He said, 'You probably got one last shot to straighten things out.' And I said, 'You know, I really want to try to.'"

David leaned forward, elbows on knees. He then bent down and began scooping chicken bones from the floor with a paper plate. The conversation lagged. Obviously, it was time for me to move on. It was time for me to go. I stood clumsily, hindered by the weight of the backpack, and stretched my legs.

"Where does this tunnel open up?" I asked him, gazing into the abyss.

Emerging from behind the blanket, David said, "It goes straight, then it turns right and goes underneath the Strip. It opens up somewhere on the other side of the street."

"What's down there?"

"A motherfucking idiot who's lived on the other end of the tunnel for five years. He's arrogant as hell, but he don't mess with me."

"Do you guys communicate?"

"Communicate? He doesn't know how to communicate. All he knows how to do is tell people how to live their lives."

"What's in the other tunnel?"

"Lots of black widows. There ain't nothing else in there. Because of the irrigation from the golf course, there's always water running through it and it's full of chemicals. There's also garbage in there. It smells like shit. But there may be somebody in the other end of it. I've never been all the way through there."

"All right, David," I said, snapping on the flashlight and turning downstream. "Good talking to you, man. Take care."

See, I got one more shot at life. I talked to a street preacher today down by the Venetian. I asked him to pray for me. I did. I'm ready. He said, 'You probably got one last shot to straighten things out.' And I said, 'You know, I really want to try to.' ~ David

"Be careful about sneaking up on that bastard," said David. "He's a weird son of a bitch. He's unpredictable. I'd worry about him pulling a shank or something on me."

Spooked by David's warning, I swept the beam across the tunnel. The darkness retreated, unveiling a shopping cart angled against the east wall; it contained empty plastic bottles, which were used by David to transport water to his camp, and a cardboard box full of clothes. Faded stenciling on the west wall read, "10 x 6 x 6 1-27-95 HCC." A mosaic of glass glistened on the floor.

Crunching across the glass and glancing back at David's silhouette, it finally hit me: *This* is his home sweet home. This is where he "hangs his hat." This is where he "rests his head." This is where he returns after a long day on the streets. This is where he relaxes. This is where he eats. This is where he sleeps. This is where he dreams. This is where he wakes.

When I came up with the idea of exploring the storm drains, I didn't consider that they might be inhabited. I couldn't make that connection; it was too remote for a boy from the middle-class South. I expected to find concrete, darkness, and water—miscellaneous items (a wallet or a wig—ha, ha, ha), graffiti, and maybe a stray animal. But I did *not* expect to find people. People sleep in houses, condos, and apartments. They sleep in hotels, motels, and—a local favorite—trailers. They sleep in shelters, parks, and under bridges. But they do *not* sleep in dark concrete boxes that run for miles and miles and miles. They do *not* sleep in concrete boxes that fill with floodwater.

Exploring the storm drains with Josh, I found out that—in fact—they do. And as we interviewed the inhabitants, it *almost* began to make sense. The drains are ready-made reliable shanties—a floor, two walls, and a ceiling. They provide shelter from the intense Mojave heat and wind. (Remember, most desert animals live underground.) Some of the drains are dry for weeks, even months. And cops, security guards, and business owners don't dare roust anyone beyond the shade line.

But ultimately, the drains are deathtraps. They're disorienting and sometimes dangerously long. Many of them run under streets and contain pockets of carbon monoxide. They can be difficult to exit, particularly in a hurry. They're not patrolled. (Who would work *that* beat for $50,000 a year?) They're not monitored. There are no rules. There are no heroes. And, oh yeah, they can fill a foot per minute with floodwater.

Walking into a storm drain is like walking into a casino: You never know what's going to happen, but chances are it isn't going to be good.

As the tunnel trended eastward, two ceiling grates cast grids of light onto the walls and floor. I cut off the flashlight, not wanting to attract the attention of anyone aboveground. The tunnel faded to black and the grids of light came into focus. Underneath the grates, a pile of rocks and aluminum cans rose from the floor. Avoiding it, I crashed into a spider web. I quickly reversed, flicked the handle of the baton, and slashed forward, noticing a streetlight and shrubs through the rusted bars.

The bend intensified. It was now night—I entered the drain at sundown, in hopes of talking to inhabitants who may have been elsewhere during the day—

and the tunnel took on a different demeanor. The shafts of light that signaled ceiling grates, inlets, and outlets had dimmed. Darkness prevailed. Straightening up and squinting downstream, I hit my head on the ceiling. The knit cap softened the blow, but it still stung. I removed the cap and rubbed my head. No blood, no turning around.

For the first time in my life, I wished that I was shorter. Or more conveniently, I wished that the Clark County Regional Flood Control District had made this tunnel taller. What if the six-foot-three Weber had stumbled on this drain? How far could he have traveled slightly hunched over and without light? What would he have said when David asked, "Who are you?!" How would these two strange men have interacted in the dark?

Still clutching the baton, I steadied the beam on the near wall. The components of a camp gradually emerged: jackets hanging from a hook in the ceiling, an Indian-print blanket curled on the floor, a queen-size mattress.

"Knock, knock," I called out nervously. "Anyone home?"

A razor, bottle of suntan lotion, and Walkman radio were nestled in a crack between two of the concrete boxes. On the mattress lay a flattened hat and the fluffy entrails of pillows.

"Anyone home?" I repeated.

A tarpaulin emblazoned with coins and dollar bills hung from the ceiling—ironically, I noted into the mike—forming the front border of the camp. I peeked around the tarp, discovering the outlet, then aimed the flashlight into another crack. It contained an adult-entertainment flier and a toothbrush partially wrapped in a plastic bag. A spider crawled across the bristles.

Returning the baton to the sheath, I exited the tunnel. An open-air channel bordered by a barbwire fence rolled eastward about 150 feet, then swung to the north. Two hangars squatted above the far embankment. A departing airliner roared into the night.

Mandalay Bay loomed over the north bank and Luxor's beam parted the sky. Admiring the view, I turned into the west tunnel. It swung to the south and straightened, a bulge breaking the square of dim light at its opposite end. A mound of garbage, I soon discovered, created the bulge: Styrofoam containers, a shit-stained carpet, plastic bags full of bottles and cans. The smell of trash and feces made me retch.

Assuming David used this area as a garbage dump and bathroom, I narrowed the beam and returned to the opposite end of the drain. I ducked into the east tunnel, again finding it unoccupied. (I returned to the camp on several occasions, night and day, but never encountered the "weird son of a bitch.") Then I placed the flashlight in the backpack and began down the open-air channel. Around the bend, the channel straightened and ran parallel to the south end of the Strip. The hotel-casinos sparkled like Liberace. The moon punched a hole in the sky.

The Strip, of course, provided a stunning contrast to the storm drain. How could these two worlds so closely co-exist, I wondered? Then again, how could they not? In America, poverty always bows at the feet of corporate wealth.

In the 1980s and '90s, the subway and train tunnels of New York City served as shelter for thousands of people. The book *The Mole People* and the film *Dark Days* documented that desperate existence. The tunnel-dwellers lived alongside the tracks in plywood shanties, rocked by passing trains, or in elevated niches. Some simply spread bedding on the rat-infested floors.

While crude, many of the camps were relatively elaborate: king-sized mattresses, dressers, cabinets, tables, bookshelves, even artwork. The inhabitants cooked on cinderblock grills and plugged into power outlets, allowing for heaters, lamps, and household appliances. A sense of permanence was established. Some people lived in the tunnels, which were draped with icicles during the winter, for more than 20 years. Niche communities (homosexuals, crack addicts, runaways, eccentrics, and families) formed. Stray cats and dogs were adopted as pets. Babies were born.

But more typically, people *died* in the subway and train tunnels of New York City. Inhabitants, known as moles or mythically as CHUDs (cannibalistic human underground dwellers), were hit by trains or electrocuted, they overdosed on drugs or died of natural causes, they were murdered or they committed murder. According to *The Mole People*, one police officer was beaten to death in the tunnels with his own nightstick. Two other officers were killed with their own guns as they tried to clear out a Bowery burrow.

Eventually, law-enforcement sweeps and tighter security reduced the number of people living in the tunnels. But—no doubt—inhabitants remain, nestled in nooks and shuddering in the darkness.

Behind a boarded-up motel, the channel swung sharply to the east and the lights of the Strip cast a procession of shadows onto the far bank. Around the bend, the channel went dark in two tunnels. I reached for the flashlight, before realizing the tunnels opened up on the other side of a two-lane road.

Again, the channel swung sharply. It then widened, slid under another street, and tore toward the Tropicana hotel-casino.

Level with Mandalay Bay, a pipe dumped water—runoff, I assumed, from the property's fountains and sprinklers—into the channel. The water curled on the bank, rolled downstream, and melted into a black void just south of the Tropicana. I pulled up at the edge of the darkness and removed the flashlight, discovering that the stream flowed evenly into a double-barrel storm drain.

Exhaling, I swept the beam of the flashlight over the drain. It was, by far, the most intimidating I'd encountered. Wet, carpeted with algae, and fronted by a towering façade, it was similar to the drain I entered when tracking Weber's trail. But these tunnels were smaller, eight feet wide and six feet high, and shielded by an ominous grate that lay parallel to the channel floor about six feet off the ground. (I had no idea what purpose the grate served.) Shrouded in black mist, the ditch was as ugly as a Fremont Street whore.

I shifted my feet in the stream, feeling like Mallory at the face of Mount Everest. I considered turning around. No, I *seriously* considered turning around. In fact, I convinced myself that it was the logical thing to do. After all, it was 10 o'clock at night—no time to be prancing around a storm drain in one of the cruelest, most desperate cities in the world. Also, I was still within walking distance of my car (which was parked adjacent to the "Welcome to Fabulous Las Vegas" sign at the Klondike hotel-casino); if I explored this drain, which cut under the northwest corner of the airport, I'd have to catch a cab back to the Klondike. And I assumed there was nothing in this drain that would add to my book—no lost tourists, no inhabitants, probably not even a lone graffiti tag.

But I *was* curious about what access—if any—the drain provided to the airport. Post 9/11, everything is super-secure. Right? *Right?* Or was there an outlet adjacent to the runway (like at the North Las Vegas Airport)? Did manholes lead directly to the apron? Were al-Qaeda terrorists huddled in the dark, praying solemnly and devising their own Gunpowder Plot?

After five minutes of debate, I ducked under the grate and splashed into the east tunnel. It reeked of mildew. Sandbars swallowed aluminum cans and diverted the stream, which was ankle-deep in areas. I aimed the beam downward, noticing a crawfish struggling against the current. Fascinated, I stopped and stood over the

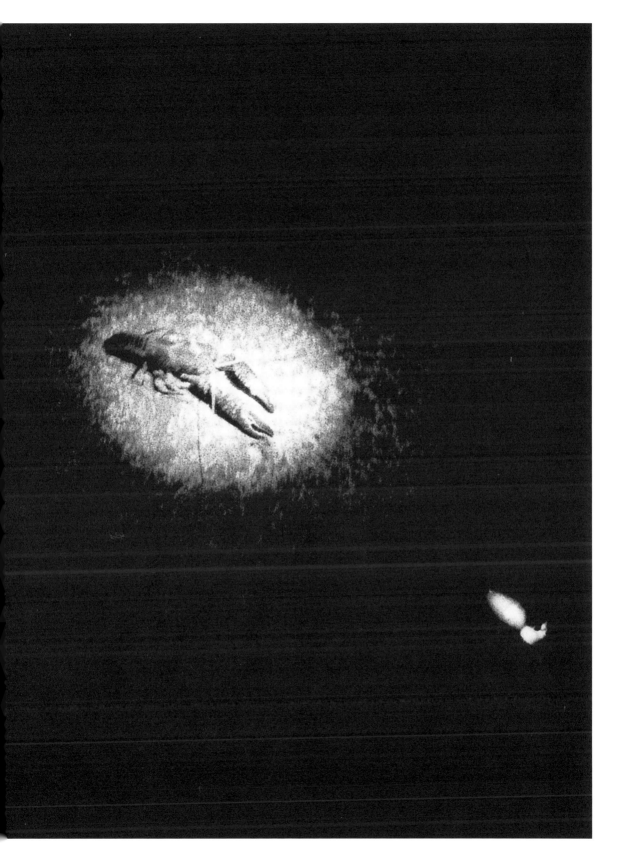

creepy little bastard. It raised its head and pincers, as if praying to the God of the Flashlight.

Continuing downstream, I noticed orange-red shells in the cracks between the boxes. It was an unnerving sight, to say the least. There were hundreds of them, maybe even thousands. The crawfish, I recalled from research, migrate from Lake Mead up the Las Vegas Wash and into the storm-drain system. I also remembered that aquariums were occasionally emptied into drop inlets, leading me to speculate about what strange species I might encounter next.

As I rounded the first bend, a red light broke my stride. It hovered in the middle of the tunnel, pulsing like a star. "What the fuck?" I muttered into the mike. Spooked and confused, I took a few steps backward. I then focused the beam and inched forward. A mountain bike with a red reflector took shape. It stood upright on its kickstand and had obviously not washed into the tunnel. Another bike emerged from the darkness, along the east wall. Two white splotches—which I eventually recognized as the bottoms of feet—floated above the bike, just beneath the ceiling.

"Hello?" I said, trying to make sense of the scene. A spectral form rose above the feet. It cowered in the light, shielding its eyes like a vampire. "Sorry to wake you," I stammered. "I'm exploring this storm drain. I was curious. But I didn't want to cut through your camp without permission."

"Go ahead," the form mumbled. "You with the county or what?"

"No," I answered, edging forward and making out a man on some sort of elevated bed. "I'm a journalist. I'm exploring the drains and working on a book."

Apparently, those were the magic words. The man turned on his side and said, "I was planning on writing a book about homelessness myself." Rubbing the sleep from his eyes, he continued: "Let me give you some background: All this homelessness really began in the 1980s. I'm not blaming Reagan or the Republicans—but if you go back and look at the passage of bills and things like that, this all started with our jobs going overseas and the turning down of low-income housing, the passing of GATT and later NAFTA. We didn't have that many homeless people before the '80s. Now, if you take away the druggies, the Vietnam vets, and the alcoholics, you still have thousands of regular families on the streets. And that don't make sense. These are everyday people who just cannot afford a place to live."

Is this a dream, I wondered? Could this possibly be real? Did I just walk into a wet storm drain in south-central Vegas and discover a man sleeping on an elevated bed? Did he wake up and deliver a well-thought-out lecture on the history of homelessness? Is his book research really that far ahead of mine?

"When did you become homeless?" I asked the man, collecting myself and approaching the bed.

"Around 1994. I had a lot of things on my mind. See, I have a really bad gambling problem. I'm working on it. I've been doing pretty good about backing off, but I still got a habit."

"Were you living in Las Vegas when you became homeless?" I said, standing beside the bed.

"No. I moved here from Kansas City a long time ago."

"What brought you here?"

"Personal reasons. I don't want to get into that." He paused, as if recalling the bad old days, then continued. "But at least here I can find work. I work through Labor Ready [temp agency]. I got a repeat ticket tomorrow. I've got to get back to sleep soon. It's a four-hour gig, janitorial work."

"What time do you have to wake up?"

"Four o'clock. I got to ride my bike to work. And I want to eat and get there early."

"How do you make sure you're up?"

A manhole rose above the bed. Jeans, workpants, and a backpack hung from the upper rungs. The man pointed at a lower rung, which supported a stack of books and a battery-operated alarm clock. It read 10:10 p.m.

"If you do your research," he continued, returning to his original point, "you'll find that everything started building up during the '80s. It was cause and effect. When you start outsourcing jobs, something's going to happen.

"Politicians, I love them. They said outsourcing wasn't going to hurt us. They said it was a blessing. They said these jobs are low-income and that our high-tech will stay. Yeah, right. All those jobs went overseas. Tell me how it's a blessing to a family whose father just got laid off. Try telling them that new jobs will come. They got car payments. They got a mortgage. That's how many people become homeless."

Leaning against the bed and setting the flashlight on the sheets, I asked the man, "How do you think local politicians are doing with homelessness?"

"Las Vegas is like a bubble," he lisped. "Las Vegas is unique. We have casinos. We have millions of tourists. You're always going to have homelessness here, because of the gambling and alcohol. Homelessness is unique here. You can't look at other cities and see how they're handling it. It's just different.

"The government can only do so much. But they're going to have to build more low-income housing. They should buy some land and build cheap steel houses on it, so a low-income family can get a place for $400 or $500 a month."

"That's an interesting idea," I said, "but the real-estate prices are working against it. There's no cheap land left in Vegas. Prices have gotten ridiculous. They want $350,000 for a stucco box in the suburbs."

"That's true. It would cost some money, and politicians can only do so much. They try to do their best. But they're frustrated, because they think we woke up one day and decided to become homeless. Please, get a grip. A person or a family doesn't just wake up one day and decide that they want to be homeless. They don't decide that they really like it on the streets and they want their children to starve. That's illogical—and I'm talking about everyday low-income people. I'm talking about people who don't have drug problems, mental problems, and Vietnam vet problems. I'm talking about low-income people who did the best they could to find a job and a home, then come to find out they have to work cheap labor. They come to find out they can't afford to pay the rent, because landlords have pumped up the prices. That's part of the reason why people are struggling to survive. That's part of the reason there's homelessness.

"It's a complicated issue," he continued. "There are a lot of reasons for homelessness, a lot of causes and effects. But one of them is not that someone woke up one day and decided they wanted to be homeless. Let's be realistic. Basically, it comes down to affordable housing and well-paying jobs."

"What happened in your situation?"

Raking his matted hair, he explained: "It has to do with depression and not understanding my gambling problem—but it's getting better. I've cut back on the gambling quite a bit. Yesterday, I decided to just play one quarter at a time. I won twenty-three dollars, and said that's it. Usually, I blow it all before I quit."

"What's your game?"

"Video slots. I don't drink liquor. I don't do drugs. A gambling habit brought me down. I'm trying to break the habit, to control it. I'm doing the best I can. I really want to get off the streets. I've done it before, but sometimes my depression gets in the way."

"I'm Matt," I said, extending my hand.

"I'm Lawrence," said the man, shaking it.

"I'm thirty-three, Lawrence. How old are you?"

"I'm fifty-four."

"I'm from Atlanta. Where you from?"

"I was raised in Omaha, Nebraska."

"Do you have a trade?"

"I cook. I write poetry and short stories."

"Have you published anything?"

"I've come close," he laughed.

"I know how that goes."

"Yeah, I do some writing," he continued. "I do research. I go on the Internet at public libraries and study. I can research and tell stories."

"You got any poetry you could share with me?"

"I just sit here and think of stuff as it comes. Give me a word."

"Um, sticking with the theme, let's go with 'tunnel.'"

Lawrence set his head on a pillow and stared at the ceiling. His nose was boxer-flat. Scars ran across his forehead and a goatee partially concealed his harelip. After a dramatic pause, he began:

"I look upon the night

and sometimes wonder

what kind of tunnel

I dug for myself:

dark, lonely, cold, and damp.

It has to do with depression and not understanding my gambling problem—but it's getting better. I've cut back on the gambling quite a bit. Yesterday, I decided to just play one quarter at a time. I won twenty-three dollars, and said that's it. Usually, I blow it all before I quit. ~ Lawrence

I long for the warmth.

Sometimes I see the light

far, far away,

at the tunnel's end—

but it's only an illusion.

My mind is dreaming.

Where does it begin

and where does it end?"

"That was cool," I said. "I liked it, particularly that you were able to do it impromptu."

"What I do is go through the alphabet and take a word that begins with each letter. Then I practice rhyming with the word, like 'hate': 'Hate is a gate for the late. It's fate. I once loved. I once understood God. But the gate closed. And my heart feels hate. It's gone cold. I'm getting old.'"

I laughed. "Damn, your stuff's pretty dark."

"I do some lighter stuff, too. But yeah, basically it's really dark."

"That's probably because of how you're living right now."

"I agree."

"So who are your influences?"

"Edgar Allan Poe. I like his poetry. He's really dark."

"Yeah, very Gothic," I agreed. "This tunnel would make the perfect setting for one of his short stories. In fact, I think 'The Cask of Amontillado' was set in some catacombs. That's a crazy-ass story."

In the story, a man named Montresor seeks revenge against his friend Fortunato for an unspecified grievance. Encountering Fortunato at a carnival and aware of his passion for wine, Montresor explains that he recently bought a pipe of Amontillado—but now doubts its authenticity. The proud Fortunato offers to sample the wine for his friend, and the two men venture into the Montresor family catacombs (which serve as vaults). Drunk and blinded by the darkness, Fortunato is lured into a remote recess, shackled, and walled in with stone and mortar.

"I also like Joseph Conrad," Lawrence continued. "There's a black author named Baldwin I like."

"James Baldwin?"

"Yeah, something like that. And I like the guy who wrote *The Hunt for Red October*, Clancy. I really like that book."

"All right," I said, still thinking about "The Cask of Amontillado." I couldn't ignore the similarities between the story and my circumstance: two men, bone-colored walls, and the "supreme madness of the carnival season" (i.e., the Strip) overhead. I could only hope that my fate would prove better than the unfortunate Fortunato's.

"Those are some of my influences," said Lawrence. "I learned their style from reading their works. I like to keep my stories short, my descriptions short and realistic. That's my style."

"Have you been productive lately?"

"No, I haven't," he answered ashamedly. "I have a lot of things I want to write about, but this year I'm mainly doing research. As I said, I want to write a book

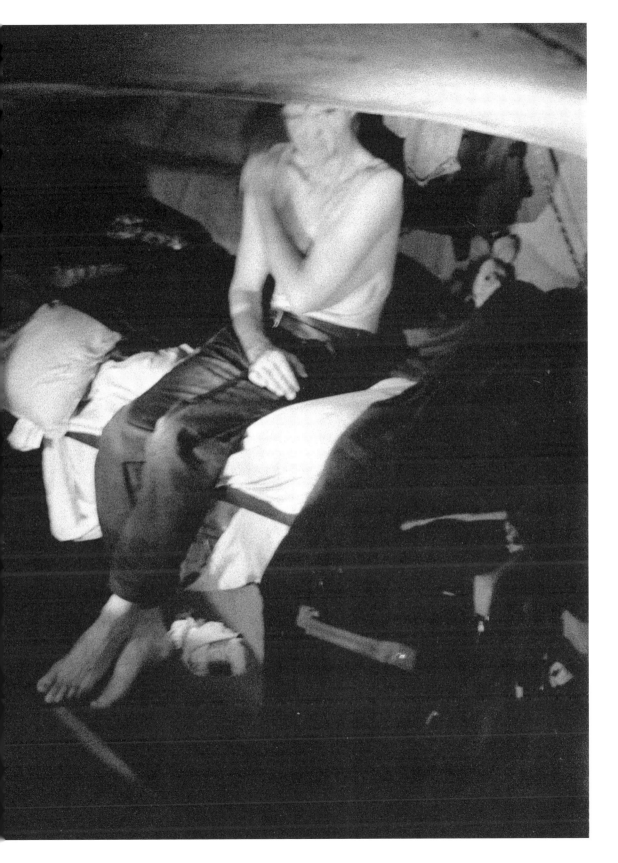

about the causes and effects of homelessness. I'm just trying to decide if I want to do it as history, sociology, or what."

I glanced at the books on the rung, which included *The Jewish New Testament* and *Receiving the Holy Spirit Today*. "Is that your whole collection?"

"Nah. I got more than that. I read a lot."

"Do you ever write about living in this tunnel?"

"Nah. Basically, I don't even think about it. I don't even worry about it. This is a temporary situation." Patting the bed proudly, he continued: "I designed this. I built it after reading about mountain climbers. This is how they sleep when they stop and rest in the middle of a climb. It's the same idea."

I played the beam over the bed, which was about four and a half feet from the floor. It was made of couch cushions, a steel frame, and a door that provided additional support. Baling wire looped around the head and foot of the bed, angled tightly through the manhole, and wrapped around the rungs. Backpacks hung from the side on hooks.

I squatted and swept the beam under the bed. It was legless. No steel poles, no wooden beams, no milk crates—nothing. A square-shaped wire dangled from the side, serving as a stepladder. Except for the bikes, the whole camp was at least three feet above the stream.

"This is brilliant," I said. "This is *absolutely* brilliant. It would take a hundred-year flood to reach up there."

"Not even a hundred-year flood would do it," corrected Lawrence. "The water never gets this high in this tunnel. It gets up to your kneecap and that's about it. I just listen to the sound. If I hear a high-pitched sound, I don't even try to get out. I don't even worry about it."

"Have you waited out floods in here?"

"

The drawback of living here is that I can get depressed, and I'll sit here
for a week and not leave. I fight mental depression sometimes.
I'm a Vietnam vet. I won't go into it any further than that, but
sometimes I just get tired of it all. Then I tell myself, 'OK, either put
up or shut up. Let's get going.' ~ Lawrence

"No, not in here. But I have in the other tunnels."

"The tunnels I just walked through, the ones near the 'Welcome to Fabulous
Las Vegas' sign?"

"Yeah, I used to live up there. A bunch of drug addicts starting moving in, so
I moved out. I brought everything down here."

"I only saw two camps up there."

"This was a long time ago. They built a police station right above the tunnel
and everyone moved out." He laughed at the recollection.

"How long did you live in that drain?"

"About five years."

"How long have you lived in here?"

"I was staying here when I moved to Denver about two years ago. I didn't
come back to Vegas for a while. Now I've been down here about five months."

"Why do you live in here and not aboveground?"

"I'm safe down here. It's peaceful. It's quiet and cool. When you go underground,
the temperature becomes constant: about seventy degrees. And in the wintertime,
it's bearable.

"The drawback of living here is that I can get depressed, and I'll sit here for
a week and not leave. I fight mental depression sometimes. I'm a Vietnam vet. I
won't go into it any further than that, but sometimes I just get tired of it all. Then

I tell myself, 'OK, either put up or shut up. Let's get going.'"

"Why'd you pick this drain? It's wet and has crawfish in it."

"Think about it."

I paused. "Because nobody will come in here and disturb you—except nosy insensitive journalists?"

"Exactly," he laughed. "Rarely will people walk where it's wet. They don't want to mess up their shoes. It's a psychological thing."

"How do you get in and out without getting wet?"

"I ride my bike. I ride it right out and I ride it right back in. My feet never touch the ground.

"But really, I got to get myself out of here," continued Lawrence, head reuniting with the pillow. "I've done it before and I can do it again, if I really set my mind to it. I'm working on it. I'm dealing with it. I'm tired of gambling to the point where I end up starving and have to go dumpster diving. I'm tired of that shit. I've just got to say: 'Enough is enough. Get a grip.'"

I glanced downstream. A mound of wet newspapers rose from the floor and cobwebs decorated the walls and ceiling. The tunnel trended to the east, then disappeared into a heavy black mist. The Montresor family catacombs couldn't have been any creepier.

"What's down there?" I asked.

"Negative. Nothing," Lawrence answered. "You don't even want to go back there. It's all mud and water. It bends all the way around there, gets low, and ends on the other side of the airport. You can't get out. It's covered with a big iron gate that's chained to the wall."

That was all I needed to hear. In fact, it was exactly what I wanted to hear. I'd experienced enough weirdness, enough surrealism, for one night in the storm drains. It was time for me to walk back to my car. It was time for me to pop the trunk and strip out of my gear. It was time to call my friend Adam, tell him I made it out alive, and share the stories. It was time to shower, eat, and set *my* head down on a pillow. It was time to dream the most bizarre dreams imaginable.

"I should let you sleep, Lawrence," I said, pushing off the bed. "Sorry about waking you up."

"No problem. Take care."

"You too," I said, splashing back toward the inlet and marveling at life. Through cold, heat, drought, deluge, addiction, loneliness, love, and war, it somehow endures—one heart beating, like a neon sign, beneath the back lots of the Las Vegas Strip.

"Good night," I said.

"Good night," said Lawrence.

Cappadocia is a *National Geographic* photographer's wet dream. It's a Roman centurion's worst nightmare. It's a museum, an art gallery. It's a church, a time capsule, an archeological dig. It's a sculpture, an earthwork, and a painting. It's a masterpiece—and a disaster. It's beautiful. It's ugly. It's the ultimate geologic freak show.

Millions of years ago, volcanoes in what is now central Turkey spewed lava across the land. It hardened into tuff, overlaid in areas with stubborn basalt. The canvas set, nature went to work. Intense heat and cold ate away at the earth. Rivers carved into the tuff, creating profound canyons and basalt-topped plateaus. Wind and floodwater sculpted dome-shaped hills and freakish cones and columns, now known as "fairy chimneys."

The region resembles the Southwest United States in areas, the moon in others.

Humans also cut into the rock. Fearing religious persecution by the Romans, early Christians migrated to the region and dug chapels, churches, and monasteries. Later, the rise of Islam forced Christians back into this underworld. Generations of townspeople expanded the network, digging cities of several levels connected by miles and miles of tunnels. The cities featured air shafts, stables, wineries, and wells. A typical dwelling included a communication shaft (which allowed people on different levels to talk to each other), a kitchen, and a toilet. A wheel-shaped rock served as a rolling door.

Today, Cappadocia has more than 400 underground cities and 3,000 churches. Some locals still live in the underworld, which is cool in the summer and relatively warm in the winter. Abandoned dwellings serve as storerooms, tourist attractions, and hideouts for adventurous children, who crawl into the entranceways in the cliffs and discover the ultimate playground.

"The result is a fairytale landscape," one guidebook gushes, "a child's delight, where dwarves, elves, fairies, and other supernatural beings seem to have just stepped round the corner, or perhaps vanished through a little doorway in the rock."

Las Vegas has its own Cappadocia. No, it's not the latest themed resort on the Strip—fake fairy chimneys, bellhops in traditional Turkish garb, and underground high-roller suites would be blasphemous (of course, that's never stopped the casino syndicate before). It's a flood plain in the southwest valley along the Flamingo Wash. Sand hills camel-back across the plain, cliffs stare down at the wash—a swath of gravel, sand, and shrub—and mesas back up against trailer parks.

But this is no "fairytale landscape." As I crossed the flood plain one hellish afternoon, about a week after exploring the "Welcome" Drain, it read more like a horror story. Creosote bushes clawed at blankets. Couches, cushions, and mattresses were camouflaged amid the shrub. Clothes dried on skeletal branches. Walking down the wash, the backpack slung over my shoulder, I sensed that I was being watched not by dwarves, elves, and fairies—but by street people with nowhere better to sleep.

At the east end of the plain, the wash goes under Decatur Boulevard in a triple-barrel storm drain. I pulled up in front of the drain and removed the bottle of water from the backpack. It was 108 degrees … in the shade. Sweat stung my eyes. My throat was as dry as the Ancient Mariner's. Sipping from the bottle, I flashed back to the summer of 2002.

• • •

"Come on, man," I said. "One more stop and we're done."

Hunched in the passenger seat, drenched in sweat, Josh glared at me menacingly. In three hours on that Saturday, I'd gone from a chauffeur to a storm-drain-seeking madman. Josh and I had a story; I could smell it. Now was not the time to go home, stretch out on the couch, and watch another art-house movie.

Strip malls and fast-food joints blurred by the windows. The car went dark under the Union Pacific railroad tracks. Budget Suites … Arville Street … the Orleans hotel-casino. After exploring the pipe in the southeast valley, Josh and I'd just emerged from a storm drain near Tropicana Avenue and Valley View Boulevard. We were blazing west on Tropicana.

"All right," Josh finally said. "But we have to go to Café Espresso Roma after this. I need a fucking iced mocha."

I pulled into a Home Depot at Trop and Decatur, opposite the flood plain. Josh scooped the flashlight and kukri knife from the floorboard. Then we stepped out into the heat, cursing it as we crossed Decatur and angled into the wash.

Standing in front of the storm drain, a concrete slot machine with 10-by-10 reels, Josh and I were in awe. It was the biggest drain we'd seen and, in contrast to the plain, seemed ridiculously dark. Garbage bags and shopping carts cluttered the inlets. We thought we heard voices coming from the dark. Wait, we *did* hear voices coming from the dark.

"Come on in, boys. We'll be waiting for you."

There was a whole new world behind the black curtains, Josh and I realized, a world that neither one of us could ever really understand. We shifted our feet in the gravel. Jeers from inside a storm drain, rustling in the dark—for two reporters used to covering politics and pop culture from behind their desks, it didn't get any creepier than this.

"There is a valley in central Turkey called Cappadocia," wrote Josh in the first *CityLife* story, "where ancient Christians dug hundreds of miles of catacombs to hide from the Romans, who were quite intent on nailing them to trees. Some of these catacombs run for thirty miles or more. As you crawl through them, you find friezes of the Virgin Mary and the occasional coin with the face of Augustus—strange reminders that some poor bastard actually lived here, hiding from the Man (personified in the third century by the local Roman legion).

"Looking into the tunnels, it wasn't hard to imagine what it might have been like to be the poor son-of-a-bitch centurion who had to go into the catacombs and roust the Christians. Standing at the mouth of a cave, listening to the inhabitants move about. Christ. It doesn't matter how old you are or how well-adjusted you may be. You *will* be afraid of the dark."

• • •

Shaking free of the memory, I returned the bottle of water to the backpack and stared into the storm drain. It was bigger and darker than I'd remembered. Weeds and plastic bags were wrapped around the dividers, as if the last flood had never subsided. There were no cruel taunts, no strange rustling—but I was still creeped out. I just couldn't stop thinking about the bad craziness that Josh and I'd experienced in the drain.

I removed the flashlight from the backpack and approached the south tunnel, the same one that Josh and I'd entered. Two men sat in the shade of the inlet.

Beyond the men, deeper into the shadows, a woman was sprawled across the floor.

"How's it going?" I said, stepping into the shade.

"You going all the way through?" immediately asked one of the men. He was sitting in the middle of the tunnel, wearing a baseball cap, T-shirt, and jeans. His face was sunburned and dirty.

"Yeah, I'm going to try to."

"Why?"

It was a legitimate question, one I'd asked myself several times while crossing the flood plain—one I'd asked myself a thousand times already this summer. "Mainly out of curiosity. I explored a few drains in the summer of 2002, and I've always wondered what else is down there. I finally worked up the nerve to find out. A few weeks ago, I explored a drain that started downtown and opened up near Palace Station. Last week, I explored one that cut under the south Strip."

"You made it out?" asked the man rhetorically.

I smiled. "Yeah, I made it out."

Squinting in the half-light, I surveyed the inlet. A purple-and-silver graffiti tag, which I couldn't decipher, burned across the north wall. Beneath the lettering, empty beer bottles stood like sentries.

"What are you guys up to?" I asked, hoping to strike up a conversation. I wanted details about the drain, updated info that would give me some idea of what lurked in the dark.

"Drinking," said the man.

"Living, bro, living," slurred his companion, reclining against a wall. He was dressed in an unbuttoned shirt, cargo pants, and black boots. Sweat and grease dripped from his shoulder-length hair.

"We don't actually *live* in here," clarified the man in the cap. "We live over there." He pointed toward the flood plain, which shimmered in the heat waves.

I glanced at the woman. She lay facedown on faded newspaper pages, the wall twisting her body violently. She was barefoot, still. It was as if she'd been swept away by a flood and came to rest, lifeless, on this very spot. "Is she OK?" I asked the men.

"Yeah, she's all right," said the man in the cap. "She's just passed out."

"Do you all ever sleep in here?"

"Every once in a while during the day, because it's cooler."

The man's response reminded me of the insulated underworld of Cappadocia, but the thought was short-lived. I was much more concerned with the Las Vegas underworld. What's in *this* tunnel, I wondered? What's in *this* drain? What's waiting for *this* poor son-of-a-bitch centurion?

"What's down there?" I asked, peering into the abyss.

"I have *no* idea," said the man. "I've never gone back there. I just stay *right* here." He patted the floor in a manner that seemed to comfort him, but did little for my composure. I *wasn't* going to stay *right* here—and I was getting some really bad vibes about this drain.

"Back where?" asked his companion, shaking from his stupor.

"Back there," I said.

"Dude, it's a drainage ditch. What do you think's down there?"

In retrospect, I should've answered: "I don't know. Maybe a double-murderer on the lam, a spider the size of a compact car, a hygienic man with multimillionaire relatives, a Vietnam vet who recites poetry—pretty good poetry, in fact—upon request. Dude, the possibilities are endless." But I simply said, "I'm just curious if anybody's back there. I don't want to sneak up on anyone."

The man cupped his hand around his mouth and turned toward the darkness. "Hey!" he yelled. His voice echoed in the depths of the drain. "Hey! Hey! Hey!"

What a prick, I thought. What a certified jackass. Has he not learned any manners in the gutters of Las Vegas? Great. Now every fugitive, junkie, and madman in the drain is awake and on edge. They're stashing their drugs. They're sharpening their shanks. They'll be waiting in the shadows and lateral pipes, anxious to pounce on the inconsiderate bastard who interrupted their first sleep in three days.

"I don't think anyone's back there," said the man in the cap.

"Well, I guess I'll find out," I said, giving up on the men and starting downstream.

"Be careful in there. Be *real* careful in there."

As I melted into the semidarkness, the two men watched quietly and intently. It was as if they expected a great tragedy to befall me right there, 20 feet into the tunnel—a savage beast to suddenly emerge, kill me for food, and drag me into its lair. But they had no such luck. There was no free freak show that afternoon, no cheap thrills. I walked down a straightaway, hit a bend, and disappeared into the sunlight-orange mist.

Around the bend, I cut on the flashlight. Visibility was low—real low. In fact, I couldn't see a goddamn thing. I closed and opened my eyes, hoping it would help them adjust. It didn't. Continuing downstream, right arm extended, I felt as if I were wading through a London fog.

Finally, the backlight faded and the beam of the flashlight came to life. A stream of runoff trickled down the north side of the floor. The walls were gray and grimy. The ceiling, originally flat, now arched in a Gothic style.

The tunnel swerved, then straightened. An intense darkness crashed down on me, like a wave of ink. My eyes were still screwed up, but my ears were working just fine (thank you). Five hundred feet into the tunnel, I could hear the men at the inlet.

"Metro undercover," said one of them, obviously referring to me.

Sweeping the beam across the tunnel, I noticed a hole in the base of the north wall … and then another … and another. These holes, known as equalizers, are designed to evenly distribute floodwater in each tunnel of the drain—and apparently to scare the shit out of alt-weekly editors. Man, were they creepy! I aimed the flashlight into the first one, illuminating the middle tunnel and a matching set of equalizers in its north wall.

The holes looked like the doorways of Cappadocia's rock dwellings—and I was feeling more and more like a sucker centurion.

Beyond the equalizers, the south tunnel connected with a 25-foot-wide arching tunnel that would not have looked out of place in the bowels of Hoover Dam. The tunnel was massive, super-dimensional, much bigger than any I'd encountered in the first two drains. I cast the beam down it, futilely.

"Hello?" I said, startling myself.

"Hello? Hello? Hello?"

I ducked through one of the equalizers and began back toward the inlet in the middle tunnel. Rounding a bend, I splashed through a pool of sludge. Sunlight colored the walls gray, revealing Jackson Pollock-style piss and shit stains. The stench was overwhelming. I gagged, then buried my nose in the sleeve of my shirt.

Exiting the drain, past a 20-foot-tall rain gauge, I took in some fresh air and looped into the north tunnel. Slabs of carpet cluttered the floor. As I stepped over a mound of clothing, a grocery cart materialized along the south wall; the cart contained cardboard boxes stuffed with newspaper. Another cart materialized along the wall; empty plastic bottles and a shopping bag full of broken glass

occupied its well. The scene didn't strike me as a permanent campsite, but as a refuge or the scattered ruins of a camp.

The ceiling went from concrete gray to soot black. Eerie graffiti—"The Eyes Are the Window to the Soul"—covered the walls and tumbleweeds were scattered across the floor. An image of Jesus and the Virgin Mary was plastered to the wall. The image triggered another flashback.

· · ·

After being spooked by the equalizers, Josh and I began down the wide arching tunnel. The flashlight flickered like a candle and offered about as much light—but it was our only hope. If the batteries had died or if Josh had dropped it, all hell would've broken loose. Panic, groping, screaming—we'd probably still be in the storm drain, eating raw crawfish and drinking runoff with cupped hands.

Wide-eyed and arms locked, Josh and I inched down the tunnel. Our hands trembled. Our heads were on a swivel. Soon, the ceiling began to drop. When it got down to four and a half feet, we turned around. As we did, we heard a splash in the depths of the drain.

"There's somebody down there," Josh whispered. "Let's get the hell out of here."

I didn't protest. In fact, it sounded like a brilliant idea. Josh and I picked up our pace. We weren't running, but we weren't lounging around the place either. We ducked through both sets of equalizers and began back toward the inlet in the north tunnel. Suddenly, I smelled smoke.

"Do you smell that?" I asked Josh.

"Yeah," he said.

As we continued toward the inlet, the smell got stronger.

"This is strange," I said.

And Josh had to agree.

The tunnel swung to the south and a long row of shopping carts appeared around the bend. The carts were placed along the wall in perfect order, as if still in front of the supermarket.

"Holy shit," said one of us—or maybe it was both of us.

"Ellis, what *is* this?"

"It's the Blair Witch, man. I have *no* idea."

Josh slowed down and played the flashlight over the carts. We couldn't make out much of what was in them. One contained a leather satchel, another faded T-shirts. There were shoes, household appliances, and God knows what else. We certainly didn't take inventory.

Beyond the carts was a hut—I repeat, a hut. Made of rotting plywood, it had three walls and

Beyond the carts was a hut—I repeat, a hut. Made of rotting
as a curtain. Bicycles, Coleman lamps, and a cinderblock
soot black. On the south wall, the image of Jesus

a ceiling. An Army blanket served as a curtain. Bicycles, Coleman lamps, and a cinderblock grill surrounded the hut and the ceiling of the tunnel was soot black. On the south wall, the image of Jesus and the Virgin Mary blended into the graffiti.

As Josh and I tiptoed past the hut, he angled the beam through the curtain. Two men lay on a futon mattress, wearing only boxer shorts. Josh and I jumped, then began to run as fast as the flashlight would allow. At the front of the camp, we encountered another improvised curtain. As Josh ducked under the curtain, its steel rod caught on his trench coat and scraped loudly across the walls.

"Who's there?" shot a voice from the darkness.

"Sorry," said Josh.

"We're reporters," I said. "We were just passing through."

A man emerged from the hut, like a ghost from a grave. "You see how clean it is here?" he said. "If you want us to leave, we will."

"Oh, no," said Josh quickly. "We're journalists. We're doing a story on the storm drains."

The man approached the front of the camp, rubbing the sleep from his eyes. He was short and thin and his hair was ruffled. "We keep everything very clean," he continued.

"We're with *CityLife*," I said. "I'm Matt. This is Josh."

"I'm Ron," said the man, extending his hand over the curtain.

I shook it and asked, "How long have you lived down here?"

"About a year," answered another sleepy voice.

"That's John," explained Ron, as another short and thin and ruffled man emerged from the hut. The man sat on the edge of the mattress and lit a cigarette.

It turned out that Ron and John had lived in the storm drain for 15 months. They worked odd jobs during the day and returned to the drain at night. They cooked on the grill. They pissed in plastic cups,

plywood, it had three walls and a ceiling. An Army blanket served
grill surrounded the hut and the ceiling of the tunnel was
and the Virgin Mary blended into the graffiti.

which they emptied outside. They kept their tunnel as clean and organized as a suburban tract home, as far as Josh and I could tell.

"Does Metro ever mess with you?" asked Josh.

"No," said Ron. "They know we're in here. They come and check on us, make sure we're OK every so often."

"What about flooding?" continued Josh. "This tunnel must fill up quickly when it rains."

"Metro comes and warns us."

"Sorry to sneak up on you guys," I said. "We didn't know anybody was in here. We were farther back in the drain, just looking around."

"Did you see the troll?" asked Ron matter-of-factly.

"The *troll*?" I repeated, hoping I'd misunderstood him.

"Yeah, there's a troll who lives back there," he continued. "He's been back there forever. But he doesn't mess with us and we don't mess with him."

"And he can see in the dark!" John added, with great effect.

Josh and I fell silent. We looked at each other, then back at Ron and John.

"He has a real long beard," continued Ron. "You don't want to run into him. He can see in the dark. He hides from people. We were walking down there one time and we thought we heard something. I looked into one of those holes in the wall and there he was, looking right at me."

"You're shitting me," said Josh.

"Nope. He was carrying a crowbar and he swung it at me."

"A *crowbar*?" I asked, cringing at the thought.

"Yeah. You don't want to surprise him. He'll bash you with it."

"I *knew* it," said Josh. "I *knew* I heard someone back there."

"He's fucking crazy," said John. "Hey, does one of you have a cigarette?"

After talking to Ron and John for 10 or 15 minutes, Josh and I hustled out of the drain and hurried to the car. We were horrified, exhilarated, and—most of all—curious. A "troll" who lives in the depths

Did you see the troll? ~ Ron

of a drain? A long beard? A crowbar? Could any of this possibly be true? Or were Ron and John just trying to scare us, so we'd stay away from their home? Either way, it didn't matter. Josh and I had a dramatic conclusion to our first story: We'd return to the drain and search for the troll.

．　　．　　．

Following a night of fragmented sleep, I woke early the next morning. I rolled onto my back and stared at the ceiling. For more than 18 hours, I'd been unable to shake the image of the troll—stringy hair, scraggly beard, hairy chest, bent back, and pale skin. I imagined Charles Manson after 15 years of hard storm-drain living.

After showering, I drove to the Home Depot. I roamed its marathon aisles for more than an hour, finally emerging with an armful of items that included a hard hat, a headlight, a Mag-Lite, a Mini Mag-Lite, a clothesline, a snap hook, a four-pack of AA batteries, and a four-pack of D batteries. The cashier eyed the items suspiciously.

"I'm doing some underground work today," I explained, as I handed her my debit card. "Just want to make sure I'm prepared."

Next, I drove to an EZ Pawn. I'd put considerable thought into what weapon to take back into the drain, but had yet to be inspired. A stroll through a Vegas pawnshop, I figured, would spark my imagination. Since Josh and I'd ruled out a gun, noting the ricochet factor and the amplified acoustics, I headed straight to the knives section. It was woefully depleted.

"Do you carry any swords?" I asked a salesman in a professional tone.

"Nah," he answered, as if ashamed. "I'm sorry. We don't."

On my way out of the pawnshop, I cut through the sports section. There, amid scuffed-up fishing poles and pool sticks, I came across a bag of golf clubs. An iron, I immediately realized, was the perfect weapon to take into the drain. It could be used as a walking stick, to flip debris out of my way, to knock down spider webs, and to test the depth of the water. It wasn't as intimidating as, say, a chainsaw and it had at least a foot on any crowbar I'd seen.

When I picked up Josh at 7 p.m.—we'd decided to enter the drain at nightfall to add to the drama—I was wearing a long-sleeve T-shirt, cargo pants, and combat boots. He was dressed in the trench coat, a black tee, black jeans, and black boots—storm-drain Gothic. As he climbed into the white-boy Camry, I handed him a sheet of paper.

"Sign this," I said, cranking up the Stones and backing out of the driveway. It was a disclaimer, hastily written after a conversation with the company attorney. It read: "I, Joshua Ellis, enter this dark and mazelike storm drain on my own accord. I am researching this story without editorial direction or pressure from *Las Vegas CityLife* or its parent company. The publication is not responsible for any foul or evil misfortune that may befall me during the research. Right hand raised, Joshua Ellis."

I'd written the disclaimer mainly for effect, to fuck with Josh, to get a reaction. And, indeed, it did. He smiled uncomfortably as he read it, as if reviewing his own will, and a bead of sweat splashed down on the sheet. After attempting and failing to secure a higher word rate, he signed it reluctantly.

Fifteen minutes later, I pulled into the Home Depot. *CityLife* Photo Editor Bill Hughes—who'd agreed to follow us into the drain after two freelancers backed out of the assignment—was waiting in his truck, sucking on a cigarette. I jumped out of the car and opened the back door. A waterfall of gear spilled to the asphalt. I picked up the Mag-Lite and put it in a top pocket of my pants. I dropped the Mini Mag-Lite into a side pocket, then picked up a piece of clothesline, threaded it through the eye of the snap hook, and tied it loosely around my neck. I looped the string handle of my tape recorder over the hook. The hard hat found my head. Finally, I gripped the iron and took a few wild practice swings.

"Fore, motherfuckers!" I yelled, prepared to go Tiger Woods on anyone and anything in the drain.

Following a photo session at the inlet, Josh and I entered the north tunnel. Bill, weighed down with gear, followed closely. We immediately encountered two men and a woman sharing a 32-ounce bottle of beer.

"Do you think we'll find anything back there?" I asked them.

"If you're talking about dead people, no," said one of the men.

"We're talking about people *living* back there."

"Just the two guys who live up the way, but they're not home. I don't know where they're at."

"Ron and John?"

"Yeah. You know them?"

"We talked to them yesterday." I paused. Then risking ridicule, I asked: "Do you know anything about a 'troll' who lives in the drain?"

"A troll?" said the man. "Nah, that's bullshit."

"There aren't any weird fuckers living back there?" asked Josh.

"Fuck no."

"That's what Ron and John told us," Josh said.

"You can't believe anything those guys say. There ain't nobody back there."

Josh and I started off into the darkness. Reaching the front of Ron and John's camp, we called out their names. There was no response. Cautiously, we ducked under the curtain and approached the hut. The bikes were gone, the hut was empty, and the ashes of the grill were dead and dusty. I suggested that we wait for Ron and John to return, so we could question them further about the drain and the troll, but Josh surged downstream. Bill and I followed him. Approaching the equalizers, Josh finally slowed down.

"Anyone home?" I asked, kneeling in front of one of the holes.

"Anyone home? Anyone home? Anyone home?"

"We're journalists exploring the storm drains. We're not looking for any trouble."

"We're journalists exploring the storm drains. We're not looking for any trouble."

Josh squeezed through one of the equalizers. It didn't sound as if he got crowbarred to death by a vicious troll, so Bill and I followed. The three of us then looped into a wide arching tunnel that ran parallel to the other arching tunnel. Josh cut off his flashlight.

"Matt," he said, "cut your flashlight off." I did, and the tunnel went dark. "Do you hear that?"

A faint ticking sound echoed in the tunnel. It sounded like a drip or maybe even a clock. I cut on my flashlight and inched downstream. The ticking got louder, but I couldn't place it. It seemed to be coming from all directions.

Bill bailed out, explaining that he wanted to check if Ron and John had returned. Josh and I continued downstream. The ticking got louder and louder. Finally, the beams of our flashlights met on a wind-up clock that was wedged between a rock and a wet piece of cloth. I picked up the clock and wiped off its face. It read 9:35 p.m. I removed my cell phone from a pocket: 9:35 p.m.

"Tick, tick, tick."

•   •   •

Josh and I pushed deeper into the drain, deeper into this mysterious new world. The ceiling rose and sank like a rollercoaster. We smelled smoke—but it wasn't coming from Ron and John's camp. It was nearby, somewhere in the depths of the drain, somewhere in the dark. I ducked through an equalizer and turned upstream in a rectangular tunnel. The smell of smoke grew stronger.

A bowling ball splattered with mud sat in the middle of the floor. Josh and I froze and stared at the ball, as if it were the head of a witch. Honestly, we didn't know *what* to make of this. Perhaps someone had accidentally rolled the ball down a drop inlet, thrown a *gutter* ball—literally. Or maybe a flood had washed it into the drain. Those, of course, were the logical explanations. But why had the ball stopped there, in the middle of the tunnel, unimpeded? And was it a coincidence that the finger holes were facing up?

Questions without answers—that, it seems, was what Josh and I found in the storm drains of Las Vegas.

The sun had fallen behind the mountains and the eastern sky was getting darker. In front of us, across Industrial Road and Interstate 15, stood Bellagio and Caesars Palace, awash in neon. The fabulous Las Vegas Strip, where so many dreams are found and lost. The Strip, where it's never really nighttime at all. ~ Josh

"A souvenir," said Josh, picking up the ball.

"You're going to carry that thing all the way through the drain?"

"Yeah. Why not? I could always take up bowling."

Continuing upstream in the tunnel, Josh and I discovered the ashes of a campfire. A tombstone-shaped piece of plywood, which apparently served as a bed, lay next to the ashes. A piece of rebar stretched across the wood.

"That looks a hell of a lot like a crowbar," I stammered, flashlight fixed on the rebar. Then I announced, "We're journalists. We're not here to mess with anyone. We're just looking around."

"We're average American citizens, just like yourself," Josh muttered.

Kukri knife and golf club poised, we entered a low and wide chamber. Ghoulish graffiti covered the walls. Through square equalizers, we could see into dark and spacious side rooms.

"I'm going to have a cigarette," said Josh, collapsing against a wall. He set the trench coat, kukri, and bowling ball in a pile and lit up.

"This area is creepy, man," I said, sitting next to him and angling the beam through an equalizer. The interior of the drain was a concrete labyrinth, with pipes and tunnels and chambers leading in all directions. Its Minotaur was nearby. Josh and I could sense the beast just beyond the range of our flashlights.

"Hey, listen," said Josh. "We know you're in here. We're not going to bother you. We're just doing a story for a newspaper. If you want to talk, cool. We'll get your story out to the public. If you don't want to talk, that's all right. We won't bother you."

Silence ensued. Apparently, whoever or whatever lived in this area of the drain wasn't interested in publicity. He, she, or it probably had enough problems without the press snooping around.

After hanging out in the chamber for 10 minutes, Josh and I continued downstream. We ducked through an equalizer and found ourselves in a long, long tunnel. Finally, as we turned a corner, we saw a dim light in the distance. The silhouette of a man sitting on a milk crate broke the light. As we approached, he looked at us with a remarkable lack of surprise.

"We're reporters with *CityLife*," I said. "How's it going?"

"Fair," replied the man.

"Sorry to bother you. We walked all the way from the other end of the drain." I extended my hand and introduced myself.

"I'm Eddie," said the man. Josh introduced himself and offered Eddie a cigarette. He politely declined.

"When's the last time you had traffic coming from the direction we just came from?" I asked Eddie.

"About four days ago."

"The guys at the other end of the drain said they hadn't had any traffic in more than three months," said Josh.

"I'm surprised to hear that. A lot more people enter the tunnel from that end than this end. That wash is like a recreation area."

"The guys at the other end said—and I quote—there's a 'troll' living in there," continued Josh, "a guy who hasn't left the tunnel for years and can see in the dark."

"That's possible, but I've never seen him."

Understandably, Eddie was nervous. Josh is six-foot-four in boots and weighs about 300 pounds. I weigh about 200 pounds. Josh was carrying a bowling ball and a knife that could gut a shark. I was clutching a golf club. We appeared at Eddie's back door, as it were, breathing heavily and sweating

like galley slaves. He had every right to assume we were madmen, assassins hired by the casino industry to get rid of the riffraff.

But Eddie eventually relaxed. He told us that he was a "gambling degenerate" who'd lived in the drain for about a year and a half. He even gave us a tour of his camp.

After talking to Eddie for a few more minutes, Josh and I mumbled our goodbyes. We'd had enough. We just couldn't take any more darkness, drama, and confusion. We began down a tunnel, toward the light. Finally, we ducked out of the drain.

"The sun had fallen behind the mountains and the eastern sky was getting darker," wrote Josh. "In front of us, across Industrial Road and Interstate 15, stood Bellagio and Caesars Palace, awash in neon. The fabulous Las Vegas Strip, where so many dreams are found and lost. The Strip, where it's never really nighttime at all."

• • •

Recalling the whole ridiculous adventure—the conversation with Ron and John, the search for the troll, the tombstone-shaped piece of plywood—I washed the beam of the flashlight over the tunnel. The image of Jesus and the Virgin Mary was all that remained of Ron and John's camp. It had been burned out, dismantled, or simply washed away.

Exhaling, I continued into the north tunnel. The walls and ceiling returned to their natural color and, beyond a manhole, the tunnel trended to the east. A row of burned and rusted shopping carts—the same row that Josh and I'd encountered, I assumed—ran along the wall. Glass crunched beneath my boots. The darkness closed around me. The beam cut through it, unveiling the equalizers. I thought I heard footsteps. Wait, I *did* hear footsteps—the crunching of gravel, sand, and newspaper. I cast the beam down the wide arching tunnel. The next few minutes possessed a dreamlike quality: A spectral form stepped into the light. … It took shape as a shirtless, pale, and haggard man. … Head down and arms flailing, he progressed toward me.

"Are you OK?" I asked the man, actually concerned about my own well-being. Was he Ron or John, I wondered? An early Christian? The "troll"?

Mumbling, the man kicked a rock across the floor. It slammed into a pile of aluminum cans, creating a metallic boom.

"Are you OK?" I repeated, reaching for the baton.

While exploring the storm drains—and while lying in bed late at night—I was haunted by my fears. Naturally, I worried about being trapped in a tunnel and a rainstorm sneaking over the mountains. I worried that I'd catch a waterborne or mosquito-transmitted disease, like West Nile Virus or something even deadlier. And I worried—really, really worried—about encountering a madman in the middle of a drain. I was so consumed by this fear that I'd practiced holding the flashlight in my left hand and swinging the baton with my right, in my living room and to the detriment of more than one lamp. Now, it appeared, I was going to put that practice to use. Now, it appeared, my worst fear was being realized.

Drawing near, the man looked up. "What?" he grumbled.

"Are you *OK*?"

"Yeah. It's hot outside."

I paused, interpreting the random statement. "Yeah, it feels pretty good in here."

The man pulled up beside me. He was about six feet tall—all bones and muscle—and wore jeans, a belt, and dirty white sneakers. His sharp nose supported square-framed glasses.

"Do you need some water?" I asked the man.

"I have water," he said.

"Do you live down here?"

"Why? You the police?"

"No. I'm just curious."

"About homeless people?"

"About what's underneath the city."

"It's about a fifteen- to twenty-degree difference," said the man. I couldn't tell if he was drunk, high, mentally ill, or some combination of the three. "Heat rises."

"Yeah, you can really feel the difference."

"At Christmas, I was stupid," he continued. "I stayed down here and the floodwater pushed even the bricks. There was about this much water in here." He motioned toward his hairy chest.

"On Christmas?" I asked, stunned by the cruel irony.

"Remember Christmas? It rained all day long. The water pushed me from here to about fifty yards down there. I hit a sandbar and went to Arville on my knees. I had quarter-inch lacerations."

"Where were you camping?"

"In the middle tunnel."

"You didn't know the rain was coming?"

"I did, but I messed around. It took both my carts away. I was doing about twenty-five miles per hour. Every time I tried to stand up, it knocked me down."

"You rode the flood all the way to the other end of the drain?" I asked incredulously.

"Yeah. I got down to the end and pushed off one of the walls. When I got about seventy-five feet out of the tunnel, I was grabbing bottles, sand, and rocks. I finally made it over to the embankment."

"And you still live in here?"

"As soon as I see clouds and it starts raining, I get out."

"What do you do at night, when you can't see the clouds?"

"I listen. I can hear the rain. I'm not saying I wait till the wall of water comes, but I can hear it when it goes through the manholes and the pipes. You can hear it dripping."

I aimed the flashlight down the wide arching tunnel. Water stained the walls, creating a procession of ghastly shapes and figures. A stream of runoff parted the floor, which was otherwise dusty and dry, then disappeared into the darkness.

"Another tunnel runs on the opposite side, right?" I asked the man, explaining that I'd explored the drain a few years back.

"Yeah, look," he said, accessing an alley between the three 10-by-10 tunnels and the two wide arching tunnels. He removed a flashlight from a pocket and aimed it down the south tunnel. "Even the Mormons have been in here."

"Missionaries? When?"

"Last year."

"Were they trying to convert people?"

"No, no, no," said the man, walking back to the north tunnel. "They just wanted to see what was down here. They can't convert me. They can't get past Revelations Nineteen and Twenty. Revelations Nineteen and Twenty say that anything added to or taken away from the book of life is a lie. It's the synagogue of Satan. Well, their book has been added to."

As I tried to make sense of what he'd said, the man began walking down the tunnel. I followed him. Sure, he seemed a bit odd and perhaps even psychotic— but any company, even a mumbling madman, was welcome in *this* storm drain.

"Does anyone else live in here?" I asked, still wondering about the troll.

"This one guy who babbles to himself. He's got a beard and his name is Moses. He's a paranoid schizophrenic."

"Sounds dangerous."

"The only dangerous people down here are the cops."

"How often do they come down here?"

"Only when they're looking for somebody, a dangerous criminal or a rapist. They came down here once looking for this black dude named Donte. They took a sample of his DNA with them."

Before I had a chance to ask about Moses and Donte, and their concrete inferno, the tunnel swung to the north. Three shopping carts, one of which was covered with a blanket, appeared around the bend.

"Is this your stuff?" I asked the man.

"Yeah."

"What's in the covered cart?"

"A dead body," he snarled. I laughed uneasily.

The man approached the cart and pulled back the blanket. The well contained canned goods, bottles of water, and a stack of adult handbills. A silver baton sat in the seat.

"Is that an expandable baton?" I asked. "For protection?"

"No," said the man, stepping between two of the carts and rounding a futon mattress. "But check this out." He reached behind the mattress and removed a steel staff that was six feet long, three inches thick, and very medieval. "I'm going to kill that motherfucker up there."

"Who?" I asked, backing away.

The man didn't respond and I didn't pursue the subject. I didn't want to get too nosy. I didn't want to know too much. That, it seemed, is a good way to go missing in the storm drains of Vegas.

"So this is where you sleep?"

"I got to watch people," he said, alluding to the camp's strategic location on the bend. "I don't trust these fuckers in here."

As my flashlight followed him, casting grotesque shadows on the wall, the man placed one of the carts parallel to the foot of the mattress. He angled another cart at the head. Finally, he set the last one along the side. This created a bunker of sorts, depicting how he sleeps.

"You must get spooked in here," I said, looking up and down the tunnel. There wasn't a beam of sunlight within a quarter-mile.

"Why? I can hear every noise in every direction. The only thing I worry about are the drunks and the idiots who come down here to see if they can victimize somebody. That's the only reason someone would be down here: alcohol, drug addiction, or mental illness."

"What's your name?" I asked the man.

"Jim," he said, extending his hand.

"I'm Matt." I shook his hand and finally felt somewhat at ease with the man. He wasn't a madman, a Christian, or a troll. He was just some dude named Jim.

After putting the carts back in their original position, Jim offered to escort me to the other end of the drain. I gladly accepted, suggesting that we follow the route he washed along on Christmas Day. He set off immediately. As we approached a foot-high sandbar, he slowed down.

"Here's the sand dune I hit," he said. He pointed at a divider that split the tunnel. "My bed hit there and I pushed off the wall."

"The flood swept you *and* your bed away?" Visions of Tom Sawyer danced in my head.

Jim nodded, then entered the south tunnel. The ceiling dropped to five feet, forcing us into a crouched position.

"It must've been hell coming through here," I said, breathing heavily.

"I tried to stand up and stop—but the water pushed me over, even with all my experience in here."

"How long have you lived in this drain?"

"About two years. Drugs and alcohol have kept me down here."

Another divider split the tunnel and the ceiling dropped even lower. Sunlight angled through a grate, illuminating a low and wide chamber. I recognized it as the chamber that Josh and I sat in while searching for the troll.

"What happened to Ron and John?" I asked Jim, passing an equalizer. While less than five feet high, the drain was at least 50 feet wide. It was a stark contrast to the first two drains I'd explored, which were relatively tall and narrow.

"They moved out," said Jim.

"Do they still live underground?"

"No. They moved to Green Valley or somewhere like that. Then John died. I think Ron moved back East."

"How'd John die?"

"I think his heart just stopped. He just slowly deteriorated and died."

The ceiling began to rise and the chamber tapered into a 10-by-8 tunnel. "Why'd they move out?" I asked Jim, following him into the tunnel.

"They ripped off a bunch of people in here. I don't care if you are a cop. That's what happened." He stopped under a vaulted section of the ceiling. "Here's the Orleans," he said, looking up.

Somewhere overhead, sunburned tourists lounged by the pool and sipped margaritas from oddly shaped cups; silver-haired women tugged on slot-machine handles, while smoking cigarettes and sucking oxygen from wheeled tanks; and baggy-eyed men beneath big hats consoled each other in the sports book. Millions of dollars a day were being exchanged above Jim's $2 camp.

"How'd you discover this drain?" I leaned against a wall and reached for the bottle of water.

"I was coming up here to go to Tropicana, because I usually go down Trop to hit the Strip. I look for [slot-machine] credits. Anyway, where I was living at the time, I kept getting messed with by the police. I just got tired of it. So when I saw this tunnel, I decided to give it a try. I found it by accident, really."

"You've obviously become acclimated to it," I said, noting that his flashlight was off when we met.

"That's because I could hear you. I don't have infrared eyes or anything."

"Who did you think I was?"

"You sounded like a cop. 'Are you *OK*?'" he mocked, continuing downstream.

As Jim and I rounded a bend and began down a straightaway, a faint light appeared in the distance. Jim disappeared through an equalizer in the south wall. I followed him, entering another 10-by-8 tunnel.

"So how'd you end up living down here?"

"I abused drugs and I didn't do anything with my life. I kept doing dope. I didn't make a decision to stop. I finally quit smoking crack, because I almost died. Now I got to get off the meth.

"I'm not a derelict," he continued, pulling a T-shirt from his back pocket and slipping it over his shoulders. "I'm not an ax murderer or anything like that. I don't hurt anyone. I just didn't make a decision to quit all the drugs and move on with my life. I'm not ignorant. I'm not stupid. All this is common sense: If I quit the drugs and alcohol, I get out of the tunnel.

"I've worked. I worked for Valley Bank. I worked for Steve Wynn's Golden Nugget, Caesars Palace, Holiday Inn. I serviced fire extinguishers. It's not like all of a sudden I wound up in the tunnel and I've never worked a day in my life. That's what some of these other idiots in here will tell you about themselves.

"It's all about motivation, about going to school. I want to be a veterinarian, but I have to get off my lazy ass and make a decision to do it. I have to say, 'Hey, enough is enough. Fuck the drugs. I don't need this shit.'"

A divider split the tunnel, creating two smaller tunnels. The sunlight silhouetted grocery carts, cardboard boxes, bicycles, headboards, and dressers—a storm-drain skyline. Jim veered into the south tunnel.

"Hey there," he said, approaching a headboard. A man in boxer shorts was stretched across a queen-sized bed, eyes closed. "Don't bother him. Let him sleep." The bed was complete: frame, box spring, fitted sheets. It looked like it had been wheeled out of a five-star resort and straight into the storm drain.

The ceiling of the tunnel began to drop. I heard the rush of traffic overhead on Arville Street. Then tall weeds and a rock embankment came into focus through the outlet. Finally, Jim and I exited the drain.

The sun was psychedelic, an intense shade of yellow. The sky was an exaggerated blue. I shielded my eyes with my right hand, cowering like a vampire out of the coffin, and squinted to the east. The wash straightened toward the Rio hotel-casino, then disappeared around a bend. To the west, on the other side of Arville, stood the Orleans.

"The water came through the wash all at once," said Jim, continuing his tale. "It carried me about seventy-five feet out of the tunnel."

"Which tunnel did you come out of?" I asked, scanning the drain's seven outlets.

> **"**

I'm not a derelict. I'm not an ax murderer or anything like that. I don't hurt anyone. I just didn't make a decision to quit all the drugs and move on with my life. I'm not ignorant. I'm not stupid. All this is common sense: If I quit the drugs and alcohol, I get out of the tunnel. ~ Jim

Jim walked over to one of the middle tunnels. "This one right here. I had my bag over my shoulder. I had my flashlight. I had to let go of two other bags. I was grabbing boxes, beer bottles, anything—on my hands and knees in the water—just trying to get over to the bank. The water was coming through here real strong." He ducked into the tunnel and started back into the drain. "Anything else you want to know?"

"Do you think any of the other guys would talk to me?"

"Maybe those guys over there." He pointed at the north wall. "Some of the people down here are cool. Just don't shine the flashlight on them."

Jim and I walked deeper into the drain, deeper into the shadows. We entered a 10-by-8 tunnel, then ducked through another equalizer. He pulled up at the edge of the darkness.

"It's pretty neat down here," he concluded, in true tour-guide fashion. "It's cooler than outside. It gets too hot out there. And you're not in anybody's business, hanging out or loitering. I'm not saying that I woke up one day and decided, 'Hey, I think I'll live in a tunnel for the rest of my life.' I'm here by choice. I just have to make the best of it."

With those words, Jim disappeared into the darkness. I cracked a smile. I couldn't help it. An hour ago, I was convinced he was a madman, a lunatic, some kind of feral beast. But as he cut on his flashlight and began back toward his camp, I realized he was just another person trying to make it in the world—just another

Vegas gold miner who'd only found dust. Just another person who eats and sleeps, who thinks and feels, who dreams and doubts. Just another person who laughs and cries, who loves and hates, who lives and dies.

Turning toward the light, I noticed the silhouette of a man standing in one of the tunnels. He was short and thin. A piece of wood supported by rocks—apparently some kind of makeshift dam—obscured his legs. He appeared to be looking in my direction.

"How's it going?" I said, approaching the man.

"All right."

"I'm Matt. I'm a journalist exploring the drain. Jim showed me around a little bit."

"I'm Eddie." Eddie was dressed in a T-shirt, blue jeans, and sneakers. He had a beard and was balding. I recognized him as the "gambling degenerate" Josh and I'd talked to before exiting the drain. He also remembered me.

"How you been, man?" I asked him.

Glancing toward the light, Eddie stepped over the makeshift dam and escorted me into the shadows. "The past two Saturdays," he whispered, "the cops came down into the wash around four-thirty in the afternoon. The first time it didn't seem like much. But yesterday they seemed mad and I think they pinched somebody—you know, shook them down and made an arrest. First, they put up standing 'No Trespassing' signs on each side of the wash. Then, about a week ago, they stenciled 'No Trespassing' on the front of the tunnel. They're really starting to put the pressure on us."

"Why?"

Eddie paused. "I'll get to that later."

"Did they actually come into the drain?"

"No. They just walked along the front, but they were yelling threats." Again,

Eddie glanced toward the light. "I think it's OK," he said, starting back downstream. "I just don't want the cops to hear us." He stepped over the dam and entered the camp. I followed him, sweeping the beam of the flashlight over a row of shopping carts along the wall.

"There's nothing illegal here," said Eddie, rummaging through one of the carts. "I don't even remember what half of this stuff is. I got food and clothing and stuff like that. Nothing of real value."

A mattress sprawled across the north side of the floor. A pillow, which partially concealed a wooden club, sat atop the mattress. Noticing the beam fixed on the club, Eddie explained: "Every hobo and his grandmother has some form of self-defense, just in case someone creeps up on them in the middle of the night. I usually don't keep it near me, though. If Metro comes in here, I'm hiding it."

A cardboard partition stood at the head of the mattress. "I'm nocturnal," said Eddie. "I go to bed around sunrise and I just got up about ten minutes ago. That keeps the light off me when the sun comes up."

Beyond the partition, along the front border of the camp, was a wooden pallet. "If it rains hard enough, the water will come over the dam and I can throw the mattress on top of the pallet. The relatively small amount of water that comes over won't be higher than the pallet and the bed won't get wet."

"This is interesting," I said, surveying the camp. "This is *really* interesting. Do you mind if I hang out for a while?"

Eddie leaned closer. "Here's what we're up against. If Metro does what they've done the past couple of weeks, they'll be here around four-thirty. I don't want to be sitting here chatting when they start yelling into the tunnel." He removed two milk crates from the well of a cart. Handing me one of them, he stepped over the dam and shuffled off into the shadows. Finally, about 150 feet upstream, he set the crate on the floor of a tunnel and sat down. I sat across from him, holding the flashlight between us.

"At the tail end of 1992, I overextended my gambling problem," began Eddie in a baritone voice. "It's just that simple. I actually lived in a cave at Charleston and Hualapai. I lived in a little cave in a wash for several years where a school is now located. I went back to L.A. when they bulldozed that area and stayed there for a couple of years.

"I came back to Vegas in July of 2000. I lived behind a store at Jones and Trop for several months, until I started having problems with people vandalizing my camp. Then I moved into this tunnel, but toward the other end. I had a camp on this side of Cameron [Street] for a while. There was a drainage grate overhead for the water to come in from the street. Light would come in through there in the daytime—but at night it was pitch black, except for a little street light.

"We had a heavy storm at the end of February of 2001. It came through so heavy that it washed everything out, including the sandbar I was living on. It was the biggest rain we'd had in a while. I was in my camp, figuring I'd be safe up on the island. It was about a foot high. I had my bed and other stuff on it, a whole bunch of milk crates filled with everything I owned. But the water kept rising and rising. It got real bad. The entire island and everything I owned—including my eyeglasses, which I had in a crate—washed away. It got so heavy I was trapped in there for about two and a half hours. I was thinking about climbing up to the grating and screaming for help, because the water was getting deeper and deeper.

"There's a law of physics that says the faster water moves the more buoyant it makes you. I'm not sure what the name of that law is, but it's true. That's why cars wash away when they try to cross flash floods that don't look that deep: the swift horizontal movement adds lift. Well, every time I tried to walk out of the tunnel, I found myself going buoyant. I didn't want to get horizontal and get washed out. So I ended up standing against the wall for two and a half hours, holding onto these metal loops."

"How high did the water get?" I asked.

"The water was never more than knee-deep. But when it hits you at that velocity, it splashes way up and it has the effect of being waist-deep. Plus, it adds buoyancy and makes you feel like you're lifting right off your feet—which you are if you're trying to walk in it."

"So what happened?"

"I waited until the water went down, then walked out of the tunnel."

"Was it tough starting over after losing all your stuff?"

"Like everything in the grocery carts, about ninety-nine percent of the stuff that washed away I found in dumpsters. You'd be amazed at what they throw away. There's more stuff in our dumpsters than there is in all the houses and closets of Third World countries.

"Anyway, I got out of the tunnel and walked around to its east end. Then I spent the rest of that night curled up in front of a building. When the sun came up, I figured the business was open. I got up and moved somewhere else, just waiting for the rain to stop so I could start setting up a camp. When the rain finally stopped, I came back to the tunnel.

"Where my dam is now, there was originally a different dam. It was two four-by-fours with a bunch of rocks and gravel behind it. Those rocks and gravel were what was left of my island and the four-by-fours came from construction they were doing on the tunnel near my camp. It all washed eastward, making a nice natural damn there.

"Well, I walked to the front [of the drain]. It wasn't raining, but there was still water running through it. There are seven tunnels up front and six of them still had water trickling through—but I noticed one of them hardly had any at all. I walked in it and discovered it was the one with the dam. I settled there with a cardboard box that I got out of a dumpster and some plastic to use as a blanket. Then I just went from there."

"How long have you lived in that spot?"

Eddie paused. "About three and a half years. I've lived in this drain for almost four years total."

Noticing the beam beginning to fade, I cut off the flashlight. The tunnel went dark. As my eyes adjusted, the walls gradually turned gray and Eddie's small silhouette reappeared.

"How'd you discover this drain?" I asked him.

"I started sleeping behind an antique store at Jones and Trop. I had a camp set up right outside the back door. Luckily, they didn't open until around ten a.m., so I didn't have to get up that early. But once I did get up, I'd have to leave because they would see me as soon as they opened the door. I simply had to be gone before they opened and I wouldn't have a problem with them. I had to have someplace else to go.

"OK, let me say this now," he digressed. "I'm prone to skin cancer, so I can't be out in the sunlight. I should be out in it as little as possible.

"So I was living behind an antique store and needed someplace to go that was in the shade. I would just come and hang out at the other end of this tunnel during the day. Then I would go out and hit the dumpsters and do whatever else I needed to do. Finally, I'd crash behind the store. That was my oddball routine. That's how I knew the tunnel was here."

"How'd you end up on the streets?"

"Mainly by chasing gambling losses, going broke, and just not having the common sense to plan for the inevitable. I could see it coming. Thousands of dollars in advance, I could see it coming. But I was too dense to do anything about it."

"Why live in here and not behind a business or in a homeless shelter?"

"My main concern right now is staying out of the sun. If I were to go out there right now and take a forty-five-minute walk around the neighborhood, I'd have some scary stuff flaring up on me. I got melanomas and stuff. I don't know if it's in remission or what, but you can hardly see them now—especially in the dark. But if I go out in the sunlight, they really flare up.

"I've had health problems for the better part of ten years, but just recently they've elevated and I'm getting concerned about it—concerned to the point that I don't want to go find out what's wrong. As long ago as '97, I was having symptoms of pancreatic cancer. I'd look at a medical book—it gives you a whole list of symptoms—and I'd have like five out of seven of them at a time. It was scary.

"But in the past two months, the bottom has really fallen out. I don't know what's wrong with me. I'm dragging at half-speed. But since there's no serious pain, I don't even want to know what's wrong. If I ever start really hurting or my ass is dragging so bad that I can't get around, I'll go to UMC [University Medical Center] and see what's up."

Eddie's arms, which had moved to the rhythm of his words, fell still. His head dropped. "What was your original question?" he asked, looking up.

"Why in here and not aboveground?"

"What makes the tunnel different from most places that homeless people live is there's a certain amount of security here. It's a place you can go every night and know it's going to be there. Any place else you go, you're always subject to being

> What makes the tunnel different from most places that homeless people live is there's a certain amount of security here. It's a place you can go every night and know it's going to be there. Any place else you go, you're always subject to being booted by the owner or a security guard or having kids wander by and tear your camp apart. ~ Eddie

booted by the owner or a security guard or having kids wander by and tear your camp apart. [Aboveground] I've been ripped off. I found a bullet in my pillow at one camp. I've been burned out or have had my camp torn up numerous times. Even in here, I've been ripped off a couple times. But in three-years-plus, that's not bad.

"In other places we try to sleep, almost any other place you can imagine, somebody's going to mess with you in one way or another—whether it's a business owner, a security guard, or kids. Kids just have to mess with you. The few kids who've gone by the front of this tunnel and have seen us, they automatically started throwing rocks. It's strange. It's just an instinct sort of thing, I guess."

Eddie's answer reminded me of a *National Geographic Adventure* article I'd read during my research. Headlined "Off the Face of the Earth," the article detailed the desperate existence of Ukrainian Jewish families who found refuge from the Nazis in a system of caves.

For more than a year and a half beginning in 1942, the families—which included toddlers and grandmothers—survived in the gypsum grottos of western Ukraine. They slept on wooden-plank beds. Underground pools supplied water, until becoming contaminated or depleted. At night, risking execution, the men crawled from the caves and scavenged the fields for potatoes.

In the spring of 1944, after discovering a message in a bottle that read "The Germans Are Already Gone," the families finally emerged from the underworld. Some of them had not seen the sky in almost a year.

"Long ago, people believed that spirits and ghosts lived in ruins and in caves," wrote one family member of the refuge. "Now we could see that there were none here. The devils and the evil spirits were on the outside, not in the grotto."

Jews in Warsaw, Poland, suffered through a similar experience.

In April 1943, the Germans began liquidating the Warsaw Ghetto. They planned to do so in only three days, using machine guns and cannons and tanks—intimidation and brutishness and savagery. But the Jewish Fighting Organization (also known by its Polish initials ZOB) was having none of it. Mostly men and women between the ages 18 and 21, with crude weapons and little fighting experience, the ZOB held out for almost a month. Finally, the frustrated Nazis began bombing the ghetto. The battle lost, the buildings reduced to rubble, Jewish survivors took refuge in the sewers.

The sewers of Warsaw were, of course, dark and wretched and miserable. Sewage was waist-deep in areas. While the main line was about six feet high, the tributaries were much smaller and had to be crawled through. Clogs and dead ends were common. Footsteps and splashes drew grenades and gunfire from Germans guards, who were stationed atop the manholes.

Nonetheless, the sewers of Warsaw were safer than the streets. At least they offered *some* protection. At least they offered *some* hope of escaping to the countryside. At least they offered *some* semblance of shelter, as the Allies marched toward the city.

This storm drain is Eddie's rock dwelling, I thought. It's his grotto. It's his sewer.

"When your camp was washed away and you moved to this end of the drain," I continued, "did you have the place to yourself?"

"When I first moved down here, I was the only person on this end. A few days later, somebody showed up in the north tunnel. He was only there a couple days. Then about a month later, a guy moved into the tunnel next to mine. After a few weeks of ignoring each other, he finally came in and introduced himself. His name was John. He claimed he was a chef who worked in some of the bigger hotels making good money. He ended up on the streets because he had a drinking problem. He was living in here, but he had no trouble walking out and going to any bar or restaurant and getting a job. He was qualified for that sort of work. But he kept getting fired, because he'd get drunk and wouldn't show up a week or two into a new job."

"What are the current living arrangements? It looks pretty crowded down there, no vacancies in any of the tunnels."

"It's getting odd. I don't know what's up with that." Eddie glanced toward the light. "I'm the senior guy in here. My friend Charlie, who lives in the far south tunnel, has been in here for two years. Then there's Frank, who lives in the far north tunnel. He's a horseplayer. He only sleeps in here. He gets up in the morning and goes to the casino, plays the ponies, then comes back here at night.

"That was the living arrangement before these other guys started moving in. You had Frank in the north tunnel, Charlie in the south, and me in the third one from the north. We've survived in this tunnel for so long by keeping an extremely low profile. In other words, we'd never leave the tunnel unless we had to. Our main concern was to not get in bad with the people who work at the businesses right outside. It wouldn't be good for us to get in bad with them, because all it takes is one phone call to get us kicked out of here.

"But recently, the other people who've moved in, they hang out all the time. They go back and forth between each other's tunnel, keeping a real high profile. They leave the tunnel and the wash all the time—and I think the people working at the businesses are getting sick of it. I think that's why the cops are putting pressure on us."

"Who else lives down here?"

"Two tunnels to the south of me is a guy named Phil, who I know fairly well. I knew him before he moved into the tunnel. We used to run into each other at the same dumpster, looking for food. He claims he's been shot twice, under what circumstances I have no idea. In the tunnel just north of me, there are anywhere between one to five people on any given day or night. And Phil rotates friends who spend the night with him."

"Have you approached the new guys and explained the situation?"

"Me and Charlie told Phil when he first moved in several months ago that we've managed to last so long by keeping a low profile. We asked him to tell that to the other guys. Finally, Phil asked the new people—nicely, I imagine—to tone it down and to stop going in and out so much. And, basically, they've been doing that. It's really quieted down the last few days."

"What's Jim's deal?" I asked, still unsure of what to make of the strange man I met in the dark.

"Is that his name? The guy in the glasses? We call him Elvis, because he reminds us of Elvis Costello when he was a skinny nerd."

I laughed. "What's his reputation in the drain?"

"He's very odd. He's a wacko—and he knows it. As far as his reputation: a total pain in the ass. When they put up those 'No Trespassing' signs, we got concerned that the more people they saw coming in and out of the tunnel, the worse it'd be for us. Well, he has this thing. Even though he lives way on the other end of the tunnel, he just has to come in and out of our end. He comes in and out more than me, Charlie, and Frank combined. Plus, he's noisy. He thinks nothing of pushing a shopping cart full of stuff through our tunnels.

"The first time I saw him, he was walking from his end of the tunnel in this direction and he went right through my camp and started shining his flashlight on my carts. That didn't go over real well. That's how we got acquainted. I chased him down and asked him not to walk through my camp anymore."

"Stuff like that must get old. Are you anxious to get out of here?"

"Why this routine? Why aren't I screaming and scratching and clawing and biting, trying to get back into everyday life? Why am I in this mess?"

"I mean, aren't there things you *don't* like about living in this storm drain? Aren't there things that bother you or scare you?"

"The weird people," said Eddie. "There was this one guy who would come from the other end of the tunnel late at night, whooping it up and making oddball noises. He was totally whacked-out—a combination of stoned and mentally ill. I would see him with his little wimpy flashlight. He would put it on the ground and start dancing around and making strange noises. I have a four-cell Mag-Lite. I'd pop it on and shine it into the tunnel, and he'd cut loose with this bloodcurdling Indian war whoop.

"There've been similar instances," he continued. "When you hear something coming from the other end of the tunnel, you can hear it when it's a long way off. The one thing that gets me is when I hear rowdy-sounding stuff coming and it takes forever to get here and you just don't know what to expect.

"One night, before I was living on this end, I had a camp set up in the middle tunnel. Before I lived on that sandbar, I lived a couple hundred feet on this side of

Cameron on a mattress. Well, three or four rowdy-sounding black guys came into the tunnel. I'm lying in bed. It's about two in the morning. I hear loud voices coming from this direction, the east end of the tunnel. It sounded like three or four guys, and at least two of them had flashlights. I'm thinking my ass is grass if they stumble on me: rowdy black guys and I'm a little honky all by myself in the dark.

"But nothing came of it. Apparently, they went all the way up to Cameron, just past me, then cut across to the far tunnel and headed back east."

"They never came into the middle tunnel?"

"Nope. They never did."

"What do you think they were doing down here?"

"I couldn't say. I'm just glad it didn't involve mugging little white guys."

Eddie and I laughed, then stood. He stretched his arms high in the air. I stretched my back and legs. Then we scooped the milk crates from the floor and began walking back toward his camp.

"You seem comfortable in here, established," I said. "Where would you go if the cops flushed you guys out?"

"Charlie and I have told each other over and over again that this is the end of the road for us. Each of us has lived in several other places. We have nowhere else to go. If the cops kicked us out of here, I would tell them to take me to UMC or stick me in the jail infirmary. I'd probably die in jail, but I'd have no place else to go."

Squinting toward the light, Eddie stepped over the dam and entered the camp. I followed him, taking one last look at his home—a mattress, a sunshade, and a row of shopping carts full of "nothing of real value." One flash flood could take it all away.

"So how much longer do you think you'll live in here?" I asked him, as I placed the crate into a cart.

"I'm turning into such a zombie," he said, escorting me toward the light. "The barebones nature of this routine is getting to be too much of too little, if you know what I mean. And the truth is I'd love to get out of this tunnel, but I don't know *how* to get out.

"See, what we need instead of stupid stuff like St. Vincent and other shelters is a work program you can get into with some dignity and work your way out of the situation. Picture, for example, a cheap motel that a guy can stay in and also have a job. You could subtract the cost of his room from his paycheck and then just work the other things out from there. What screws people up is when they don't have a permanent address, a place to bathe, or a phone. When they don't have those things, they don't have a place to start."

According to county officials, the homeless population in the Las Vegas Valley is about 12,000. That number, courtesy of a one-night census conducted in January 2005, is low—*way* low. See, the census only counted people who were *visible*. Street people, of course, are largely *invisible*. Some are embarrassed by their situation. Others fear their children will be taken away from them. Most, however, simply hope for some sense of permanence and don't want to be pushed along from place to place.

But they are there … on park lawns in Henderson, in parked cars in Boulder City, under railroad culverts in North Las Vegas, along natural washes in Las Vegas, and in the Cappadocia-like storm drains of unincorporated Clark County.

T o understand the topography of the Las Vegas Valley, look at the palm of your hand. The mounds on the outside of your palm are the mountain ranges surrounding the valley: the Spring Mountains to the west; the Desert, Sheep, and Las Vegas mountains to the north; Sunrise and Frenchman mountains to the east; and the River and McCullough mountains to the south. The concave interior is the basin floor. The lines are flood channels—the more prominent ones representing primary washes—widening and deepening over time.

Like your palm, the 600-square-mile valley is enclosed—except for a shallow groove at its southeast edge. The Las Vegas Wash, which winds across the basin and marks its lowest elevation, escapes through this groove. It empties into Lake Mead, the reservoir created when Hoover Dam plugged the Colorado River in the mid-1930s.

Located in the heart of the Mojave Desert, Las Vegas is devastatingly hot and dry. Its average high temperature in the months of June, July, and August is 101.6 degrees. In the summer of 1944, it suffered through 66 consecutive days of triple-figure temperatures. Its average yearly rainfall is 4.49 inches. (Los Angeles, by comparison, averages 13.15 inches of rain a year; Seattle averages 37.07.) And it often goes months without any measurable precipitation.

But during the spring and summer, air from the Gulf of Mexico produces thunderstorms that release significant amounts of rain in short periods of time. The hardpan desert floor—and all the asphalt and concrete—allows little infiltration. The slopes of the basin carry the water to the lower and more urbanized elevations, destined for the Las Vegas Wash, at speeds sometimes exceeding 25 miles per hour.

Fall and winter typically feature lighter, steadier storms originating over the Pacific Ocean. But those seasons are not immune to flooding.

In 1985, following a series of summer floods that crippled Las Vegas, the Nevada Legislature authorized the creation of the Clark County Regional Flood Control District. The goals of the District, which is governed by a board of directors, included developing a master plan to reduce flooding, regulating land use in hazard areas, and helping fund the maintenance of channels. This was the valley's first serious and coordinated approach to flood control, which had been done piecemeal by various Southern Nevada entities.

Clark County voters—traditionally reluctant to support flood control, while casting ballots under clear skies—approved a quarter-cent sales tax to fund the Flood Control District in 1986. The following year, revenues arrived. Finally, in 1988, construction began on the first project: the channeling of the Las Vegas Wash between Craig Road and Civic Center Drive.

The District has been playing a spirited—and unwinnable—game of catch-up ever since.

Along with the valley, which had a population of 750,000 in 1990 and is now home to more than 1.8 million people, the flood-control system is in constant growth. An intricate web that spans from mountain range to mountain range—like the lines of your palm—it consists of 73 detention basins and 446 miles of channels, an estimated 65% of which are underground. (It's separate from the sewer system.) Another 62 basins and 413 miles of channels are planned over the next 30 years, the culmination of the Flood Control District's master plan, at a cost of about $1.7 billion.

·　·　·

One Saturday night in the summer of 2002, I received an unexpected phone call from Josh. He said that he wanted to explore one of the system's detention basins—the Tropicana Detention Basin and its drainage tunnel, which we'd scouted out earlier that week. He said it would be fun—yes, *fun*—to explore the tunnel at night. Also, he added, we'd be able to climb the fence surrounding it without fear of being seen.

Stretched on my couch and staring at the TV, I remembered the tunnel well. Indeed, it was difficult to forget. Located at the base of a 40-foot-high embankment, it was surrounded by a steel fence that looked like a total bitch to climb. A trash rack—a specialized grate designed to keep debris from blocking the inlet—covered its mouth. Weeds, cobwebs, and police tape draped from the beams.

"Are you insane?" I asked Josh. "It's eleven o'clock."

Josh laughed his maniacal laugh and persisted. Obviously, he was bored or high or simply going mad. He'd lost all control of the assignment.

After some resistance, I agreed to drive Josh to the detention basin and pick him up if he needed a ride home. But, I told him, I was *not* going into that tunnel at this time of night. I just didn't have it in me. I just wasn't feeling it.

Around midnight, I pulled into a stucco strip mall on Decatur Boulevard south of Russell Road. I parked and popped the trunk. Josh scooped his backpack from the floorboard. Then I climbed out of the car, changed into my boots, and removed the Mag-Lite from my backpack, leaving the rest of the gear behind.

Josh and I crossed Decatur and a patch of raw desert, headlights casting our shadows across the scrub. We climbed a chain-link fence, walked down a bank, then angled into an open-air channel, which slithered across the basin like a concrete snake and led to the drainage tunnel. Breathing heavily, Josh stopped in front of the steel fence and tossed his backpack over it. Then, using my hands as a stepladder, he climbed the fence with a grunt and disappeared beneath the trash rack.

"Poor bastard," I mumbled, leaning against the fence and staring into the Great Nothing. I hung around for five minutes, listened for screams, then headed back to the car.

Throughout the night, Josh called me on his cell phone with updates. During the first call, made about an hour after he entered the tunnel, he described a crude camp at the inlet and a stunning view of the Strip at the outlet. The second call detailed a conversation he had with a man named Ernie, who'd lived in a pipe under I-15 for several years. Finally, around 3 a.m., he woke me with tales of low ceilings and mysterious shafts beneath the Strip, then provided a live account of his escape from the system near the Hard Rock Hotel—more than four miles downstream from the basin.

Josh's solo exploration was not included in the *CityLife* stories, as we had plenty of material and a shortage of time and space. But his rambling breathless updates—and the mystery that surrounded them as I lay in bed—stuck with me. I'd always regretted not following him into the tunnel that night. I'd always regretted missing out on that storm-drain party.

• • •

A few weeks after exploring the Cappadocia Drain—I'd transcribed more than 16,000 words of notes, written the rough draft of Chapter Two, and explored three other drains—I decided to follow the trail blazed by Josh. It was Saturday night, Fourth of July weekend. The moon was full. The sky was clear. The pulse of the Strip was palpable from my downtown apartment.

Around midnight, my friend Angela pulled into the strip mall across from the detention basin and parked. I told her the route I planned to take—along I-15, under the Strip at Tropicana Avenue, to the Hard Rock (where my car was parked)—then gathered my gear from the floorboard.

"Thanks for the ride," I said, kissing her on the cheek.

"Be careful," she said. "And give me a call when you get out."

The moon floated in a midnight-blue sky and the Strip strutted across the horizon. In the foreground, embankments sloped toward desert shrubs and water-depth poles and illegal dumpsites. I angled into the open-air channel, following it downstream. Christ, I thought. Just walking across a basin at this time of night is creepy enough. There's no telling what I could encounter: a deranged junkie, a vagrant rattlesnake, a dead body. Where's Josh when I need him? (Probably the same place I was when he needed me.) Is Angela still around? Should I call her on my cell phone and tell her the party's over?

Approaching the tunnel, I noticed that the steel fence was gone. This was a relief. I nearly broke my damn neck climbing the chain-link fence, and I wasn't looking forward to another clumsy attempt. The beams of the trash rack glistened in the moonlight. Crickets chirped in chorus. As I cut on the flashlight and approached the rack, which was supported by three-foot-high concrete columns, something rustled in the dark. It was Cappadocia all over again. Oh well, send in the sucker centurion.

"Knock, knock," I said, kneeling between two of the columns. "Anyone home?"

I angled the beam through a four-by-four inlet, which was designed to slowly drain the basin, illuminating a spacious tunnel. I crawled into the tunnel and stood. A soccer ball sat in the middle of the floor, atop an island of sand. A soccer ball—the ultimate icebreaker, a classic symbol of youthful innocence. But in this dark and dreary tunnel, it was as creepy as a witch's head. I considered kicking it downstream and screaming, "Goooaaal!" Instead, I shuffled around it as if it might bite me and started off into the darkness.

The tunnel swung sharply to the north. I expected a square outline to emerge around the bend, the familiar shape of a campsite, but discovered a long and empty straightaway. Soot stained the walls. Rocks and pieces of plywood sprawled across the floor—the ruins of a camp, I assumed, perhaps the one that Josh had encountered. About 150 feet downstream, an unidentifiable object protruded from the wall and stretched across the tunnel.

The object, it turned out, was a metal strip wedged between the wall and a drainage pipe. It pierced a piece of Styrofoam and nearly touched the opposite wall—a swinging gate crafted by floodwater, I could only assume. Fascinated, I walked around it and into a sharp eastward turn.

Strange shadows lurked beyond the bend. I progressed tentatively, discovering a ceiling grate. The moon drifted above the bars, and the top of a chain-link fence was also visible. Curving with the tunnel for more than 100 feet, the grate—the longest I'd seen in the system—finally yielded to a ceiling black with soot. The grid of a grill leaned against a wall. Obviously, someone had been cooking down here. A soccer ball and a grill, I thought lightheartedly. Now all I needed to find was a Lee Greenwood CD and my Fourth of July weekend would be set.

The next half-mile proved particularly creepy and uncomfortable. I crashed through cobwebs, which tickled my face and hands. The ceiling dropped. The temperature rose, providing the sensation of walking through a heating duct. Every little noise was amplified. The crickets, for example, sounded like a high-

school marching band. I longed for the comforting shafts of light present during the day, but only found dim manholes and shadowy ceiling grates. Every 10 steps, I cast the beam over my shoulder—convinced that someone or something else was in the tunnel, that someone or something else was following me.

Eventually, the rush of fast-moving vehicles drowned out the crickets. The ceiling rose. The temperature dropped. The rush became a roar, as if the tunnel emptied into the Las Vegas Motor Speedway. I could distinguish passing motorcycles, cars, and tractor trailers.

Finally, around another bend, a rectangle of light appeared in the distance. It expanded with each step I took, revealing an open-air channel and vehicles streaking south on I-15. The ceiling, like a concrete curtain, slowly unveiled the

Strip: the orange, blue, and gold turrets of Excalibur; New York-New York's multicolored skyline; the bright-white Monte Carlo. I crouched at the outlet, which was littered with beer bottles and cardboard mats, feeling like Dorothy arriving in Oz.

Snapping off the flashlight, I exited the tunnel. The channel swung to the north and straightened, running parallel to the interstate and the Strip. The contrast was staggering, more intense than the midday Mojave glare. Mandalay Bay, Luxor, and Excalibur soared above the channel's east wall. Bellagio and Caesars Palace stood to the north. Admiring the view, I forgot that I was in a flood channel. A nest of debris along the west wall quickly reminded me.

At the end of the straightaway, a divider created two open-air channels. I angled into the east channel, which burrowed under the interstate in a seven-by-seven tunnel and straightened toward the Strip. My God, I finally realized, I'm about to walk *under* 2,000-room New York-New York and the 5,000-room MGM Grand (one of the biggest hotels in the world). I'm about to walk under 100,000-square-foot casinos, lake-sized fountains, and multi-deck parking garages. I'm about to walk under 12 lanes of burning asphalt—the fleets of cabs, the lumbering charter buses, the hordes of tourists. What would I find under the neon rainbow, I wondered, other than the low ceilings and mysterious shafts that Josh had mentioned? Knee-deep runoff from the fountains, sprinklers, and poker-player sweat? The decomposed bodies of disobedient mob lieutenants? Elvis?

I stepped into the shadows and snapped on the flashlight. Squinting into the

My God, I finally realized, I'm about to walk *under* 2,000-room New York-New York to walk under 100,000-square-foot casinos, lake-sized fountains, and multi-deck cabs, the lumbering charter buses, the hordes of tourists. What would I find under that Josh had mentioned? Knee-deep runoff from the fountains, sprinklers, and

tunnel, I saw the silhouette of a man kneeling along the south wall. He appeared to be dipping a rag into a pool of water.

"Mind if I cut through?" I said, above the rush of the interstate.

"Go ahead," said the man, "but you ain't going to find a whole lot back there."

"How far back you been?"

"A mile or so, I guess. I wish I had a good light, though. I'd go back as far as it goes, but it does get kind of spooky down there."

Approaching the man, who was alarmingly short and skinny, I realized that he was washing a T-shirt in a stream of runoff. He rung out the shirt, snapped it in the air, then hung it to dry on two screws in the wall.

"You know," I said, "that water has all types of chemicals in it?"

"Yeah, I know," said the man, seemingly unconcerned. "It has acid in it, too. If you wash your hands in it, you'll trip for days."

I laughed—I mean, what else could I do?—then continued the conversation. "Does anyone live back there?"

"Nope. I'm the only person who's lived in this tunnel for the last ten years. And there ain't nobody in the other tunnel, either. Trust me. I go through them every day. I don't go very far, but I go through them."

A wet sleeping bag and a suitcase full of soiled clothes, which I assumed had washed into the tunnel, sprawled across the floor. There were cigarette butts, Styrofoam cups, and empty potato chip bags—but no signs of a campsite. "Where's your camp?" I asked the man.

"Right here," he said, removing the shirt from the screws and exposing a lateral pipe. I aimed the flashlight into the pipe, which was about three feet from the floor and three feet in diameter. Its midsection was beige and contained a duffel bag, a piece of cardboard, and a candle. Thirty feet long, it dead-ended into an alcove choked with garbage bags.

In a friendly Southern twang, the man explained that he sleeps in the midsection of the pipe and painted it beige so he could detect black widows (which really give him the creeps). The piece of cardboard, he said, serves as a mattress and the candle as a reading light. The garbage bags contain blankets and winter clothes.

"Ernie?" I presumed, feeling like Henry Stanley when he met Dr. Livingstone in Africa.

"Yeah," said the man, trying to place me.

"I'm Matt. I'm a journalist with *CityLife*. A couple years ago, I co-wrote two stories on the storm drains with a guy named Josh. He came through here one night and talked to you."

"I remember Josh," said Ernie enthusiastically. "How the hell's he doing?"

"He's doing all right," I said. "He's doing OK."

I went on to explain that Josh and I'd considered expanding the *CityLife* stories into a book, but ultimately decided against it: Josh was moving to San Francisco; we had different visions for the book; and having heard of married couples who got divorced while working on books together, we figured we'd probably end up killing each other. Eventually, I explained to Ernie, Josh passed the project off to me, with the understanding that if I got a book deal, I'd give him a cut of the advance. Well, I got a deal with a local press, gave him his cut, and here I was: 1 a.m., Fourth of July morning, soaked in sweat, streaked in cobwebs, an expandable baton wedged in the small of my back, destined for the bowels of the Las Vegas Strip.

"What's the book about?" asked Ernie, who was dressed in sneakers, jeans tucked into dress socks, and a T-shirt that read "God Bless America." Noticing the flashlight fixed on his socks, he explained: "I ain't no fag. I pull my socks up like that so the black widows don't crawl into my pants."

"The storm drains," I answered. "I'm exploring the drains and writing about my experiences."

"Well," he said, climbing into the mouth of the pipe and sitting down, "what do you want to know?"

"Let's start from the beginning." I checked my hip to make sure the tape recorder light was burning. "How long you been in Las Vegas?"

"I came to Las Vegas on July 4, 1994," said Ernie, who told me he was 44 years old. "I was left at a truck stop by a man I was working with. I'm a professional jockey by trade."

"A jockey?" I asked, assuming that I'd misunderstood him. I'd met former soldiers, bellhops, truck drivers, construction workers, and businessmen in the drains—but not former jockeys. Perhaps he said "junkie," I considered. There seemed to be plenty of those around.

"Yeah, a thoroughbred jockey. And I was a pretty damn good one, too."

His 5-foot-3 and 105-pound frame seemed to validate his story, but I wasn't convinced. "When did you ride?" I asked him.

"I started in '73 and my last race was in '87 or '88."

"Did you race at any of the big tracks?"

"I've raced at tracks all over the place, man."

"What happened?"

"My wife left me. I guess she decided I wasn't what she wanted. Then I got strung out on drugs and started missing races. I've been sober about six and a half years now by the grace of God, but I smoke the hell out of some pot whenever I can afford it. And I gamble. Unfortunately, I fucking gamble."

"What's your game?" I asked, studying his features: receding hairline, protruding chin, ears as big as detention basins.

"Video poker," he said with a guilty smile, revealing that his front teeth were missing. "I'm about to get tired of doing that, though. I'm getting tired of having nothing. Gambling beats drugs any day of the week, but it's a worse habit in some ways. See, the drug man doesn't always got what you want and sometimes he's not at home. But that slot machine—trust me—is there twenty-four hours a day, seven days a week, and it will always take your money. It ain't going to give it back, either."

"

To make a long story short, it seemed like there was never anybody in these tunnels. Being a country boy—I'm from Arkansas—I decided to walk back in here and see what I could find, maybe a treasure chest or something. Coming down off the crack, I walked down here thinking I might find a big old pot of gold underneath the Strip. Instead, I found this little pipe. ~ Ernie

"You were dropped off in Vegas exactly ten years ago today?"

"Yes, sir. I was riding on a truck, moving furniture. I told the crew there was a horse running that I liked and I thought it had a good chance of winning. I asked for my paycheck. They gave it to me and said, 'You got to be back here by three o'clock.' Well, the race didn't run until two forty-five. Anyhow, I made it back at five minutes after three and they'd left all my stuff in this parking lot back here."

"Did you win the bet?"

"Yeah, about four thousand dollars. But I was broke the next day."

"How'd you discover this pipe?"

"I was smoking crack and I didn't want to be around nobody. I'd get scared. I'd get real paranoid. Well, I saw these tunnels and I crawled into one of them. Back then, the floor was all dirt. There wasn't any concrete at all. Well, I'd come back in about ten or fifteen feet and I'd take a hit. Finally, I said: 'Hey, this is pretty cool. Can't nobody see me under here.'

"To make a long story short, it seemed like there was never anybody in these tunnels. Being a country boy—I'm from Arkansas—I decided to walk back in here and see what I could find, maybe a treasure chest or something. Coming down off the crack, I walked down here thinking I might find a big old pot of gold underneath the Strip. Instead, I found this little pipe."

"And you've slept in it ever since?"

"Yep. I was living in here and I got back on my feet a little bit. But I was still smoking crack and had no way of making money, so I started stealing clothes out of stores. Well, I'm not a very good thief. In fact, I'm really bad at it. I got caught practically every time and went to jail for a total of three years. The law caught me many times back when I was doing my crimes and they always gave me the address of Tropicana and I-15. That's my address. That's my home."

"The police know you live down here?"

"They don't know exactly where I live. I just tell them Trop and I-15. But every New Year's Eve, they come down here and tell me to leave. They close these tunnels down. But they tell me I can come back the next day, so evidently they do know that I live in here."

"They close the tunnels down? For security reasons?"

"Could be. I have no idea."

"Do they close them on the Fourth of July?"

"Nope. Not since I've been in here."

"So when you're released from jail," I continued, "you always return to this pipe?"

"Right back here," said Ernie, patting the concrete affectionately. "See, I like to keep to myself. I like my privacy. Nobody comes down here and messes with me, but you can't get a girl down here. That's the only problem. You're just *not* going to get no woman to come down in here. I'm sorry. She ain't coming—not even one of these crack whores. It's kind of sad in that way, but it's a place where I can sleep and just get away from everybody and everything."

"When you go to jail, does your stuff ever get stolen?"

"I never had a thing stolen till about two months ago. They're selling crack at these motels so thick now that homeless people are starting to hang out around here. This is their area. They're in all these other tunnels around here. See, nobody used to know that I live down here. But somebody knows now, because I had my brand-new Nikes wrapped in a plastic bag and they disappeared. My electric razor disappeared, my underwear, my [marijuana] roaches, my cigarette tobacco, my rolling papers …"

"How can you afford brand-new Nikes?" I interrupted.

"By dumpster diving. I find enough brand-new stuff every day to sell and survive, to gamble and eat."

"Does your family know you're living like this?"

"Hell no! I haven't talked to them in years. Well, I talked to my mom this Christmas for the first time since 1979, but she don't know I'm down here. If she did, she'd blow this tunnel up. She wouldn't want me living like this. No way."

I nodded understandingly, then aimed the flashlight into the pipe. It was dark, dusty, and narrow. I couldn't believe that it was someone's *home*. Lawrence's elevated bed, which I'd discovered in a wet drain near the Tropicana, was shocking. Jim's isolated camp beneath the Orleans was super-spooky. But this was, by far, the most mind-blowing living arrangement I'd encountered in the drains. This was, by far, the most mind-blowing living arrangement I'd encountered *anywhere*. "You don't get claustrophobic in there?"

"Dude," said Ernie, climbing down from the pipe, "sometimes I get so fucking scared. I just stay up as long as I can, until I can't stay up no more, and then I crash. As far as just laying back and getting comfortable, I've never been able to do that."

"What about the noise from the interstate?" About 200,000 vehicles a day roll over Ernie's camp. "Does it bother you?"

"I got used to that awhile back. It's like my clock. I can tell the time of day by the sound, when the traffic's getting thick and all that. The only thing that bothers me is the pipe is starting to shake. That scares me. I don't know if it's going to cave in or what, but it's really starting to wobble."

"Were you in here during the flood of 1999?"

Despite its aridity, Las Vegas has a long and ugly history of flooding. In July 1905, two months after the city was founded, a thunderstorm soaked the dirt roads and wooden storefronts and sprawling ranches. (Minimal damage was done, as there was little developed property around at the time.) A series of floods swamped stores and homes, shorted out phone and power lines, and shut down roads and railroads in the summer of 1955. And a July 1975 flood swept hundreds of cars from the parking lot of Caesars Palace, closed down a section of the Strip, and claimed at least two lives.

Between August 1982 and December 2002, at least 19 lives were lost to floods in Las Vegas.

The city's most destructive modern-day flood occurred in July 1999, when three inches of rain fell in an hour and a half. (Remember, the average *annual* rainfall is 4.49 inches.) Sidewalks became streams, streets rivers, and intersections lakes. Washes raged, growing wider and wider as their banks crumbled. Trash cans, newsracks, cars, mobile homes, and people were swept away. The Las Vegas and Clark County fire departments performed more than 200 swift-water rescues and the water caused about $20 million in property damage. A week after the flood, President Clinton declared the county a disaster area.

"Yeah," answered Ernie morosely, "I was in here. Matter of fact, they were doing construction on the tunnel at the time. Steel beams that were telephone-pole-high washed right down this tunnel. Hell, they were bouncing off the walls."

> "It was real dark and loud. There was two people who yelled, 'Help!' But I didn't see nothing, because I got as far back in my pipe as I could. Hell, I was starting to think about trying to dig my way out. I didn't see nobody. I know I heard them, though. I definitely heard them: 'Help!' It's not my imagination and it's not the drugs. It's the truth. ~ Ernie

"You *stayed* in here during the flood?"

"I couldn't go nowhere. I was stuck. I was sleeping. Once you hear the water in here, it's too late to get out. You're trapped."

"How high did the water get?"

"It came right up to my pipe, but it never came in. If it did, I'd be dead. There'd be nowhere for me to go."

"That must've been hell," I said.

"When it first hit, I didn't think nothing about it. I'd been in here during floods before. The water sounds really scary, but it's usually only a few inches deep. I just throw a rock into it. If the rock disappears, I know not to get into the water. If I can see the rock hit the bottom, it ain't that bad. Well, that storm there was bad—real bad. I don't know how the water didn't come into my pipe. And there was no oxygen in here. For some reason, I couldn't breathe because of all the water.

"I stayed in here for two or three days. I had no food, no water. I damn sure wasn't going to drink that floodwater. I was *screwed*. You'd think I'd have something in here for emergency situations like that—but in an emergency situation, you better not be down here or you're dead.

"I've been lucky. I've been real lucky. I've been through three of the big ones in here. I've been trapped in here for days when the rain got too rowdy. I'll tell you what, Matt. I've seen God. Me and God have had some long talks, buddy."

"That must've been a brutal two or three days."

"It was real dark and loud. There was two people who yelled, 'Help!' But I didn't see nothing, because I got as far back in my pipe as I could. Hell, I was starting to think about trying to dig my way out. I didn't see nobody. I know I heard them, though. I definitely heard them: 'Help!' It's not my imagination and it's not the drugs. It's the truth."

"They were swept into the tunnel, underneath the Strip?" I asked, recalling that the body of a homeless man was recovered about three miles downstream from Ernie's camp.

"Yeah, but I couldn't do nothing about it. The water was deep and shit's bouncing off the walls and the traffic on the interstate was real loud. It was scary, bad scary. I'm a good swimmer, but there's no man alive—not even Arnold Schwarzenegger—who's going to make it out of here when the water's coming through like that. Mark Spitz ain't going to do it, neither."

Ernie's experience reminded me of another Holocaust survival story, one with echoes of western Ukraine and Warsaw.

In the summer of 1943, when the Germans began liquidating the ghetto in Lvov, Poland, about 500 Jews found refuge in the sewers, which harnessed the Peltew River and doubled as a flood-control system. That number quickly dwindled to less than 100, as survivors returned to the streets starving, were shot as they tried to float to freedom in the Peltew, or drowned. Rats, diseases, and freezing temperatures didn't make things any easier.

With the help of a Polish sewer inspector, who smuggled in food and information about the war, one group of 10 Jews managed to survive in the sewers for more than a year. Initially, the group lived in a dry tributary tunnel. But after being discovered by a curious civilian, they were forced to relocate to a remote storm basin.

One morning in the spring of 1944, a thunderstorm swept through Lvov. The streets flooded, the runoff raced to the drop inlets, and the basin began to fill. The survivors tried to dam the inlet pipe with pots and clothing, but the water pressure was too powerful. They tried to staunch the flow by pressing their backs against the pipe. This, too, proved ineffective. Finally, all they could do was try to keep the outlet pipe—which attracted a variety of debris—unclogged … and pray.

As the water level approached their chins and the air pocket shrank—indeed, it appeared the Nazis had won again—the rain slackened and the flow from the inlet pipe gradually diminished. The outlet pipe continued to perform. Finally, the floodwater drained away—leaving behind a thick blanket of mud, but taking no lives.

"Obviously," I said to Ernie, "this is a really dangerous place to live."

"A lot of people have brought that to my attention," he said. "Yeah, it's pretty darn dangerous."

"So why don't you move out?"

"The old story is when I hit a royal flush I'm going to leave town," he said. "Well, I haven't hit a royal in five years. So as far as that goes, I may end up staying here awhile longer. But yeah, that's been my goal: Get eleven hundred or twelve hundred dollars and get the hell out of town.

"If I get that kind of money, I'm going to go back to the racetrack. I have no problems on the racetrack. I can explain myself to the people. 'Where've you been, Ernie?' they'll ask me. And I'll say, 'I've been in Las Vegas, living it up in a pipe underneath the Strip.' They ain't going to believe it, but it's a true story."

• • •

The tunnel rolled downhill, as if destined for the center of the earth. The air was heavy and still. I had a long walk ahead of me. I could sense it in the first few steps I took from Ernie's camp, after thanking him for his time and telling him to stay dry. As I weaved around the sleeping bag and suitcase, the beam of the flashlight sparkled in a pool of water that smelled like raw sewage—Ernie's toilet, I assumed. I stuffed my pant legs into my socks, then—holding my breath—waded through the mire. It swallowed my boots and left a watermark across my shins.

The floor dried and I found a long straightaway. White stalactites hung from the ceiling and the walls were wet and grimy. Am I in a storm drain or Carlsbad Cavern, I couldn't help but wonder? What next? Boot-piercing stalagmites? A swarm of bats? Actually, something much more disturbing: '80s-themed graffiti ("Mötley Crüe" and "Love Hurts" and that cheesy Van Halen symbol). Another scrawl, accompanied by a phone number, read: "To Lick Dick Call Jason." I removed the cell phone from my pocket and dialed the number—not interested in the offer, please understand, but hoping to gather some background info on the tunnel and tags. The number rang several times, then transferred me to voice mail. I hung up quickly and continued downstream.

The ceiling dropped to six feet and the tunnel trended to the east. An equalizer punched a hole in the north wall. I ducked through it, entering the parallel tunnel. An equalizer in its north wall exposed a third tunnel and its equalizer a fourth.

The tunnels were each eight by six, wet, and crawling with cockroaches. Judging from the walls and floor, which was footprint-free, no druggies or This was the system's South Pole, its Sahara Desert. No punks or drunks

I returned to the south tunnel and continued into the darkness, trying to keep my knees bent and back straight. But inevitably, my knees straightened and my back bent. (Survival—not posture—was my main concern.) A car seat wrapped in police tape leaned against a wall. I froze in horror. This was either the most bizarre crime scene I'd ever encountered or the mischievous work of floodwater. Assuming the latter, I shuffled around the seat. The walls closed in on me. The ceiling sank. It felt as if the entire weight of the Strip was pushing down on me.

Beyond a mural-like pattern of mold, the south tunnel merged with the parallel tunnel. I aimed the flashlight up the parallel tunnel, discovering a ladder. The ladder, wreathed with debris, led to a 15-foot-high manhole shaft cluttered with cobwebs. Standing beneath the shaft, I thought about the survivors of Lvov.

In the summer of 1944, after the Russian army pushed the Germans out of the city, the sewer inspector told the survivors they could exit the system. They crawled through the outlet pipe of the storm basin, squeezed into a lateral pipe, then climbed an opened manhole. The sunlight stung their eyes. They felt for the rungs with their hands and feet, which were severely swollen.

In an apartment courtyard, a crowd gathered around the manhole. Additional spectators looked on from the doorways and balconies. Straddling the manhole and smiling proudly, the inspector pulled the survivors out one by one.

"To the collective sounds of a mixture of horror and amazement," wrote Robert Marshall in his book *In the Sewers of Lvov*, "Socha [the inspector] reached down into the hole and pulled out a dark-colored, filthy creature: an emaciated, foul-smelling, crooked hag, her back hunched over, her hands covering her face from the glare. Behind her, another: smaller, a child, a girl. Again, the back doubled

gangbangers or disillusioned teens had explored this area of the storm-drain system. were allowed. This area was reserved for madmen, maintenance crews, and the dead.

over. Blind. Clothes dark with grime. Then another child: smaller still, a boy, with a look of utter terror on his face."

The survivors entered the sewers on June 1, 1943. They exited on July 28, 1944. They lived in the dark and damp underworld for 13 months—about eight and a half years less than Ernie.

I stared up the shaft. Through the finger hole of the cover, I could see the sky—but nothing else. The only sound I heard was water splashing somewhere in the depths of the drain. All I smelled was mildew. Assuming that I was still west of the Strip, I returned to the confluence of the tunnels and continued downstream. Rusted pipes punched holes in the ceiling and dumped water onto the floor, creating a two-inch-deep stream. I followed it into the darkness.

Judging from flood-control maps and my own sense of direction, I was under the Strip just north of Tropicana. However, the 10-by-8 tunnel provided few clues of what loomed overhead. I saw concrete shafts (plugged manholes, from what I could gather) … not winking neon. I heard gargling water … not the horn blasts of cabs. I smelled mildew … not the exhaust fumes of charter buses. Like the main characters of Jules Verne's *A Journey to the Center of the Earth*, I felt entirely disconnected from the terrestrial world.

Spooked and disappointed, I surged deeper into the drain in search of an outlet. The stream persisted. The graffiti disappeared. (The Crüe rocked and all, but not enough to justify spray-painting its name in *this* ghoulish dungeon.) Judging from the walls and floor, which was footprint-free, no druggies or gangbangers or disillusioned teens had explored this area of the storm-drain system. This was the system's South Pole, its Sahara Desert. No punks or drunks were allowed. This area was reserved for madmen, maintenance crews, and the dead.

The sound of music pulled me from my thoughts. I froze and tilted my head, then inched downstream. The music got louder. Initially, I assumed that someone in the drain was listening to the radio or a CD. (Many of the camps I'd encountered were equipped with battery-operated boomboxes.) But eventually, I fixed the flashlight on a lateral pipe in the south wall. I approached the pipe and put my right ear to it; a pop-country tune eased from the cobwebs, dust, and darkness, as if from a Bose speaker. Assuming the music came from a Strip courtyard, probably on the MGM Grand's sprawling property, I nodded my head to the beat and did a little two-step downstream.

I danced under a vaulted section of the ceiling, sidestepped a divider wrapped in debris (which cut an outline as tall and wide as a grizzly bear), and stopped beneath a ceiling grate that exposed the frail limbs of a tree. Only the sound of rustling leaves trickled into the tunnel, confirming that I was east of the Strip. I slalomed through a chamber that was supported by columns, encountered three 10-by-6 tunnels, and entered the south tunnel. The roar of crashing water greeted me. Startled, I scurried to a nearby manhole and aimed the flashlight downstream. At the end of the beam, I could see water pouring from a pipe in the wall. It sparkled in the light, slammed into the opposite wall, then disappeared into the darkness.

Beyond the pipe—a geyser of sorts that spit out water at random intervals—I discovered a sharp turn. As I began to wonder if it was going to carry me in a circle, as I actually began to get dizzy, it straightened and I heard the rush of traffic. A faint light appeared in the distance. The floor went soft with mud and mosquitoes buzzed in the beam of the flashlight. Through the outlet, which was covered with a hinged grate, I saw two white ducks and the midsection of the Hard Rock Hotel.

I pushed open the grate and splashed into an open-air channel that was about 50 feet wide. The ducks flapped wildly downstream. Above the south wall of the channel, cars flashed by on Harmon Avenue. A man and woman on the sidewalk, cameras dangling from their necks like jewelry, glanced down at me with a remarkable lack of surprise. It was as if they'd seen this kind of shit all weekend long in Vegas.

Gathering my bearings, I turned around. The Fairfield Resort towered over the triple-barrel storm drain and, farther west, stood the Strip. I stared at it in awe, the stream pressing against my boots. Four hours and four miles ago, in the Tropicana Detention Basin, I'd viewed the Strip from the southwest: Mandalay Bay, Luxor, Excalibur. I now viewed it from the east: Aladdin, Paris, Bally's. It was a strange sensation, as if I'd crossed a great river or mountain range and was looking back at it triumphantly.

Turning to the east, the stream spilled over a ledge and into a foamy pool of water. The ducks drifted in the pool, jerking back and forth in a paranoid manner. I had no idea what these beautiful birds were doing in this mud hole—but, I conceded, their presence certainly made a hell of a lot more sense than mine.

Unable to determine the depth of the pool, I climbed out of the channel and walked along the north bank. My boots were as heavy as cinderblocks. My neck and armpits were cold with sweat. The sky was black, the moon shining down on me like God's flashlight.

After rolling under a driveway, the channel disappeared beneath the Hard Rock in three 15-by-6 tunnels. The stream trickled into the south and middle tunnels. I entered the north one, discovering couch cushions and cardboard mats. Farther downstream were mattresses and sleeping bags and mounds of clothing. I weaved around the bulges, looking for bodies. I found one along the south wall, wrapped in blankets and as still as a mummy. Near the outlet, I discovered another—shoes stuffed under its pillow, so they wouldn't be stolen.

Beyond the shadows, on the other side of the Hard Rock, an open-air channel swung to the east and slid under Paradise Road. I glanced up at the sky, which was turning purple, then looped into the middle tunnel. Champagne bottles, hypodermic needles, and empty cigarette packs were strewn across the floor. Blankets and towel-pillows formed makeshift beds.

This was the meanest, most brutal skid row I'd ever seen—and right beneath the hippest hotel-casino in Las Vegas.

I weaved into the third tunnel, a breeze drying the sweat on my face. The stream dribbled along the south wall, sadly. Tumbleweeds, newspapers, and aluminum cans were swept across the north side of the floor. As I approached the outlet, glass crunching beneath my boots, a blue laser beam shot from the darkness and blinded me.

"OK," I said, lowering the flashlight. "Now we're even." The beam disappeared and my eyes slowly adjusted. Continuing downstream, I noticed a man along the north wall peering out from underneath a blanket. "Sorry to bother you," I said. "I'm not a cop. I'm a journalist. You got a second?"

"I don't know," said the man, setting something off to the side.

"What's that?" I asked him, making out what appeared to be the blade of a kitchen knife.

"That's for protection. I'm just putting it away." The man rolled over on couch cushions and stopped on his side. "Yeah, sure. I got a second."

Approaching the man and sitting on a nest of newspapers, I introduced myself.

"I'm Cary," he said, "like Cary Grant."

Compared to Ernie, Cary seemed like a giant. His midsection bulged beneath the blanket and his feet hung off the makeshift bed. His nose was hooked and prominent, his head big and balding. "I look Italian," he later told me, "but I'm actually Jewish."

"Do you live in here?" I asked Cary, noticing a book and bottle of cologne at the foot of the bed.

"Yeah."

"For how long?"

"I stayed in another tunnel for a while, then moved in here about nine months ago."

"What other tunnel?"

"The one across from Starbucks [at Paradise and Flamingo Road]. It's right up the street."

"Do people live in that drain?"

"Yeah, a whole bunch of druggies. Some guy told me the cops are down there all the time, because the people are doing drugs and causing a commotion. But I think they cleared a lot of those people out. They did the same thing down here. The cops don't come down here often, but they did a few weeks ago. A bunch of people moved in and were living right at the front of the tunnels. I guess Hard Rock security called the cops and those people were forced to move out."

"How many people were in here?"

Cary counted aloud, stopping at 15.

"How many are in here now?"

"About eight. But three or four of them are heroin addicts, so they're only in here every few days. I don't like it when they're around. They leave their needles and everything out. They don't ever clean them up. I almost stepped on one once when I was barefoot. The cops call this place 'Heroin Alley.'

"I used to live down here with my old lady, but we split up about two months ago," continued Cary in a New York accent. "She turned into a crack whore and I sent her on her way."

"The two of you lived in this drain together?"

"Yeah. We used to live on the other end of the drain in a different tunnel, but then a guy named Dale moved in. My old lady and I used to screw down there, so we moved over one tunnel."

"Do you do drugs, too?"

"Yeah. Don't everybody?"

"What do you do?"

"I smoke crack. But I need to get off that shit, so I'm going to move to a place where they don't have so much of it. I need to get away from Las Vegas for a while. When I get cash in Vegas, I just want to do drugs. It's a rush. My body starts shaking and I got to have it. I can have no money on me all day and I won't get high. But as soon as I get ten dollars, I go running for it. That's the thing about crack. You can smoke it all day long. There's never enough. Even if you're a millionaire, it'll break you.

"I've done a lot of different drugs over the years, but I don't drink. I got involved with her because I was in love, and I ended up doing drugs. Now it's over with her. I'm just waiting to get an ID. I'm supposed to get it Monday. I'll be out of here soon."

"You're leaving the tunnel?"

"Yeah. I'm going to get a job and find a better place to live."

"What arc you going to do?"

"I'm going to work banquets. I've also played poker and claimed credits."

"What do you do for money now?"

"I look for credits on the machines."

"I hear you can make pretty good money doing that."

"It varies. But lately, it's been terrible."

"Why's that?"

"They have these new machines that make it tougher to leave credits behind. Also, you end up getting eighty-sixed out of a lot of these casinos. It's not easy. But at casinos that get a lot of foreign tourists, like Paris and Bally's, you can make big money. No kidding. They'll leave eighty, a hundred, sometimes a hundred and fifty dollars in a machine. They'll hit a jackpot and leave four or five hundred dollars behind. They don't know what the hell they're doing."

"What's the biggest score you've had?"

"The biggest one recently was eighteen hundred dollars. It wasn't here, though. It was in Laughlin. I take trips down there sometimes. Somebody in the Flamingo hit a jackpot and just walked away. The machine wasn't making any noise, but I saw that it read 'Jackpot.' Then I looked and saw that it wasn't paid out. I didn't have my ID, though, so I called my old lady over and she claimed it."

"What's your biggest score in Vegas?"

"The biggest one I caught here was a thousand dollars. It was at New York-New York. I walked in there at about three in the morning. I was looking for my old lady, because she was out running around. A grand was sitting in one of the machines. Someone had hit the bonus and walked away.

"Let's say they're playing the Wheel of Fortune machine," continued Cary, right arm under his chin. "They hit the bonus spin for a thousand dollars and they still have eighty credits sitting in the machine. The attendant hand-pays them a thousand dollars cash. And when they get paid, they walk away all excited and leave the credits behind."

"When you're claiming, do you get dressed up so you don't stand out?"

"Not everyone does, but I do. I change my clothes. If you don't dress nice and you're in the Bellagio or Caesars Palace, you really stand out. Security can tell the difference between a five-dollar shirt and a five-hundred-dollar shirt. Also, I try to shave every day. I comb my hair.

"But this weekend, security's too busy to worry about credit hustlers. When they're bored, they come after you—and they know who you are. But if you're cool and you don't bother them or the guests, you'll be all right. The problem is some credit hustlers steal purses and rip off the guests. They're asking for trouble."

"What casinos do you hit?"

"I walk from casino to casino. If one's dead, I go on to the next. If it's busy, I stick around. I start here at the Hard Rock and go all the way down to Mandalay Bay. I put my headphones on and get ready to walk a long way. You also got to know how to make all these other moves: sneaking into buffets, getting free coffee and soda, stuff like that. The Four Seasons gives out free coffee and cake every morning. That's where I get my newspaper. Later this morning, I'll get up and go to the Hard Rock. They give out free breakfasts. I walk in there, act like I know what I'm doing, and they don't know if I'm a guest or not."

Voices echoed in the tunnel. I turned toward the outlet, discovering a dark-blue sky and a group of tourists on Paradise Road. I cut off the flashlight and moved closer to Cary. "You're one of the few people I've met who's lived in a drain with a woman. How'd she react to being down here?"

"She actually showed *me* the drains and how to live in them," said Cary. "Here's how it was. We used to make really good money and get a hotel room. Then she got hooked on crack and stopped wanting to spend money on a room. Even when we were living down here, we'd get a room once or twice a week when we made a score. She didn't even want to do that anymore. She didn't want to go to the movies anymore. She didn't want to eat with me anymore. All she wanted to do was drink beer, smoke crack, and play the machines. I was so in love with her that I went along with it—until it got to the point where I thought, though I didn't really want to believe it, she was doing all these other things for crack.

"I kept hearing rumors on the streets. I asked this one guy about it, but he lied to me. Turns out he was one of the guys she was getting together with for the crack. But a few of the hookers told me what was going on. They told me what was up. They were like, 'Yeah, you didn't know?' And that was it. I was finished with her."

"She was hooking for crack?"

"Yeah, that's what she was doing when we were running around. That's what she was doing when we were together." Cary's head dropped. He stared at one of the couch cushions and picked at some lint. After flicking it to the floor, amid the glass and dust and broken dreams, he looked up.

"She showed you the drains?" I said.

"Yeah. I didn't even know about these damn things. She showed me that one up the street.

"See, I went to jail for twenty-one days for trespassing. I would've been out in a couple days, but I had to open my big mouth to the judge. When I finally got out, she met me and said: 'Let me show you where I'm staying. We can stay there for free.'

"At first, she was staying in this big box behind a hotel. But then management discovered us, so she took me down to that drain and said: 'Let me show you another spot.' She walked right into the tunnel."

"Isn't that drain wet?" I asked, recalling its algae-lined outlet.

"Not all the way back in one of the tunnels," said Cary. "You have to find the right spot in there."

> **"**

One night she said she heard something. She said she heard
something moving around in the dark. I'm going, 'You're crazy.
There ain't nothing in here.' Then I cut on the flashlight and saw
all these little lobsters swimming around. You ever seen them?
The crawfish? They get pretty damn big. ~ Cary

"What'd you think when she walked into the tunnel? I would've freaked the hell *out*."

"I didn't have any money when I got out of jail, so I said: 'OK.' And we weren't staying there that often. We were getting hotel rooms a few nights a week. But then it got worse and worse. She just wanted to spend all our time and money on crack."

"Why'd you all move out of that drain?"

"One night she said she heard something. She said she heard something moving around in the dark. I'm going, 'You're crazy. There ain't nothing in here.' Then I cut on the flashlight and saw all these little lobsters swimming around. You ever seen them? The crawfish? They get pretty damn big. Well, that was it. We got the hell out of there, and she ran right over to the Hard Rock. She was hustling over here. I came looking for her and I saw this drain."

"What was her hustle?"

"She had a really good hustle," said Cary, succumbing to a smile. "She probably still uses it today. She would tell people that she came to Las Vegas to get married and that her fiancé left her here. She had no money, she would say. She needed to get back home. A lot of people would give her twenty, forty, fifty dollars. One day, a college kid at the Bellagio gave her two hundred dollars."

"How'd you all meet?"

"I was playing poker at Boulder Station and she was working at the Burger King there. I asked her, 'How much money do you make a week?' She wasn't even making two hundred dollars. I said, 'Come live with me, sweetheart. I'll give you two hundred dollars a week—and that's just spending money.'

"I took her out of there. I was in love. I don't know what it was about her. She wasn't even that pretty then. I bought her clothes and made her grow her hair out and all that stuff. And there's a twelve-year difference in age between us. She's younger than me. I'm almost fifty now."

"Where were you living at the time?"

"I was living with my mom in a mobile home, but I was making pretty good money playing poker. She moved right in with me and my mom. That's how the relationship got started. That's how we started going out."

"How long did you all go out?"

"Seven years. Seven years we were together. But she's hooked up with some older guy now, who I guess she's having sex with. I assume they're having sex, because he's been giving her money for dope. But she's just using him. I know that for sure. When she first hooked up with him, she'd come down here and bring me dope. She even said, 'I'm just using him.' She came down here because she missed me."

"When was the last time you talked to her?"

"About three weeks ago, but I hear about her all the time. She's always asking about me. She wants to get back together. She wants to keep doing what she's doing and also be with me."

"Do you think you all will ever get back together?"

"I'll probably love her for the rest of my life," said Cary, as the rectangle of light at the end of the tunnel grew brighter and brighter. "But I told her, 'If you keep doing what you're doing, we'll never get back together. We'll never be like we were. We'll never be close.'

"So, yeah, I think it's over. I think it's over because she doesn't want to change her ways. I think it's over because I want to get off the drugs and off the streets. I think it's over because I want to get my life back."

As I stood and stretched my legs, I secretly doubted that Cary would get his life back anytime soon. He was in as deep as anyone I'd talked to in the drains: unemployed, no ID, a police record, drug-addicted, heartsick. He'd broken a golden rule—never fall in love in Las Vegas—and he was suffering the consequences. From his crude camp underneath the Hard Rock Hotel, he could see everyday life flashing by on Paradise Road—credentialed conventioneers, uniformed casino workers, rush-hour traffic—but it was all much farther away than it appeared. You don't just walk out of the storm drains of Vegas and find a nine-to-five. You don't just drop the kitchen knife, roll off the couch cushions, and shed 30-year addictions like old skin. You don't just lose the woman you love to the streets and forget about it the following morning. These things haunt. These things scar. These things take months, years, *lifetimes* to leave behind.

I considered all this as I wished Cary well, shuffled upstream, and climbed out of the open-air channel at the driveway bridge. As I found my way onto Harmon Avenue, reached for the cell phone, and dialed Angela's number. As the sun broke over the mountains, the cabs streaked by like comets, and the bright lights of the Strip finally began to fade.

T he flood-control map nailed to the wall above my desk was beginning to look like a Jackson Pollock painting. Three-foot-by-three-foot and curled at the corners, it was a swirl of colors: red, blue, green, and yellow creating a variety of shades. Streaks, drips, and spatters formed intricate patterns. To the untrained eye, the map was an ugly accident … an art project gone awry … a meaningless abstract. To me, it was a masterpiece.

Courtesy of the Regional Flood Control District—which had no idea I was actually *exploring* the storm-drain system—the map featured channels, basins, flood zones, streets, and local landmarks. A faded yellow represented the flood zones. Dark blue represented channels and basins that had been completed, light blue channels and basins under construction, and red those to be built in the next 10 years. A grassy green, the legend showed, represented channels and basins proposed in the Flood Control District's master plan.

I'd added my own colors to the map, which was creased and riddled with nail holes along the edges. The Strip and Fremont Street Experience were highlighted pink, so I could get a better sense of what storm drains ran underneath them. The Tropicana, Flamingo, and Las Vegas washes were highlighted blue. (These primary washes, I assumed, would feature the biggest drains.) Red checks—more than 20 total, most of them central, some scattered about the outskirts—marked channels and basins I'd explored. The final touch, the signature of this painting, was a light-brown coffee cup ring (applied when the map was sprawled across my kitchen counter) that circled the Regional Flood Control District logo.

Finishing the rough draft of Chapter Three, I stood and stared at the map. I moved about its edges, like Pollock around the canvas. I zoomed in. I zoomed out. I tilted my head to the left. I tilted it to the right. Finally, I focused on a channel in the south-central valley that merged with the Tropicana Wash at I-15 and cut under the Strip. I was drawn to the channel for a few reasons: Josh and I'd explored a section of it, and I was curious about the rest; I'd just explored the south tunnels under the Strip at Tropicana Avenue, but had seen little of the north tunnels (which were a continuation of this channel); and Ernie said motels in the area were selling crack "so thick" that addicts were living in the surrounding tunnels.

Intrigued, I leaned closer to the map and studied the channel. It was dark blue and green, indicating that part of it was manmade and part of it was natural (but would probably be channeled in the future). Running parallel to Tropicana, it snaked and straightened toward the interstate. Checkmarks—some eating through the map's heavy stock—surrounded it. I removed a notepad from my back pocket and a pen from my front. "Southwest corner of Trop and Valley View," I scribbled on the pad. "Cuts under Valley View and Industrial Road. About a mile long. No lateral channels."

Closing the notepad, I walked into the kitchen and made lunch: a veggie sandwich, cashews, and a glass of iced tea. I ate at the kitchen counter, quietly and solemnly, the bread of the sandwich struggling down my throat. Then I removed a bottle of water from the fridge, carried it to the living room, and turned on the TV. While watching sports highlights, I stretched on the floor. My muscles were tight. Even though I'd just eaten, my stomach felt hollow. My mind wandered, coming up with all types of wretched possibilities: getting jumped by crackheads; drowning in floodwater (though the Weather Channel didn't show a trace of rain within 200 miles); getting lost in the system (though this channel didn't look complicated on the map); running out of drinking water; stumbling on a pocket of poisonous air. …

Breaking free of the thoughts, I told myself that everything was going to be all right. That I was being ridiculous. That there was nothing to worry about: You can outrun most crackheads—even while carrying a flashlight, weighed down with gear, and checking the floor for rocks and slick spots; it's not going to rain today, tomorrow, the day after tomorrow, maybe in the next three months; you've studied the system and the channel, you've taken notes, you've done your homework; you'll have plenty of drinking water; and the manholes and drop inlets ventilate the tunnels. Then, getting all FDR with it: The only thing you have to fear is *yourself.*

While swimming through the darkness, cowering beneath five-foot-high ceilings, and walking straightaways that felt like concrete treadmills, I'd faced my worst enemy. I'd confronted the one person in the storm-drain system who could do me the most harm. The one person who could make the shadows come alive. Who could force me to turn around. Who could make me move when I needed to rest—or rest when I needed to move. The one person who could cause me to panic. Who could turn friends into enemies. Who could leave my blood on the tunnel walls. The one person in the system who could cause some *real* serious problems.

Me.

After stretching, I walked to the bedroom and changed into a long-sleeve shirt, cargo pants, and thick socks. I removed the backpack from a closet, dusted it off, set it on the bed. Unzipping the main pouch, I tested the Mag-Lite against a wall. The beam was dim, so I replaced the batteries. Returning the flashlight to the pouch, I took inventory: Mini Mag-Lite, expandable baton, sheath, knit cap, and fresh D and AA batteries.

Exhaling, I unzipped the backpack's secondary pouch: tape recorder, tapes, holster, wire microphone, and fresh AA batteries.

I put on a canvas belt, threading it through the sheath and holster. I stuffed the notepad and pen into my pockets. Finally, I placed the bottle of water in one of the exterior pouches and started for the front door.

Parking on a side street near Trop and Valley View—since the channel was only about a mile long, I didn't arrange for a ride—I popped the trunk and climbed out of the car. The sun sat high in the sky. The heat was brutal, as if a fire-breathing dragon was perched on my shoulder. I changed into my boots, sheathed the baton and recorder, and clipped the mike to the collar of my shirt. Then I slung the backpack over my shoulders and started off into the harsh Mojave glare.

Heat waves blurred the landscape—sand hills, scrub, and a wash—and railroad tracks, chain-link fences, and storage yards lined the horizon. It was as industrial an area as I'd seen in Las Vegas, a city that only produces hopes and dreams. I angled into the wash, which swelled and dipped like the surface of an ocean. In the ruts, I discovered rusted barrels and shattered wooden pallets and gutted kitchen appliances. Farther downstream there were sleeping bags and plywood huts and the desperation and sense of defeat that fill every crack of the Las Vegas Valley. Gravel and high grass crunched beneath my boots. The smell of fire and urine hung in the air.

Just west of Valley View, the wash leveled off and turned toward a double-barrel storm drain. The north tunnel, which was about 15 feet wide and five feet high, was black with soot. A blanket covered the inlet of the south tunnel. Approaching the drain, I flashed back to that Saturday morning in the summer of 2002 when I picked up Josh at his house.

• • •

Since Josh lived in the southeast valley, we decided to search for drains rumored to be near the intersection of Boulder Highway and Russell Road. Blazing south on Boulder Highway, we passed trailer parks and neighborhood casinos … dive bars and no-cover-charge strip joints and acres of desert that even the valley's insatiable developers had deemed useless. Just north of Russell, we crossed a wash. I tapped the brakes, pulled into a convenience store, and parked.

After walking across Russell and a plot of desert littered with beer cans, car tires, and Styrofoam cups, Josh and I pulled up at the edge of the wash. It was 50 feet wide and 15 feet deep. A piss-colored creek wound through its bed. The wash rolled to the northeast about 500 feet, then snaked and disappeared. To the west, it cut under Boulder Highway and was swallowed by shrubs.

With no map, no drinking water, and no expectations, Josh and I crossed the snake-carcass-covered highway and followed the wash west along a chalky path. Josh complained bitterly about the heat—and with good reason. It was hotter than hell's kitchen. I looked around for rattlesnakes and dead bodies. This stretch of scorched earth—sand dunes, tumbleweeds, and cactuses (cattle skulls were the only thing missing)—could be home to nothing else, I'd already decided.

Around a bend, the wash transitioned into an open-air channel. Josh and I descended into the channel, discovering a six-by-four tunnel in the west bank. As we approached the outlet, a shuffling sound shot from the darkness. We flinched, then identified ourselves as journalists. Echoes were the only response.

Confused, Josh and I crouched at the outlet and squinted into the tunnel. The floor was swept with sand. Official measurements, which looked like hieroglyphics to us, marked the walls. We had no idea if the tunnel was 50 feet—or five miles—long.

"I'm going to check it out," said Josh, cutting on his Mag-Lite.

"All right," I said, backing away from the outlet. I didn't even consider following him into the tunnel. It was low, dirty, and dark; I was tall, clean, and without a flashlight. There was no way in hell I was going to crawl into that glorified snake hole.

Handing me his trench coat, Josh shuffled sideways into the tunnel. His left hand held the flashlight. His right hand tickled the kukri, which dangled between his belt and the waist of his pants in the small of his back. He disappeared into the darkness. I heard shuffling, grunting, and cursing. Then there was silence.

I leaned into the tunnel. "Josh?" There was more shuffling, grunting, and cursing, then Josh—dusty and sweaty—broke through the darkness.

"There's nothing down there," he said, breathing heavily. "It dead-ends. The sound we heard was an echo."

Exiting the tunnel, Josh collapsed on the bank. Sweat showed through his clothes and his chest rose and sank violently. I thought that he was going into cardiac arrest, that he was going to die right there on the glass-covered bank of a flood channel in southeast Vegas. What in the *hell* have I gotten myself into, I wondered? Isn't there a hard-hitting political story we could be covering? What are we doing here?

"Are you OK?" I asked Josh, glancing upstream. The channel tore northward for a quarter-mile, then swung to the west. "I'm going to jog ahead and see what's beyond the bend," I said. "I'll wave you on if there's anything interesting."

As I started upstream, two bicycles appeared around the bend. They weaved up and down the banks, cutting through the creek and leaving behind tires tracks. Finally, I could see that three boys were on the two bikes. One of them had blond spiky hair and appeared to be about 14 years old. The other two, who were sharing a bike, looked like brothers—one about 12, the other eight.

"Do you all know if there are any tunnels around the bend?" I asked the boys.

The boys skidded to a stop and straddled the bikes. The blond pointed upstream. "Yeah," he said. "There's a big one back there. It's pretty long, I think. Some kids I know have gone in there, but not all the way."

"How far around the bend is it?"

"Not far."

I turned around and waved to Josh. He struggled to his feet, picked up his trench coat, and started upstream.

Rounding the bend, Josh and I saw the boys loitering in the shade of an overpass. The blond was straddling his bike. The other two were on foot, scurrying up and down the south bank like sewer rats. Drawing near, we noticed a gaping hole in the bank. It threatened to swallow the boys if they made one little misstep.

Crossing the creek, Josh and I approached the hole. It was more than five feet in diameter and cradled yellow-green standing water. It burrowed northward for about 30 feet, then jerked to the west. A pissy stench drifted from the darkness. To my surprise, the smallest boy scurried into the pipe. He quickly reemerged, wide-eyed and pale, as if he'd been greeted by a ghost.

"There's a flashlight in there that's on," he said.

"What?" I asked.

"Where?" said Josh.

"In the water."

Josh whipped out the kukri with a flourish. The boys backed away from the pipe. Handing one of them his trench coat, he cut on the flashlight and approached the outlet with purpose. It was as if all of his energy had suddenly returned. I also felt reenergized. I mean, if there was "a flashlight in there that's on," as the boy had said, I sure as hell wanted to see it.

To avoid stepping in the water, Josh and I walked with our legs spread and our feet on the sides of the pipe. This was terribly awkward—it looked like we were straddling invisible bulls—but better than sloshing through the muck, which was more than a foot deep in areas and appeared corrosive. We crashed through a cloud of mosquitoes. We stepped over a milk carton, car battery, and flashlight (that wasn't on). Resting, I glanced between my legs. A reflection of the three boys peering into the pipe rippled in the water.

Negotiating the bend, legs cramping, Josh and I discovered a circular light in the water. We stared at it in awe. We couldn't make *any* sense of it. It seemed to shoot from the murky depths and pierce the top of the pipe. Is this the flashlight the boy was talking about, I wondered? If not, what kind of bizarre alien beast is lurking beneath the surface? Suddenly, there was a loud rush overhead. A metallic boom shook the pipe. Cowering, Josh and I noticed that the light disappeared and quickly reappeared in sync with the boom. We looked up, discovering a manhole. A beam of sunlight angled through the cover's finger hole and dissolved into the water.

Realizing that a car had run over the manhole, Josh and I limped deeper into the pipe. He slashed through a cobweb with the kukri, the blade scraping against the concrete like a fingernail on a chalkboard. Goosebumps rose on my back and neck. About 50 feet beyond the bend, the water disappeared and the pipe narrowed to four feet. I glanced over my shoulder. The backlight had faded. Facing forward, I saw Josh's silhouette in the depths of the pipe.

"Slow down," I said. "I can't see shit."

Feeling like a hamster in plastic tubing, I caught up with Josh. The glow of the flashlight revealed

We'd found very little in the pipe, I admitted: a car battery, a flashlight, a strange foulness of the runoff that goes untreated into Lake Mead, the valley's main source of or tourists—knew anything about. In a city constantly featured in movies, TV shows, (literally and figuratively) that United Artists, E!, Frommer's, and *Maxim* had that the pipe continued to narrow and appeared to climb into the heavens—no dead bodies, no live bodies, nothing.

• • •

After making the long walk back to the convenience store and finding refuge in an adjoining fast-food restaurant, Josh and I drove crosstown on Tropicana. The drive gave me time to reflect on our first exploration. We'd found very little in the pipe, I admitted: a car battery, a flashlight, a strange beam of sunlight. Certainly nothing newsworthy (though I *was* surprised by the foulness of the runoff that goes untreated into Lake Mead, the valley's main source of water). But, I realized, we'd discovered an area of Las Vegas that few people—locals or tourists—knew anything about. In a city constantly featured in movies, TV shows, books, and articles, we'd stumbled on virgin territory—an underground world (literally and figuratively) that United Artists, E!, Frommer's, and *Maxim* had overlooked while focusing on poker rooms and the breasts of showgirls.

Encouraged, I turned south on Valley View and parked on a side street (in the same spot I'd park two years later). Josh and I opened the car doors and stepped out into the heat. Cursing Bugsy Siegel, Hank Greenspun, Howard Hughes, and all the other crazy white men who helped establish this city, we walked to the wash (which I'd discovered while researching a story on homelessness) and started downstream.

I'd, of course, seen storm drains throughout the valley. Some of them are visible from the streets and sidewalks. Others can be seen from the washes, which also serve as recreation areas (though I wouldn't recommend walking a dog or throwing a frisbee in any of the central channels). But I'd never paid attention to the drains. I didn't know their official name. I didn't know their specific purpose. They were just another part of the valley's sprawling infrastructure that I took for granted, just another thing in this world that I unconsciously ignored. But standing in front of it with Josh, I couldn't ignore *this* storm drain. Its face was white, clean, and about 10 feet tall. Its walls were smooth and strong, making it look more like a sculpture buried in dirt than some kind of flood channel.

Josh and I had no idea who or what lurked in the dark—but he wasn't taking any chances. He drew the kukri, wriggled into the trench coat, and tied its belt tight. We then ducked into the south tunnel, discovering two men sitting in the shade surrounded by empty beer bottles. Surprised—though probably not as surprised as the men, considering Josh's startling silhouette—we explained that we were journalists curious about what was in the drain. Nothing really, said the men. It's just a refuge for people who live in the wash. It gets too hot out there. But no one, they said, actually *lives* in the drain. It's too dangerous. That floodwater comes like a thief in the night. It will take you away and won't ever bring you back.

After talking to the men briefly, Josh and I shuffled deeper into the drain. The dividing wall disappeared, yielding to an arching tunnel that was about 20 feet wide and five feet high at its apex. Sand and rocks were scattered across the floor. The walls and ceiling were clean.

About 300 feet downstream, Josh and I discovered another divider. It created two 10-by-5 tunnels that straightened into perfect darkness. Josh aimed the flashlight into the north tunnel, which was choked with rocks and blocks of concrete—testaments to the awesome power of floodwater. We considered exploring the south tunnel, which was less cluttered than the north, but ultimately decided against it. We assumed the tunnel was long, low, and dark. We assumed it was crawling with spiders, scorpions, and maybe even snakes. We assumed it was suicide.

Two years later, I'd returned to find out if we were right.

•   •   •

Pulling up in front of the storm drain, I put on the knit cap and tightened the straps of the backpack. My head was light. My throat was dry. I felt like an athlete before the Big Game. No matter how many drains I explored, no matter how well I prepared, I was *always* nervous before stepping into the shadows. Exhaling, I surveyed the façade. It was as black and grimy as a New England chimney. The walls were chipped and scarred with spray paint. The blanket covering the south tunnel billowed in the wind, exposing the bottom of a folding chair and love seat.

I was stunned by how much the drain had changed in two years, by how quickly it had been claimed by the graffiti artists, street people, wind, sun, and rain.

"Hello?" I said, standing in front of the south tunnel.

The wind died down. The blanket straightened. There was no other response.

"Anyone home?"

The sun looked down on me with scorn. My neck began to sting. Finally, I heard movement behind the blanket. "Yeah?" someone mumbled.

I pulled back the blanket. Squinting into the tunnel, I noticed a man lying facedown in the inlet. He had long greasy hair and wore only cargo shorts. His skin was red, splotchy. He was surrounded by the folding chair, the love seat, and a makeshift coffee table (a piece of plywood balanced on a milk crate). Slabs of carpet covered the floor. The man looked drunk, tired, and pitiful—but I hoped he could answer one question that the flood-control map, which didn't indicate what was aboveground and what was underground, couldn't.

"Do you know where this storm drain ends?" I asked the man. He turned his head toward me slowly, painfully, and opened his eyes. The rest of his body remained still.

"It goes all the way down to the Budget Suites," he said, a beard concealing his lips and providing a hint of ventriloquism.

"Can you walk all the way through?" I continued, remembering the low and cluttered tunnels that Josh and I'd encountered.

The man propped himself up on his elbows, like a boxer struggling from the canvas, and squinted down the wide arching tunnel. "Yeah, you can walk all the way through or you can go around on Tropicana and come in the other end behind Budget Suites."

"I think I'll walk all the way through. Do you mind if I rest in the shade a minute? It's hotter than hell out here."

"Nah. That's all right. I'm just trying to get me a little rest, too."

I ducked into the tunnel, shook out of the backpack, and sat against the dividing wall, opposite the man. His upper body reunited with the floor and his eyes closed. He didn't seem at all concerned with my presence. I could've been a county employee, a cop, or a serial killer targeting drunk and bearded homeless men, but none of this seemed to matter to the man.

I removed the bottle of water from the backpack and glanced downstream. Blankets, suitcases, and garbage bags were strewn across the south side of the tunnel. "Is that your stuff down there?" I asked him.

"It was everybody's stuff at one time," said the man, who introduced himself as Phillip. "It all got washed down there during the rain we had a few days ago, but it's all right. It didn't get too wet."

"How many people live in this drain?"

"There was a bunch of people living in here, but some of them moved out."

"Why'd they move out?"

"They were just going different places. They got different things going on. One

137

guy's girlfriend got pissed off and burned everybody out of the other tunnel."

"I noticed the soot as I was walking down the wash."

"Did you see all those hooches they built out there?"

"Yeah. I don't know how they live out there in the summer. It's *so* damn hot."

"I got another camp not too far from here. It's a little tent behind this building. It's all right, but I can't sleep there during the day. Like you said, it's just too hot."

"How long have you lived in this drain?"

"About a year."

"Does anyone else live in here with you?"

"Right now, it's just me. But there are some people on the other end of the tunnel, too."

"How many?"

"About five, I guess. Maybe more."

"Are they cool?"

"Yeah. They're all right. In fact, there was a couple girls living down there. They got a nice little hooch. They got a bunch of mattresses and …"

Hearing voices outside the drain, Phillip hesitated. The gravel and high grass crunched, gradually growing louder. The blanket billowed in the wind.

"Hello there," said someone on the other side of the blanket. "It's Tyrone."

Fighting off a yawn, Phillip lifted his head from the floor and glanced toward the inlet. "Hey, Tyrone. Come on in."

A man with dark-black skin and braided graying hair pulled back the blanket. Shockingly thin, he wore a long-sleeve shirt, faded jeans, and combat boots. "I asked my mom to stop in here for a minute, because it's cooler," he said, ducking into the tunnel and sitting on the love seat. "It's just too hot out there."

A woman in a white visor, plaid vest, and long denim skirt rolled a suitcase into the tunnel. She propped it against a wall, then removed her glasses and wiped the lenses with a sweater tied around her neck.

"Hello," said the woman, sitting next to Tyrone.

"Hey," said Phillip. "I was just taking a nap for a minute."

"I'm sorry to bother you," the woman said. "We're just stopping in for a minute. We won't stay long."

"Ah, you ain't bothering nobody," Phillip said. "Stay as long as you want."

Stunned, I remained silent. I took a sip from the bottle of water, trying to make sense of the situation. If I'd heard Tyrone correctly, the woman sitting next to him was his mother. So, I naturally wondered, what were a mom and her son doing walking into a storm drain in south-central Vegas as if it were the living room of the family home? I felt a strong need to have this question answered, but not before I disclosed my identity. I wanted to be straight up about who I was and why I was in the drain, before things got too weird.

"I'm Matt," I said. "I'm a reporter exploring the storm drains. I peeked into this drain a couple years ago, while working on some stories for *CityLife*. Now I'm working on a book. I was just asking Phillip a few questions about the drain."

"Good to meet you, Matt," said Tyrone. "Yeah, we've had a few people come down here and ask questions about where the tunnel leads and how long it is and stuff like that. Not many, but we've had a few people come through."

I wondered if Phillip and Tyrone were the two men Josh and I talked to briefly. When Tyrone said that one of the people who came into the drain asking questions was a "big dude" with a "really long knife," it confirmed he was one of the men. Phillip, however, didn't seem to recall the encounter.

"I'm Gwen," said the woman. "I come down here every once in a while to visit my son."

Tyrone explained, "I stayed in here awhile. I never lived deep in the tunnel, because of the flash floods. Every time it rained, there was a river going by me and people sleeping all around me who were used to this and didn't even wake up. I'm like, 'Yeah, right. Not me.' I knew I wasn't going to stay in here long."

"But you were in here for a while," said the woman, shaking her head.

My God, I thought, I *did* hear Tyrone correctly. I couldn't believe it. I'd never even considered interviewing the parent of someone who lived in the storm drains. It wasn't realistic, I'd thought. It wasn't possible. Their parents were dead or unreachable or cold or didn't know they lived in the drains, the inhabitants had said. Don't even bother. But sitting in front of me on a faded love seat, her legs politely crossed, was a mother who'd actually visited her son *while* he lived in a drain. I returned the bottle of water to the pouch and made sure the tape was rolling. I was excited and nervous. I'd lucked into an interview that I never could've arranged.

"After I fell off the top of this tunnel and hurt my back, I had to stay in here," continued Tyrone. "I couldn't move. But as soon as I got up and was able to move around a little bit, I got out of here right away."

"You knew he was living in here?" I asked Gwen, more curious about that than how Tyrone had managed to fall off the drain.

"She has photographs of me in here," said Tyrone.

"I came down here last year when we first found Tyrone," Gwen said. "I hadn't known where he was for twenty-eight years, and he's my oldest child. My daughter and a friend of hers finally found him.

"I had a detective looking for him starting in 1985," she continued. "I got a folder of information on him this thick." She held her index finger and thumb three inches apart. "I've gone through 'Unsolved Mysteries.' I've gone through so many different search programs. You send them money and they send you a book of people with the same name as the person you're looking for, then you got to call all those people. I knew Tyrone wouldn't be in a cold climate, so I didn't bother calling any of those people. But I did call a lot of the other people. I still got that folder with all the stuff in it."

"How'd you finally find him?"

"My daughter has a friend who's in politics. This friend somehow found him. I don't know all the details. All I know is that she put his name into some database and it came up, because he got arrested last year. That's how I found him."

"I heard that someone was looking for me and I kept moving on," said Tyrone. "I knew that I hadn't done anything wrong, but I wasn't taking any chances. I didn't know who it was. I definitely didn't know it was my mom."

"You found him last year?"

"Yeah," said Gwen, "after he got arrested for that little thing at the convenience store."

"There was a lady working at the store," Tyrone explained, "and she was irritable because of the heat that day. I go in there every morning with my own cup, so I can get free ice. Well, I got my cup of ice and I'm on my way out and she says: 'Hey, you got to pay for that.'"

"They give him free ice all the time," added Gwen.

"Well," continued Tyrone, "the woman caught me at the door. Another customer said he would pay for the ice, but she said: 'No. I'm calling Metro.' Next thing I know, I look out the door and there's Metro. I went out there to talk to the officer and he kind of ignored me. He knows me, too, so I got really mad. I

picked up a brick—and he's watching me the whole time—and threw it through the window of the convenience store." Tyrone laughed. "The cop cut on the siren lights, drove right up to me, and took me to jail. That's when my sister's friend came across my name in that database. Next thing I know, my sister was calling me."

"Then she called me at one o'clock in the morning," said Gwen, "and told me that she'd found him."

"How long have you been on the streets?" I asked Tyrone.

"I moved to Tucson awhile back," he said. "I was going to school there. Then I came up here to work, earn money, and then go back to Tucson. I was sleeping in a car and walking twelve miles from Washington Park to the Aladdin to work. Finally, I found a place to stay. Everything had kind of settled down. Then I took a leave of absence from work, accumulated time off. When I came back, they told me I was fired. I've been on the streets ever since.

"But as I was just explaining to my mom, this is kind of where God put me. I was going to go back to Tucson and go back to school, but for some reason I stayed here."

"Do you like Las Vegas?"

"The only thing I have a real problem with is the heat. That's all. I keep telling myself and other people on the streets, 'Drink fluids and stay on top of your diet.' People just don't realize how extreme the heat is here. Living outside, you have to be more aware of the fluids you put into your body. People on the streets don't drink the right things. They gamble and drink all that free alcohol."

"Do you drink or do drugs?"

"I've drank and I've smoked weed. But I'm really careful about the alcohol, because that's what killed my father. I try not to get under its influence too much, maybe every once in a while on a weekend when I let my hair down a little bit. But that's OK."

"We've been trying to get him to leave Las Vegas," said Gwen, noting that she raised Tyrone and his three siblings in upstate New York, "but he keeps saying that this is where God put him. Personally, I wish he would leave. But if he wanted to stay here and live inside, that would be fine with me. I just want him to be safe. I just want him to be happy. It breaks my heart to see him living like this. We do what we can for him. We really do. We offer him help, but he just won't take it. He doesn't want to come live where we live, in Atlanta, and I can understand that. But him living like this, in the tunnels and in the wash, it just breaks my heart."

"Where do you live now, Tyrone?"

"Further up the wash. I built a shack out of wooden pallets. It's temporary, but I had to get out of here."

"Last summer," said Gwen, "I was here one day when it rained a whole lot. We had just found Tyrone. Well, some man got washed away in one of these tunnels and they couldn't find him. They were looking for his body, but they never did find it. Maybe it washed into Lake Mead or something. I don't know. But you just can't get out of these tunnels fast enough when the rain's coming down."

"She really worried about that," said Tyrone, "and I did, too. Since I can't swim, I would stay up all night paranoid about the water. It would be going right by all these people, making all kinds of noise. There was a river on that [the north] side of the tunnel and over here we were high and dry, but I'd stay up all night worried about it. I kept waiting for it to come and get me."

"He was worried about the spiders, too," his mother added.

"Oh yeah, those spiders were eating people up. I couldn't deal with that. There was this one spider. People were just watching it like it was a piece of art. I'm saying, 'Kill the spider! Kill the spider! Kill the spider!' But they just kept on watching it. The spiders multiply in here this time of year. The moisture makes them breed and move around more. I had to get out of here. It was just too much."

"Did you ever see his camp down here?" I asked Gwen.

"I've seen it ever since I've been coming down here to visit him. I couldn't believe it. I was just devastated. I hated to see him living like that. I encouraged him to move out of here. I told him it was dangerous. But he's an adult now—sometimes I forget that, because he was gone for so long—so I just say my piece and let it be. I don't want him to get mad at me. I don't want him to not want to see me anymore. I want to keep coming to see him, no matter where he lives."

"When did you move out of the drain, Tyrone?"

"About three weeks ago. We're in the monsoon season now and we had this one storm where the water just kept coming and coming. In other words, we had to really work to keep this tunnel from flooding. That's when I said: 'I got to get out of here. I can't take this no more.' I wanted to move further up the wash anyway. I already had a spot picked out. So I just came down here, got my stuff, and moved out.

"In the tunnels, you're out of the sun and it's a lot cooler. That's what attracts people to them. But the water's real dangerous. I've seen Phillip, though he probably doesn't remember it, get swept away in here. I'm hollering at him and the water's almost up to the ceiling. He's barely got his head above it all. He's at the wall down there that divides this tunnel, just holding on for his life. He held on until the water went down, then walked back up here."

"Do you remember that, Phillip?" I asked, unsure if he was awake.

"Yeah," he said. "I had a hell of a time getting back up here. It was real rough."

"Are you all able to monitor the weather down here?"

"I would usually check with this one Oriental guy who lived down here," said Tyrone. "There are certain people who read the paper and can tell you the weather forecast. I would check with them. If they said it was going to rain, I'd sleep on the hill outside. If they said it was going to be dry, I'd stay in the tunnel."

"That reminds me," said Gwen, turning toward Tyrone. "I brought you an umbrella. You can use it in the rain or the sun. Also, I brought you a backpack, a flashlight, and some new boots. Make sure I give you all that stuff when we get to your campsite.

"We're about to go to his campsite now," she said, facing forward. "I brought him a bunch of stuff. I brought plastic bags for him to put his stuff in, so it won't get wet, and a suitcase for his winter clothes."

I was moved by Gwen's thoughtfulness. In fact, I'd never seen a mother do anything quite like this for her child. She'd traveled to Las Vegas from Northern California, where she lived during the summer. She'd bought gifts for her son—her first child—to help him survive on the streets. Carrying these gifts in a suitcase, she'd somehow made her way to the intersection of Tropicana and Valley View.

Then, in 112-degree heat, she'd rolled the suitcase across rough and dangerous desert terrain, down into a wash, and into a storm drain. She did all this for a son who apparently remained distant and complex.

"You have an incredible mom," I said to Tyrone. "Why don't you accept her support?"

"I appreciate her support," he said. "I really do. But I need to work these things out on my own. I don't want to lean on her for support. Sometimes I forget that God is showing me different things and leading me in different directions. Sometimes I stop and wonder if I'm still in God's will. Sometimes I look around and ask myself: 'What am I doing here? Why now?'

"Well, I lost my father when I was young. I never completely got over it, but I've come to accept it and understand the circumstances around it. There are other people on the streets who lost their father at an early age. Some of them have hidden this or tried to ignore it. Some of them have accepted it. Some of them are trying to deal with it and can't.

"Anyway, I think that God is using me to help these people accept the fact that their father passed away and not to let it bring them down. I try to tell them to accept it and keep on living. One guy told me I've been instrumental in that way, that I've helped a lot of people out. I don't know. I just hope that God has a plan for me and that I've at least helped a few people out."

"When his father passed away," said Gwen, leaning forward on the love seat, "I didn't realize how much it affected him. I didn't know until he was an adult that it was something that bothered him. I remember one time when we were having problems, I got some counseling for him. They came to the house when he was in high school, but they didn't know what was wrong with him. Then three months before graduation, he dropped out of school. That really bothered me. I didn't know what was going on. He's a very smart person. He could've gotten all kinds of scholarships. But there was something going on with him."

"It wasn't just my father passing away," Tyrone explained to his mother, seemingly for the first time. "It was that the world itself seemed to be falling apart."

"Then he went to Vietnam," she said, leaning back, "and came back a totally different person."

Tyrone didn't respond and his mother didn't elaborate. I stared at my boots—dusty, mud-caked, and scuffed—not wanting to pry too deeply into their family affairs. The wind blew, hot and dry. The blanket billowed, licking at the folding chair and love seat. Tyrone turned to his mother. "You ready?"

"I'm ready when you are."

"OK, we're going to take off." Tyrone stood and stared into the depths of the drain. "There are people who prefer to live in the tunnels," he said. "But I prefer to duck into one for a while, then find a safer place to stay. See, these catacombs go all the way down to Harmon Avenue. That's where they come out. I actually know people who've been washed from here all the way down there and lived to tell about it."

"I would hear all these stories when I came to visit him," said Gwen, retrieving the suitcase and shaking her head. "I just thought to myself, 'Oh, Lord. Please look after him.' But I still have to come see him. He's my child. He'll always be my child."

Tyrone ducked out of the drain and disappeared behind the blanket. His mother tightened the knot in her sweater, snapped the handle of the suitcase into place, then rolled it into the sunlight. As the sound of crunching gravel and grass grew softer and softer, I brushed the dust off my lap and stood. "OK, Phillip," I said. "I'm going to move on and let you get some sleep. I've bothered you enough. Sorry about that."

"No problem," he said, lying motionless on the floor. "I'm just going to rest for a while. I'll probably go out in a bit, get me something to drink, piddle around, or whatever. But like I said, it's not too far down to the other end. The tunnel goes right, left, and then right. No, I got it backwards. It goes left, right, then left. There's one little blind spot down there—you got to be careful there—but you can see the rest of the way. There's light from the manhole covers."

"Thanks, man," I said, not bothering to explain that I had a flashlight. "Sleep tight."

Carrying the backpack by its top loop, I started downstream. The slope of the wide arching tunnel carried me into the semidarkness. As the backlight faded, I removed the flashlight from the main pouch and swept the beam about the tunnel. Obviously, a lot had gone on down here in the past two years. The ceiling was black with soot, I assumed, from makeshift grills and furnaces. Graffiti covered the walls. The floor was littered with shoes, jackets, garbage bags, spray-paint cans, and broken beer bottles. The whole scene reminded me of a punk-rock club on a Sunday morning.

Reaching the divider, I aimed the flashlight into the north tunnel. The rocks and blocks of concrete remained, joined by suitcases and four-by-fours and bicycle frames. The south tunnel was still less cluttered than the north, but it wasn't exactly a red carpet. Gravel and glass covered the floor and pieces of plywood leaned against the walls. I now remembered why Josh and I'd turned around. This

Josh and I'd found questions in the storm drains of Las Vegas; I was determined to find map. They weren't always found on the Regional Flood Control District's Web site. outlets. Oftentimes, these answers lurked in the most remote regions of the storm-drain

drain wasn't designed for graffiti artists, gangbangers, or novice urban explorers. It wasn't designed for the mildly curious or slightly disturbed. Only those with a specific reason—to score drugs, to get away from the cops, to avoid armed enemies on the streets—would even *consider* crawling into one of these tunnels. I, of course, had my own reason: Josh and I'd found questions in the storm drains of Las Vegas; I was determined to find answers. And these answers, I'd discovered, weren't always found on the flood-control map. They weren't always found on the Regional Flood Control District's Web site. They weren't always found in basins and open-air channels or around the inlets and outlets. Oftentimes, these answers lurked in the most remote regions of the storm-drain system—in dark and dusty recesses that few, if any, people had passed through alive.

Knees bent and back straight, I entered the south tunnel. Flashlight arm extended, I took long strides that whisked me through the darkness. I ducked under a spider web and stepped over a pool of muddy water. Things went well for the first 50 feet. Then I felt the silky threads of a cobweb stretch across my face. … I stepped onto an island of gravel, which made the tunnel feel about four feet high. … My ankles twisted on the rocks. … My knees straightened. … My back stooped. … The backpack scraped against the ceiling, slowing my pace.

About 150 feet into the tunnel, the divider disappeared and I found myself in a wide and comparatively clean tunnel. The ceiling, however, remained low. Surrounded by darkness—this must've been the "one little blind spot" that Phillip had mentioned—I lunged downstream, boots sliding on the gravel. My back began to tighten. My neck grew stiff. I considered kneeling on the floor and

answers. And these answers, I'd discovered, weren't always found on the flood-control
They weren't always found in basins and open-air channels or around the inlets and
system—in dark and dusty recesses that few, if any, people had passed through alive.

taking a break, but the sparkling glass spurred me on.

Around a bend, I found refuge in a manhole. I stood upright in the shaft, stretching my back and rolling my neck. Though only three feet wide and seven feet high, it felt as spacious as the Sistine Chapel. I wallowed in the sunlight and fresh air. My breathing echoed in the tunnel. Catching my breath, I ducked out of the manhole and continued downstream—knees and back bent, head down.

Lifting my head, I noticed a flicker of light in the distance. The tunnel snaked, eclipsing the light, then straightened. I staggered onward, leg and back muscles burning. The tunnel widened. The light grew brighter. Finally, the outline of a camp—grocery carts, a mattress, a futon couch—came into focus along the south wall. Two silhouettes sat on the couch.

"Do you all mind if I cut through?" I asked, approaching the camp and breathing heavily.

"Nah," said one of the silhouettes.

"I was just talking to Phillip and Tyrone on the other end of the drain." I entered the camp and knelt a safe distance from the couch. "Phillip told me which way the tunnel turned, but he forgot to mention that it was a half-mile long and only four feet high. I think I ruined my back for good."

"I always carry a milk crate with me," slurred one of the silhouettes, a man with a paunch.

"What for?"

"So I can stop and sit down on it." Leaning forward on the couch, the man flicked a lighter. The flame danced in the semidarkness. "I hope you won't be offended," he said, raising a glass pipe to his lips.

"No, not at all," I said, again feeling the need to disclose my identity. "I'm just exploring the drain. I've explored about twenty or twenty-five of them so far this summer. I'm working on a book about the drains and the people who …"

"We don't want no pictures taken," interrupted the man, exhaling.

"I'm not taking any pictures. I'm just exploring the drains."

"Well, this one opens up right here." The man motioned toward the outlet, which was about 50 feet downstream. It was 35 feet wide and four and a half feet high, emptying into a wash strewn with debris. "It stays that way till you get to Industrial, then it goes underground and gets real low in two tunnels that open up on the other side of the street. There are two other tunnels that run alongside I-15, four total."

"And they all go under the interstate and the Strip," I added. "I explored the two other tunnels a couple weeks ago, but I haven't explored these two. That's what I'm going to do today."

The man passed the lighter and pipe to the other silhouette, a skeleton of a woman with her hair in a bun. She flicked the lighter, illuminating her gaunt and dirty face.

"What are you all smoking?" I asked, assuming it was crack.

There was silence. "Crack," the man finally confirmed.

"I hear that's a rough drug," I said, recalling my conversation with Cary. "I hear that's a tough drug to quit."

"Nah," said the man, "it ain't that bad. It's not as addictive as some other drugs. It's not as bad as heroin. It's not as bad as snorting cocaine."

Uncomfortable with the situation—I'd never been around anyone who was smoking crack … and certainly not in the shadows of a storm drain—I surveyed the camp. The mattress was pushed against the wall, which served as a headboard. The light of the outlet silhouetted milk crates, garbage bags, and mounds of clothing.

"Do you all live in here?" I asked, for lack of a better question.

"I don't," said the woman in a raspy voice. "If there was no bugs in here, I would. But there are so many of them. Did you know there's bugs in these tunnels?"

"Yeah," I said, smiling uncomfortably. "I know."

The woman passed the lighter and pipe back to the man, who leaned forward on the couch, flicked the lighter, and inhaled. I removed the bottle of water from the backpack and unscrewed the cap. The man exhaled. I took a swig from the bottle and swallowed. "Do you all mind if I hang out for a few minutes?" I asked, hoping to find out more about the man, the woman, and the drain.

"Not at all," said the man. "Just don't put my name in that book."

"No problem." I scooted closer to the couch and sat on the floor. "I understand."

The sun broke free from a cloud, illuminating the tunnel. I looked up at the man. His hair was gray and receding. His skin was pale and naked, covered only with a faded star-shaped tattoo on his left arm. His legs were dirty and indistinguishably entwined with the woman's legs. She, too, was naked. Her skin was yellow and pockmarked, and she had small sagging breasts. Her lips were a similar shade to the pipe, which was burned deep purple. She appeared to be malnourished, in the terminal stage of AIDS, or going through some other miserable experience that I was—fortunately—not familiar with.

"What's that tattoo on your arm?" I asked the man, trying to play it cool. But obviously, that wasn't the first question that came to mind. In fact, it was preceded by several others: Are they *really* naked? If so, why do they seem so nonchalant about it? Am I blushing? Can they tell just how freaked out I am? Should I sit still and try to remain calm? Or should I sprint for the outlet, screaming for the cops and my mom?

"I got it when I was eighteen. It was the first time I was in jail. It's a spider. Another inmate drew it on me with pencil lead."

"What's it represent?"

"Nothing. Nothing at all. But when I got out of jail, my grandfather asked me how come I put a swastika on my arm." The man laughed, revealing that he was missing all of his teeth. "That was like, whew, forty years ago."

"Who else lives down here?"

"No one," said the man. "It's just me. There's a lady in the right [south] tunnel down there under Industrial. You'll probably meet her. Everybody does. She's a hamburger short of a Happy Meal, if you know what I mean. Ah, I'm just kidding. She's a little bit crazy, but she's all right. She's OK. Beyond her, at the other end of the tunnel, is an ex-truck driver. And in the left [north] tunnel, there's a few other guys."

"Where do you live?" I asked the woman, who appeared to be about 30 years old.

Occupied with the lighter and pipe, she didn't respond.

"She stays down here sometimes," said the man. "She might be in here for two or three days, then I won't see her for a while. She just disappears on me. I don't know where she goes. The woman who lives down there in the right tunnel is the same way. I'll see her for two or three days in a row and then she's gone."

"Are the two of you together?"

"Nah. She just likes to take advantage of me—and sometimes I let her."

I briefly wondered if this was Cary's woman and the older guy she was "hooked up with." But Cary's camp was three miles downstream—a long way on the streets—and it's not uncommon in Las Vegas for younger women to use older men for drugs. In fact, it's an art form in the city. It happens all the time in the stucco mansions out west, the high-roller suites on the Strip, and even the storm drains.

"How long have you lived down here?" I asked the man.

"About two years," he said. "I used to live in the desert behind Mandalay Bay, but they cleaned it up and made us all move out."

"Do you know the other people in the tunnels around here?"

"Everybody knows everybody else. We may not like each other. We may not socialize. But we know each other and we look out for each other. There's good ones and there's bad ones. There's only one person around here who people don't really care about at all. I won't name him. He ain't worth mentioning. He's just a troublemaker. He's just a drunk piece of shit. Personally, I don't drink."

"But you smoke crack," said the woman out of nowhere.

"Shut up," said the man, turning toward the woman and spanking her playfully on the leg. "I'm not talking to you." He turned back toward me. "Hey, what can I say? That's just my preference."

As if reinforcing his point, the man took the lighter and pipe from the woman. He pinched the pipe with the index finger and thumb of his left hand and clutched the lighter in his right hand. Leaning forward, he raised the pipe to his lips and flicked the lighter. He then steadied the flame on the end of the pipe.

"I was born and raised in Las Vegas," said the man, leaning back and exhaling. The smoke was thin, vague, and had no particular smell—at least not one that overpowered the mildew, urine, and body odor.

"What do you think about the city?"

"I think it's a piece of shit. The year I was born was the year they opened the Flamingo [1946]. Where the Stratosphere is now, that was the southern edge of town. There wasn't anything below there. They've made the city too big. There's too many people here and it's too corporate. They let it get way too big and they commercialized it. There are people in powerful positions here who don't deserve to be. It's all about who you know—and if you don't get along with those people, they'll do anything and everything they can to get rid of you.

"I used to like a lot of things about Las Vegas," he continued, "but they don't do anything they used to do. They used to have the Helldorado rodeo. They used to have parades. They used to have all kinds of things they don't have anymore. I miss the days when the good old boys—you know, the Mob—ran the town. I don't really go to the Strip that much, but I miss downtown: the Horseshoe, the Golden Nugget, the Golden Gate."

The man passed the lighter and pipe back to the woman, who was picking her teeth obsessively. She was on her knees, back arched, staring at the ceiling. She didn't seem to know or care that she was naked. She seemed oblivious to the conversation. She seemed to be somewhere else—somewhere far, far away from this storm drain in south-central Vegas.

"I have my reasons for being down here," said the man, tapping a cigarette from a crumpled pack. "There are some things I'd like to tell you on the serious side—and they're all true stories—but I don't want them in no book."

"Don't tell me anything you're not comfortable with."

"Ah, I don't give a shit," he said, lighting the cigarette and inhaling. "You know that little girl Rose who got killed? Supposedly, she was drunk. A lot of people really cared about her. It was a big story at the time."

"Who?"

"Rose."

"No. I don't remember that story."

"Well," the man continued, "one day the cops came around asking about her.

They said, 'What do you know?' I'm an ex-felon, so I said: 'I don't know nothing.' But they didn't have to say who she was or what happened to her. We all knew who and what they were talking about."

"What do you mean?" I asked, unsure if the man was confessing, ratting on someone, or just rambling.

"There are people on the streets who are high and need money. If they have to commit a murder or whatever to get it, they'll do it. You know what I'm saying?"

Actually, I had no idea what the man was saying—and I didn't want to know. I didn't want him to tell me some deep dark secret, come down off his high, and regret it. That, I realized, could create an uncomfortable situation. That, I realized, could get ugly.

"What are some of the myths of the storm drains?" I said, changing the subject. "What are some of the stories?"

"Here's a good one for you," said the man, leaning back on the couch and exhaling. "We have all these kids that hang out around here and play in the wash. Well, this other lady used to live in here with me. She was here because—well, whatever. I can't get into all that. But we lived together and we were friends, good friends."

The man took another hit from the cigarette and continued, "Anyway, one day all these kids were out there in the wash. There were a bunch of young boys and girls. They were all looking into the tunnel, but they didn't want to come in. A couple of them asked, 'Are you all murderers? All you all rapists?' Well, she looked at me and I looked at her. Then I said, 'I'll let you handle that one. Will you show these kids what's going on in our lives?'

"We didn't have no dirty magazines or anything like that lying around, so she says: 'Come on in.' I think there was around ten kids or something. Anyway, we wanted the mystery to be solved. We wanted them to know that we weren't killers, that we weren't any of that other stuff that kids come up with. We told them, 'Be careful. We can't be responsible for anybody else in here.' Then she brought them in and showed them this, that, and the other.

"Now, they might've been in here for five or ten minutes. They had a lot of questions: 'Do you have candles? Do you need them in the daytime? Where do you sleep?' She had a flashlight and she showed them around. But when she took them back outside, every parent was standing on every balcony of the Budget Suites going all the way down the wash. The police were at the gate. The kids all looked up at their parents. Then one of the policemen said: 'What's going on here?' She said, 'Well, you can see what's going on here. The kids have been told that murderers or rapists or whatever was living down here.' Then she looked up at the policemen and all the parents and said: 'I just wanted to clear that up. I wanted them to know that we aren't murderers or rapists or whatever. We're just everyday people.' The policeman just said, 'OK, kids, now go on home.'"

The man's story seemed to contradict the one he told about Rose, but I didn't want to bring that subject up again. So I simply said, "How'd the kids react to being down here?"

"It was pretty strange," he said, slipping into a pair of boxer shorts and flicking the cigarette butt into the darkness. "The kids didn't want to leave. When the policeman told them to go home, they just stood there. I guess they felt sorry for us or something. I guess they realized we weren't murderers or rapists or whatever. But the parents made sure the kids didn't come back down here for a long time. Some of the kids used to give us ice sometimes, but just a few days ago was the first time I'd seen any of them in a while. Four of them came down here and asked if we needed a mattress. We said, 'Sure, if it's clean.'"

The man leaned forward and fished dentures from a fast-food cup on the floor. He scrubbed them with a toothbrush, then popped them into his mouth.

"Well," I said, overwhelmed by everything I'd seen and heard, "I should probably move on. I'm sorry about interrupting you all. I know you were in the middle of all types of private stuff."

"Nah," said the man, "we're just chilling. I mean, if we'd been fucking like a couple of rabbits, we might've said: 'Hey, get the hell away from here!'" He laughed loudly, showing off his fake teeth.

I returned the bottle of water to the backpack and struggled to my feet. "How far down's the next drain?"

"Maybe a couple of blocks, if that."

"Cool," I said, starting downstream. "Thanks for letting me hang out. Sorry again about interrupting you all."

"All right, buddy. Take care."

Passing the mattress, I noticed a young man tangled in the sheets. I flinched, then realized he was facedown and motionless. He, too, was naked.

"Is he all right?" I asked over my shoulder.

"Yeah," said the man. "He's all right. He just had a *real* long night."

Weaving around the grocery carts and mounds of clothing, I ducked out of the drain. The sun was still high in the sky and the heat hit me with its full force—but I didn't bitch about it. In fact, I was relieved to be out of the drain and into the open. It felt safer. It felt like everything was going to be all right—maybe. However, I was still somewhat confined. A barbwire fence stood atop the south embankment of the wash and a cinderblock wall atop the north bank.

Anxious to get away from the camp—I was worried that the man may have thought he told me too much—I put the flashlight in the backpack and surged downstream. Rocks, gravel, and broken glass bedded the wash. Desert shrubs—some more than 10 feet tall—rose from the banks, clothing and plastic bags tangled in the branches. I skipped from rock to rock, over a warped Bible and a Polaroid picture of a half-nude woman fingering herself. Budget Suites loomed over the cinderblock wall. Beyond Industrial and I-15, Excalibur shimmered like a mirage.

Continuing downstream, I thought about the conversation I had with the man. I wondered what someone his age—about 58, according to my math—was doing living in a storm drain. How was his health. Did he ever feel intimidated by the younger inhabitants? I also wondered about his drug habit: How often did he smoke crack? Where did he get the money to buy it? Panhandling? Stealing? *Murder*? And, of course, I wondered about "that little girl Rose." Who was she? When, why, and how did she die? What did the man know?

Stepping over a pool of water, I wished that I'd asked the man some of these questions. But, I realized, the flood-control system is a tough beat and exploring a drain is a tricky assignment. I never knew who I was going to run into and under what circumstances, so I couldn't prepare any questions. I wasn't interviewing public officials or local personalities who knew the protocol. The interviews weren't conducted over the phone or in a well-lit office with degrees framed on the walls. One wrong question in the storm drains of Las Vegas could get a reporter bound with his own wire mike and bludgeoned to death with his own tape recorder.

At Industrial, the wash went underground in two 15-by-4 tunnels. Jeans and T-shirts hung from the face of the north tunnel, drying in the sun. Cardboard boxes, mounds of clothing, and a bed blocked the south tunnel.

"Hello?" I called out, kneeling at the mouth of the south tunnel. I heard muffled voices deep in the drain, but no direct response.

Not wanting to enter the camp without permission, I shuffled into the north tunnel. It cut under Industrial, then emptied into an open-air channel that turned toward the interstate. I climbed out of the channel, lowered myself into a parallel channel, and approached the south tunnel.

"Who are you?" yelled a woman sitting legs-crossed in the outlet. A young man in a baseball cap sat on a patio chair deeper into the shadows and a shirtless middle-aged man reclined on a couch pushed against the wall.

"I'm a journalist," I said over the rush of the interstate. "I think I've talked to this guy before." I pointed toward the man on the couch, Mike, whom I spoke with briefly while taking follow-up notes on the adjacent tunnels.

"Hey, man," said Mike. "How's it going?" He turned toward the woman and young man. "He's all right," he said. "He's a reporter."

"I kept saying hi to you," said the woman in a shrill voice, "but you didn't say anything." She had stringy hair and hairy armpits. Muscles bulged from her slender limbs.

"I couldn't hear you over the traffic," I explained, ducking into the tunnel and kneeling next to her.

"I was cussing you out," she said, her bloodshot eyes rolling madly. "I said, 'If you can't say hi to me, you can kiss my ass.'"

"Hi," I said, smiling. "I'm Matt."

"I'm not going to tell you my name." The woman looked away. "If you can't say hi to me, you can kiss my ass."

"You been working, Matt?" asked Mike, rescuing me from the conversation.

"Yeah. I entered a drain near Trop and Valley View around one o'clock. I talked to Phillip, Tyrone, and Tyrone's mother there. Then I took the drain under Valley View and talked to an older man and younger woman for a while." Recalling what the older man said about a lady in the south tunnel under Industrial who was "a hamburger short of a Happy Meal," I turned toward the woman. "Do you live at the other end of this tunnel?"

"I did," she said, "but I'm moving out. There's too much stuff going on down there. It's getting too crazy."

"Who else lives down there?"

"A few rats. A few spiders. Everyone lives down there, baby."

"What's down the other way, under the interstate?"

"More tunnels," she said. "They all go under the Strip."

"I've explored the two tunnels that run along I-15," I said. "They empty near the Hard Rock. These two tunnels empty at that same place, according to my map."

"I ain't gone *that* far yet," said the woman, as if *I* were crazy. "They go all the way to the Hard Rock, huh? Ah, man. I'm going to get me some roller skates. I'm going to have me some fun."

"You won't get very far," I said. "It's wet and there's all kinds of debris down there."

"That's all right," she said. "If you know how to skate, you can jump over all that stuff. Oh yeah. Oh, hell yeah. That's what I want for Christmas. I want me some roller skates.

"You'll have to excuse me," she continued, as the young man rose from the chair and disappeared into the darkness. "I got to go. I got to get out of here." She patted her lap, then stood. "Where's my dick?" she said, referring to her crack pipe. "Where did it go? I need to find my dick. My dick is my pimp."

"He has it," said Mike, referring to the young man.

"Hey, man!" yelled the woman, darting off into the shadows like a demon. "Where the fuck you running off to? Get your ass back here!"

"Nice to meet you," I said sarcastically.

"Nice to meet you, too," she said, failing to pick up on the sarcasm. "Come see me some time. We'll go roller skating."

"OK," I said. "We'll couples skate under the Strip." I slipped out of the backpack and moved into the chair vacated by the young man. "Do the two of them live down there together?" I asked Mike, who was about six feet tall and 220 pounds. He was balding and missing his front teeth.

"I don't know what's going on there," he said. "She's been with everybody in these tunnels. She told me I was gay, because I wouldn't have sex with her. I said,

'No, honey, I'm intelligent. There's nothing gay about me.' I just kind of like my sex organs, Matt. I want to keep them for another day."

"How long have you lived down here?"

"About a month."

"Do you live alone?"

"Yeah. I had an apartment, but I ran out of money last month. Now I got to get my wife to love me again. Every time I call her, she hangs up on me. I moved into this end of the tunnel, because you got to hunch down to get here. Most people are too lazy to come this far under the road and they don't want to climb in and out of the channel. They do too much dumb shit that I don't want to be involved with. Hell, I do enough dumb stuff on my own."

"But you hang out with them?"

"I don't invite them in here. If they show up, they show up. But I usually throw people out pretty quickly. They make a mess. I know this isn't a house, but it is where I live. They disrespect it. They leave all their trash and crack bags all over the place. They don't care where they piss and shit. I got a bucket for that. I got toilet paper. If I have to take a dump, I roll it up in a newspaper, put it in a garbage bag, and carry it out of here. You go down to the other end of the tunnel and it stinks like hell. You got to live somewhere, so why disrespect it?

"I'm not saying I'm innocent or anything," he continued. "I do some drugs, but I don't live on them. If it stops being recreational for me, I'm not going to keep doing it."

"What's your drug?"

"If I had my choice and I had to do something all the time, it'd probably be speed. It's what I used to do in the old days, in Vietnam and shit. I've tried every drug there is at least once. I'll try anything just to see if I like it. I tried heroin once and I couldn't understand why anybody would want to take something that's going to make them puke and go to sleep. Hell, I could eat my wife's cooking and do that."

Smiling, I surveyed the camp. An ottoman was pushed against the far end of the couch and a plastic cooler served as a coffee table. A stack of milk crates topped with a videocassette recorder stood in the middle of the tunnel. A TV that was powered by a generator, explained Mike, once accompanied the VCR—but it washed away during the recent rainstorm.

"Where'd you get all this stuff?" I asked Mike, who was dressed in faded blue jeans and dirty white socks.

"Mainly out of dumpsters and from other people on the streets."

"How'd you get it down here?"

"Over the top of the chain-link fence. Then I just lowered it into the channel and dragged it in here."

"At night?"

"No. In broad daylight. I'm not trying to hide anything."

I laughed. "You're crazy, man. That must've given the tourists a jolt."

"Nobody has ever come down here and said anything to me. The cops were down here yesterday. They didn't say anything. If they ever do, I'll tell them that I'm homesteading under the Civil Rights Act as a veteran."

"How'd you end up on the streets?"

"Me and my wife own a Freightliner truck. Well, I pissed her off just before I went into a casino to use the bathroom. We were getting ready to leave town and she just drove away. I came out of the casino and my blanket and pillow were lying on the ground. She was gone."

Grimacing, Mike lifted his right hand and set it on the arm of the couch. It was red and swollen from his wrist to his fingertips.

"What happened?" I asked him.

"I don't know," he said, picking at a scab on top of the hand. "Something bit me, I think. It hurts like hell. It hurts all the way up to my fingertips. It hurt so bad yesterday I couldn't climb out of here to go get water. I was so dehydrated I was thinking about taking a rag, dipping it into that dirty rainwater, and sucking on the end of it. Last night, I actually cried it hurt so bad.

"It almost feels like a break or a fracture. It constantly burns. It hurts to even move my fingers. I can feel a fly landing on the damn thing and walking around on it. But last night I just laid here and kept my hand elevated against the wall. I think that helped a lot. If it gets any bigger, I'll probably lance it. If it's not better after that, I'll visit the doctor.

"I'm supposed to have hernia surgery soon anyway. You can see how my stomach's busted right here." He pointed at a lump next to his navel. "I have a rip in my stomach line. But when I went to the hospital last week, they said they didn't have any beds available for people who don't have insurance. So I guess I'll have to go back some other time."

While Mike spoke, I studied his facial features. He had gray-green eyes, which brought life to his otherwise dead and dirty face. His nose was flat and off-center—not from sanctioned boxing, I assumed, but from barroom brawls. A scar ran down his right cheek, showing through the dirt and stubble.

"That's my Clint Eastwood," he said, when I asked about the scar. "I was at a bar in Dallas. I had to piss and there was a really long line for the bathroom, so I went outside to pee. When I came out of the bar, two guys were robbing this one guy in the parking lot. The dumb-ass that I am, I tried to help the guy. One of the guys took a screwdriver and stuck it right in my stomach." He pointed at a circular

> *I don't know. All I know is that I'd never fight for this country again. It didn't do nothing for me. It used me, then left me hanging. I'll just defend myself and my friends from now on, nobody else. ~ Mike*

scar. "I could actually feel it hit my backbone. Then he went for my head and I put my left arm up to block the screwdriver." He extended the arm, revealing a crooked scar. "The other guy came at me with a razor blade and sliced me on my face. And then they robbed me. I guess that's what I get for butting into other people's business."

"When did that happen?"

"Probably fifteen, twenty years ago. I was bleeding so bad that blood was shooting out of my veins. They hit an artery in my arm. I still got a plastic bloodline in there. I tried to open the door of the bar, but I fell flat on my face. I woke up in the hospital."

"Sounds like you're lucky to be alive."

"I don't know. All I know is the nurse who put the catheter in me had really big breasts."

Noticing movement along the bottom of the wall, I turned away from Mike. A trail of ants weaved in and out of the camp. I followed the trail until it disappeared in the sunlight, then looked out across the interstate. Luxor and Mandalay Bay shimmered in the light. I turned back toward Mike. "You're a veteran?"

"Yeah. I did three years in 'Nam beginning when I was seventeen years old. I was there in '67, '68, '69 and a little bit of '70. I was in the Army.

"I didn't plan on going to Vietnam," continued Mike, propping his feet up on the cooler. "I went into the Army to get away from home. My dad was a violent bastard and I was always a big guy from the time I was really young. I don't remember ever being small. I could kick his ass, so there was always shit going on around the house. I went into the service to get away from all that.

"Well, my dad followed me to basic training, to AIT [Advanced Infantry Training], and we'd get into fights. So I went to my company commander and said, 'I want to get away from all this fighting. Send me somewhere else.' The smart-ass sent me to Vietnam."

"What was that like?"

"It ain't John Wayne. It ain't like the movies. It's different, much different. There ain't no heroes—except the dead, I guess—and anybody who tells you they weren't scared is lying their ass off. I pissed in my pants more than once. I'll be the first to admit it. It's really hard to take that first step when you don't know if you're walking right into it. But after a while, you get used to it. It's survive or die. You just do it."

"Did you see much action?"

"Sex or violence?" he deadpanned. "Oh, I don't know. A little bit, I guess. But that's a question I don't like to answer. I've actually had people ask me how many people I killed. I hate that question. I really do. It's not something you want to talk about.

"Obviously, you're going to see some action in Vietnam. Something's going to happen at some point or another. You're in a country where you don't know who the enemy is. They talk about baby killers and women killers—but when they got a grenade taped to their body and they're coming at you, what are you supposed to do?

"I don't know. All I know is that I'd *never* fight for this country again. It didn't do nothing for me. It used me, then left me hanging. I'll just defend myself and my friends from now on, nobody else."

"Were you a tunnel rat?"

During the Vietnam War, Viet Cong guerrillas utilized a network of tunnels that stretched from Saigon to the Cambodian border. The network—dug in the 1940s to fight off colonial landlord France and expanded over the years—connected villages, districts, and provinces. The typical tunnel complex included a storage room, conference room, sleeping chamber, kitchen, and hospital. Punji-stake traps protected the trap-door entrances.

As U.S. soldiers high-stepped through the jungles, the guerrillas—dressed like peasants in cone-shaped hats, silk pajamas, and truck-tire sandals—waited behind trees and in spider holes. They opened fire on the lead column, then scurried into the underground. Anxious for revenge, the Americans returned fire and advanced—but found no trace of "Charlie." Their sweeps also proved fruitless. It was as if the enemy had melted into the foliage. It was as if they were fighting ghosts.

Once aware of the underground network, U.S. troops tried a variety of tactics. They dropped grenades through the trap-door entrances, which—of course—did little damage. They dynamited tunnels, destroying Viet Cong documents and equipment that should've been seized. They pumped poisonous gas into the ventilation shafts—but trap doors prevented the gas from spreading throughout the multi-level complexes.

Finally, the U.S. military decided the complexes needed to be explored before they were destroyed. A special unit was formed to carry out this task. The unit was volunteer; there are some things that even the military can't make a man do. Typically, the soldiers were small (many of the tunnels were too narrow to turn around in) and introverted. They seemed to have something to prove to their commanders, fellow soldiers, and themselves. Their basic gear: a knife, a pistol, and a flashlight. Their basic rules: There's no rank in the underground; never hold the flashlight close to your body (that makes for an easy target); and always whistle "Dixie" as you exit the network, so you're not mistaken for the enemy by aboveground troops. Their nickname: tunnel rats.

"I'm a fool," said Mike, still picking at the scab, "but I'm not an idiot. Those guys would go in there with a knife between their teeth, a forty-five tied around their neck, and a flashlight in their hand. That was it. They didn't have anything else. This tunnel here is the Hilton compared to what they were crawling around in. Hell, they'd probably pay twelve hundred dollars a month for this—plus utilities. See, those guys never knew what they were coming up on. Sometimes the tunnels were empty. Sometimes there were whole battalions down there."

Indeed, sometimes the complexes were inactive or "cold." Nonetheless, the tunnel rats had to deal with booby traps and poisonous snakes and spiders … the darkness, claustrophobia, and all their worst fears. Sometimes the complexes were active or "hot." Tunnel rats often found that out the hard way—the flash of a gun, a bayonet to the groin, hand-to-hand combat in the narrow passageways. Some rats crawled and crawled and crawled, surfacing miles away in a straw hut or pigpen, hands and knees bleeding. Some were injured or killed in the complexes, then dragged out by the rope conveniently tied to their ankle. Some never surfaced at all.

"Have you followed the war in Iraq?" I asked Mike.

"Yeah," he said. "A little bit. It's the same bullshit, different country. It's the same crap, different sewer. A bunch of innocent kids are dying for bureaucracy, oil, and George W. Bush. He's just trying to make his daddy happy by getting back at Saddam. It's a grudge match. It'll be going on for a while yet. You just wait and see.

"The sad thing is," he continued, "both wars really had nothing to do with the United States. We have so much fuel stockpiled in places throughout the world, but right now I can't make any goddamn money off my truck. I got to clear over four thousand dollars a week just to take home any check at all. That's why I don't even bother calling my wife and asking her for money. Fuel prices are ridiculous. It's so stupid. We're over there killing foreigners and wasting billions of dollars."

"Are you registered to vote?" I asked Mike, wondering if he was just bitching or if he planned to participate in the next election.

"Yeah, but I don't vote. I would've voted for JFK. But after that, there hasn't been anybody worth voting for. Since I came back from Vietnam, there hasn't been anyone worth a damn. Anyway, my vote ain't going to make a difference. This country ain't run by the voters. It's run by the businessmen. They're going to put whoever they want in the White House—and the president doesn't make that much of a difference anyhow. He's just a figurehead. He ain't got a damn thing to say about jackshit. He's got a lower life than I do, except he has a nicer place to live and he gets laid every once in a while."

"Is it tough to get laid in the drains?"

"No. It's actually really easy, but some of the girls down here have AIDS."

"Do you miss your wife at all?"

"I was planning on getting back together with her soon, but she's still hanging up on me when I call. She doesn't know I'm down here. She thinks I'm still in the apartment, so it's not hurting her feelings to hang up on me. I don't really miss her anyhow. We'll have been married twenty-one years on New Year's Eve. We got married on New Year's Eve just so I'd remember the anniversary. But for ten years now we've been married in name more than anything else."

"Are you anxious to get back on the road? To get out of Vegas?"

"Yeah, in some ways. Sex, drugs, and money—that's all this place is about. Las Vegas changes people. Everybody is out for number one, at least that's what I've seen. People here don't seem to care about each other. All they care about is themselves.

"I helped a guy up there on the street the other day. I pushed his car to a gas station and helped him get it started. He said, 'All I got to give you is three dollars.' I said, 'I didn't ask you for any money. And if all you got is three dollars, partner, you better hang onto it.' I'm from the old school, man. If somebody helps you, you help somebody else. I don't ask for money. If you want to give me some, go ahead. But I don't ask these people for shit."

"How do you get by?"

"I don't know yet," said Mike, flashing a toothless smile. "I'll work on that later."

"Do you panhandle?"

"Somebody told me they make fifty dollars an hour doing that, so I went up there to Tropicana and I-15 one day. I stood there for an hour and a half and made one goddamn dollar. But I've got a new sign made up. I'm going to try it out tonight. It says, 'Vietnam Vet. Newly Homeless. Apologize for Asking. Anything Would Help.' If that doesn't work, I'll just rob a bank."

"You seem to have a laid-back attitude about all this."

"I just accept things as they are and try to make the best of it. I don't bitch about it—and this really ain't that bad: no taxes, no utility bills, it's cool at night, I got light from the Strip, I got my new TV. It's color, too. See it over there?" Mike pointed at Mandalay Bay's electronic sign. "It shows the same program over and over again, though. That's my only complaint. And there's a lot of commercials. Maybe next week they'll get a new attraction or something."

Smiling, I rose from the chair and picked up the backpack. "I think I'm going to walk under the Strip and check it out from these two tunnels. I want to get down there before it gets dark."

"If you find my old TV," said Mike, "would you bring it back up here? It's a little Sanyo."

I laughed, then ducked out of the drain. "Yeah. No problem, man."

After checking on Ernie, who wasn't around, I returned to the north channel and started downstream. It swung sharply to the east, then burrowed under the interstate in a seven-by-seven tunnel. I stepped into the shadows—out of the blue and into the black, as the tunnel rats used to say—discovering a camp made of cardboard and plastic.

"Do you mind if I cut through?" I asked a man stretched on the floor.

"No, not at all," he said, picking at the bones of a chicken breast. "Where does this tunnel lead to?"

"It comes out near the Hard Rock," I said in a weird role reversal. "I'm not going all the way through, though. I'm just going under the Strip, then coming back out this way. How far back have you gone?"

"About a quarter-mile," said the Gatekeeper of the Strip.

"Anything interesting back there?"

"Nah, not really. Just standing water."

"Well," I said, not wanting to interrupt the man's meal, "I guess I'll check it out."

Removing the flashlight from the backpack, I ducked under a piece of wood that supported the front of the camp. The tunnel was gray and slightly disjointed, as if leading to the Twilight Zone. White stalactites hung from the ceiling and cockroaches crawled along the walls like liquid graffiti. Somewhere in the depths of the drain, a manhole cover rocked a creepy lullaby.

At the end of a long straightaway, the tunnel turned to the north and the ceiling dropped to six feet. Water painted the floor black. The smell of mildew nearly knocked me on my ass. Beyond another bend, the rush of the interstate faded and an equalizer punched a hole in the wall. I peeked into the parallel tunnel, which looked a lot like the others, then returned to the north tunnel and continued downstream.

Along this stretch, I thought about the flood-control map and how the storm drains are installed. The Flood Control District's master plan dictates where drains are placed. Its engineers prepare plans and specifications, then construction companies bid on the project. The terrain is surveyed and staked. Track-hoes dig a trench. Then cranes lower the concrete boxes into the trench (or, less often, the tunnel is cast in place), bulldozers or forklifts push the boxes together, and the terrain is returned to its original condition—or as close to it as possible.

I also thought about how the boxes, which can weigh more than 50,000 pounds, are made: two open-ended cages, one slightly larger than the other, are wired together and placed in steel forms (or a "jacket"); a machine pours concrete into the forms; the jacket is removed and the box dries; it's smoothed and stenciled; then it's fork-lifted onto a truck, secured with chains or cables, and transported to the construction site.

The ceiling dropped to five feet and the tunnel trended to the east. Water gargled in the depths of the drain. With each step I took, the gargling got louder and the smell of mildew stronger. Then, at the confluence of the tunnels, the beam of the flashlight bounced off water pouring from a pipe in the ceiling.

Sidestepping the water and continuing into the darkness, I discovered more ceiling pipes. Assuming I was under the Strip, I sat on an island of dust and surveyed my surroundings: concrete, cockroaches, and a two-inch-deep stream of runoff.

"The underworld is a mirror of the world aboveground," wrote Klaus Klemp in *Underworld: Sites of Concealment*, an architecture book I read during my research.

But huddled in the darkness, the beam burning a hole in the ceiling, I found few clues of the Great Gambling Civilization overhead. I did, however, note some similarities between the storm drains and the casinos: They neutralize all sense of time; their exits can be extremely hard to find; and they're among the loneliest places on Earth.

T he words leaned and fluttered, as if rearranged by the wind. They formed crooked lines, like jail-cell poetry, and an oddly shaped stanza. Fading and surging on the sun-bleached wall of a channel near Eastern and Tropicana avenues, beyond the shadows of an eight-by-six tunnel, they read in block letters:

"THIS PLACE WAS ONCE MY HOME.
MY FAMILY ONCE LIVED HERE.
I ONCE FELT LOVE & SAFETY HERE
BECAUSE OF THE PEOPLE WHO SURROUNDED ME—
WHO I CONSIDERED MY TRUE FAMILY –
CLOSER THAN BLOOD.
I NOW FEEL ALONE AND BETRAYED.
IT TAKES MERE SECONDS 4 EVERYONE
TO TURN THEIR BACKS ON 'FAMILY.'
FROM THE BOTTOM OF MY HEART,
I MISS YOU ALL
AND WILL LOVE YOU FOREVER."

Putting on the knit cap and tightening the straps of the backpack, I stared at the words. I pressed "Play" and "Record," then reread them aloud. They were simple. They were raw. They were beautiful. In a city full of false advertising and industry propaganda—"The Loosest Slots in Vegas" … "The Hottest Ticket on the Strip" … "The Sexiest Girls in the World"—they were refreshingly honest. They felt like the first *real* words I'd read on the signs, billboards, and seemingly never-ending walls that line Las Vegas.

Clutching the flashlight, I turned toward the tunnel and squinted into the gloom. A cardboard mat sprawled across the floor, surrounded by napkins and newspapers. A cushioned chair was pushed against a wall. And a hand mirror hung from a hook in the ceiling, spinning like a disco ball and shooting light in all directions.

"Hello?" I said, stepping into the shadows and snapping on the flashlight.

A breeze followed me into the semidarkness, rustling the newspapers and stirring up the stench of urine. Graffiti—tags, gang names, and declarations of love—blistered the walls. Around a bend, a glass pipe and hypodermic needle were wedged between two of the concrete boxes. Farther upstream, beyond couch cushions and garbage bags, the tunnel bled into the darkness.

Sitting on the cardboard mat, I cut off the flashlight and picked up a newspaper. I shook a section loose, leaned against the wall, and began flipping through the pages. As I skimmed the week-old stories, my mind drifted and I thought about the previous day's adventures: After exploring a few drains near Flamingo Road and Boulder Highway, finding one isolated camp and miles and miles of algae, I followed the system southwesterly in my car using an eight-and-a-half-by-eleven rendering of the flood-control map. I cut on the hazard lights, rolled down the windows, and searched for inlets and outlets. I weaved through residential neighborhoods, parked illegally, and walked winding open-air channels until I was sure they didn't go underground. I ducked into culverts, saw sunlight on the other side of the street, and returned to the car. I consulted the map regularly, while making sudden U-turns. Body-heat steam formed on the fringes of the windshield. The floorboard was smeared with sand and mud. I was sweaty, carsick, and convinced there was no action to be found in the storm drains of the southeast valley.

Near the intersection of Eastern and Tropicana, as I unclipped the mike from my collar and prepared to head home, I noticed an open-air channel that ran parallel to a side street. I pulled over and put the car in park. Engine idling, I stepped onto the sidewalk and glanced down at the channel through a chain-link fence … discovering the eight-by-six tunnel and the cardboard mat, which stretched beyond the shade line. I parked in a nearby strip mall and scooped the flashlight from the passenger seat. Then I climbed a cinderblock wall, angled into the channel, and approached the tunnel.

As I entered the tunnel, two heads poked around the bend. In the strange and hazy half-light, the heads appeared to be floating: One had shaggy light-brown hair and a mustache; the other was round and smooth, partially obscured by a bandana and granny glasses.

It turned out the heads belonged to a friendly middle-aged couple, Bob and Jona (pronounced John-a). Bob and Jona told me that they live upstream in an open-air channel and visit the tunnel once or twice a day to get out of the sun and get high. They said street kids hang out in the area and a disillusioned teenage girl wrote the words at the outlet. The inlet, they explained, is on the other side of Eastern, and the channel goes back underground at Spencer Street.

After talking to Bob and Jona for five or ten minutes, I decided that this stretch of the storm-drain system was worth exploring. However, I was tired and thirsty and had left most of my gear in the car. So, I told Bob and Jona, I'll come back to the tunnel tomorrow afternoon and we can continue our conversation. Sounds good, they said. See you then.

About 15 minutes after I sat on the mat and began flipping through the newspaper, voices drifted into the tunnel through a drop inlet. Footsteps pattered on the roof and a flock of pigeons flew from the south bank of the channel. I lowered the paper, assuming that Bob and Jona had arrived—but a young man with greasy hair and a goatee appeared in the outlet, cradling a roll of carpet. A buttoned-down shirt and blue jeans hung loosely from his frame.

"Hey, man," I said. "How's it going?"

"What's up?" said the young man, ducking into the tunnel and dropping the carpet around the bend.

"Not much," I said. "What's up with you?"

"I'm just rebuilding my house," he said, exiting the tunnel.

Another young man entered the tunnel carrying carpet. He was about six feet tall and 175 pounds, shorter but heavier than his companion. He wore a T-shirt, baggy shorts, white socks, and black boots. Braids or dreadlocks—I couldn't tell which in the half-light—snaked from underneath his baseball cap and coiled on his shoulders. Struggling with the carpet, he dumped it around the bend.

The young man with the goatee returned, wrestling a mattress. I folded the paper and placed it on the floor. "You need some help with that?" I asked him.

"No," he said. "I'm fine." He threw the mattress onto the mound of carpet. It bounced, then settled, flattening a few of the garbage bags. Breathing heavily, the young men kicked the cushions and bags out of the way and began to roll the carpet. I stood and walked toward them, deeper into the shadows.

"Do you all live down here?" I asked the young men.

The young man with the goatee answered, "Yeah."

"The reason I'm asking is I'm a reporter. I'm working on a book about the drains and the people who live in them."

The young men continued to roll the carpet. The tunnel fell silent. "Is that what you're doing down here now?" asked the young man with the goatee, who appeared to be about 18 years old.

"Yeah. I was down here yesterday talking to Bob and Jona. I told them that I was going to come back today and talk to them some more."

The young man in the baseball cap stood and stretched his back. He lifted the bottom of his shirt and wiped his brow, which was glistening like a switchblade in an alley. "I can't roll it no more," he said, collapsing against a wall. He pulled down the bill of his cap, covering his eyes.

"It's not good that you're a reporter," said the other young man, continuing to roll the carpet. "We don't want people to know we're down here."

I sat on the arm of the chair and set the flashlight on the floor, butt end up. "The book won't be published for a while," I said. "Also, I'm being vague about names and locations. I'm only using first names and I'm trying not to give away the locations of the drains. For this one, I'll just say something like a tunnel near Eastern and Trop."

"But this is the *only* tunnel near Eastern and Trop," said the young man.

"There are a few others around here," I said, "and this one's fairly well-concealed."

The young man in the cap lay still against the wall, legs extended and hands behind his head—but he wasn't asleep. I sensed that his eyes were open, that he was listening to every word, that he was considering all options. I assumed he had a blade on him. Most street kids in Vegas do—if they're smart. Where was it, I wondered? In his sock? His pants pocket? The small of his back? I shifted on the arm of the chair, making sure that my right hand had a clear path to the baton. The young man with the goatee rolled the final piece of carpet, smoothed it out with his hands, then sat on the foot of the mattress.

"So Bob and Jona talked to you, huh?" he said.

"Yeah. I talked to them for five or ten minutes. They said they live nearby and visit the tunnel once or twice a day to get out of the sun or whatever. They said it's a hangout for street kids, but that nobody lives in here."

"That's bullshit," said the young man, lying on the mattress and staring at the ceiling. He raked his fingers through his hair and rubbed his forehead. He seemed angry, confused, *crushed*. It was as if my presence had ruined everything, all his grand plans of creating a street-kid kingdom in this dreary eight-by-six tunnel. "I wish they would've kept their fucking mouths shut," he said, "and I'll tell them that, too."

A shadow rose on the south wall of the tunnel. I flinched, discovering a sweaty balding man standing over my shoulder. He was wearing a striped short-sleeve shirt, black jeans, and sneakers. A scratch outlined with dry blood ran down the side of his face.

"Are Bob and Jona down here?" he asked quietly.

"No," said the young man with the goatee.

"How's it going?" I said, looking up at the man.

"All right," he said. "How are you?"

"This is a reporter, John," interrupted the young man.

"Huh?"

"We got a reporter down here," he repeated, as if soliciting advice.

"I'm Matt," I said, extending my hand. "I'm a reporter. I'm working on a book about the drains."

"I'm John," said the man, shaking my hand. "Nice to meet you."

"I was down here yesterday talking to Bob and Jona," I continued. "They said they were going to be around today."

"I'm trying to find them, too," he said. "They haven't been down here, huh?"

"No," I said.

"Well," he said, "I guess I'll go look for them."

And just as quickly and quietly as he'd appeared, John disappeared into the sunlight. The young man in the cap rolled onto his side, back turned toward me. The young man with the goatee lay motionless on the mattress. I shifted on the arm of the chair and stared at the floor—playing cards, fast-food wrappers, hypodermic needles. The wind whipped, creating ghostlike clouds of dust in the outlet. The tunnel moaned. A manhole rattled somewhere in the distance.

In the old and crumbling border city of Nogales, Mexico, a storm drain sits at the end of a dry arroyo. The drain, composed of two 14-by-7 tunnels, is dark and dusty. It's eerily quiet and choked with debris. It's long—several miles long—and suffocating. The drain, which empties in sister city Nogales, Arizona, is also the only hope some Mexicans have of entering the United States.

As migrant workers, smugglers, and families desperate for a better life shuffle into the drain—with money and drugs and all their personal possessions—they're greeted by gangs of street kids. The kids, high on marijuana and paint fumes, offer to escort the illegals (known as *pollos*) through the darkness for a couple hundred pesos (about $20). In the depths of the drain, the pollos are jumped and robbed. They're forced to exit on the U.S. side, bloody and naked, where they're greeted by the Border Patrol and loaded into a transport van. Welcome to

America. We hope you enjoyed your stay.

Looking around the eight-by-six tunnel—the graffiti, the drug paraphernalia, the street kids in baggy clothes—I couldn't help feeling a little bit like a pollo. I couldn't help feeling that something bad was about to go down.

The young man in the baseball cap farted, pulling me from my thoughts. He then began to laugh loudly. The young man with the goatee groaned and rolled onto his side.

"You better get your ass out of my tunnel, dude," he said. He was facing his companion, but I sensed that the words were directed at me.

"I was saving that one," said the young man in the cap.

"Man, I got to find me another roommate. If you fart again, I'm going to kick your ass."

The young man in the cap farted again.

"You motherfucker," said the young man with the goatee. "I'm going to *beat your ass*."

The young man in the cap curled into a fetal position on the floor and laughed uncontrollably. The young man with the goatee squirmed on the mattress, then laughed along with his companion. They gasped and snorted. They panted, sniffled, and damn near convulsed. Their eyes were wet. Their stomach muscles must've been sore.

Finally, the laughter faded. The young man with the goatee sat on the foot of the mattress and looked up at me.

"So you're going to wait here for Bob and Jona?" he said.

"I was planning to, but you guys are obviously not comfortable with that."

"Ah, dude," said the young man. "I didn't want to tell you this, but I *really* don't want you down here. I want you to leave—like right now."

"All right," I said, scooping the flashlight from the floor and rising from the chair. "That's cool."

"Fucking Bob," he muttered, falling back onto the mattress. "I'm going to get his ass."

"I think I'll go out this way," I said, starting upstream.

"Good luck getting through there," said the young man in the cap.

"Does it get low?" I asked.

"Yeah," said the young man with the goatee, "and there's a whole bunch of spiders down there."

Weaving around the couch cushions and garbage bags, I watched the young men closely. I was waiting for one of them to reach for a shank and come charging at me, but they lay as still as the graffiti. They just wanted me to leave, I finally realized. The sooner, the better. The same way I'd want a nosy and uninvited guest to get the hell out of my house. Actually, I was surprised I didn't get this same cold reception from more of the inhabitants. I was, after all, entering their homes and asking them personal questions—and I wasn't offering them money, drugs, or even a sip from my bottle of water. The only thing I offered them was an ear, an opportunity for their low and raspy voices to be heard amid the din of slot machines, Convention Authority ads, and posturing politicians.

Beyond the cushions and bags, the tunnel went dark. I cut on the flashlight, discovering more graffiti and a sharp turn to the west. Around the bend, which was lined with newspapers, the tunnel narrowed to six feet and straightened toward two rectangles of light in the distance. I hurried up the straightaway, glancing over my shoulder. The backlight had faded and I couldn't see a damn thing, but I heard debris rustling and the young men laughing. I assumed that they were continuing to build their camp, playing a spirited game of grab-ass, or doing whatever young men who live in drainage tunnels do on cloudless summer afternoons in Las Vegas.

At the end of the straightaway, the tunnel rolled up a ramp and split into two five-by-three tunnels—the eye sockets of this concrete skull—which were each about 150 feet long. Spider webs screened the south tunnel. I tried to enter the north tunnel sideways, but the ceiling forced me to my hands and knees. Head down and back arched, I began crawling toward the light. The flashlight clanked against the floor. The concrete, which I scanned for spiders and hypodermic needles, gnawed at my hands and knees. I felt like a pollo groveling for the promised land.

Sensing the light and hearing the cars overhead on Eastern, I lifted my head. The last box of the tunnel cradled a pool of water buzzing with mosquitoes. I turned sideways, placed my right hand on the wall, and slid through the water. Then I staggered into the sunlight and stood upright, imprisoned by the walls of a rectangular channel. The sun glared at me like a Border Patrol agent in a watchtower. The heat rivaled the Sonoran Desert.

Extracting a thorn from my hand and brushing the dust off my pants, I started upstream in the channel. A pine tree leaned over the north wall, providing a rare patch of shade, and leaves crunched beneath my boots. I glanced over my shoulder, then squinted upstream. Blurred by heat waves, the channel appeared to straighten for a quarter-mile and disappear to the south amid palm trees and Spanish-tile roofs.

Halfway up the straightaway, the south wall broke and gave way to a steep ramp. I climbed the ramp, which led to a detention basin—concrete crest and bed, rock-and-wire banks, and a drainage pipe covered with a grate. I looked out across the basin, shielding my eyes from the sun, thinking that it resembled the strangely beautiful earthworks found in the remote Mojave Desert.

Angling down the ramp, I turned upstream in the channel … and stumbled on a man crouched behind the south wall. I flinched, then reached for the baton. The man stood upright, equally surprised. Recognizing John, the sweaty balding man I'd met in the tunnel, I took my hand off the baton and exhaled.

"How'd you get down here so quickly?" I asked him.

"I went around the other way [aboveground]," he said.

"Did you find Bob and Jona?"

"Nah."

"Do you have any idea where they are?"

"No." He glanced nervously up and down the straightaway. "Uh, I was kind of in the middle of something. No offense or anything."

"No problem," I said, noticing a plastic bottle between his feet. It appeared to contain an inch of clear liquid and a hypodermic needle. "See you around."

As I continued upstream, John crouched over the bottle. "If I see Bob and Jona," he said over his shoulder, "I'll send them your way."

"All right," I said. "Thanks."

The channel swung to the south. I rounded the bend cautiously, wondering if I'd stumble on another sweaty junkie preparing to slam heroin. I sidestepped a soiled blanket and pillow, which I assumed had washed downstream. A rustling sound shot from a lateral pipe. My God, I thought as I surged up a straightaway. The open-air channels are just as creepy as the storm drains. They reminded me of downtown alleys—long, straight, and lined with graffiti—only much more secluded. I wondered who or what I might encounter next. The Jets and the

My God, I thought as I surged up a straightaway. The open-air channels are just
straight, and lined with graffiti—only much more secluded. I wondered
A pack of rabid dogs? A shirtless madman howling

Sharks? A pack of rabid dogs? A shirtless madman howling at the sun, predicting the Second Coming?

Under a canopy of pines, the channel snaked to the west and straightened. I noted the rungs on the walls—in case I needed to make a quick escape—then weaved around more blankets and pillows, wondering if there was a campsite upstream or if people were actually sleeping on the floor. Tightening the straps of the backpack, I started up the straightaway. A camp took shape along the south wall. Emerging from a hut, a man stood in the middle of the channel and adjusted a pair of overalls.

"Bob?" I said, approaching the man.

"Yeah," he said, concentrating on the straps of the overalls. "Who's that?"

"Matt. The reporter you talked to yesterday."

"Hey, Matt. How's it going?"

"All right," I said, pulling up next to him. "I was just in the tunnel where I met you and Jona. I was looking for you all."

"Well," said Bob, "you found us."

"Is Jona in there?" I pointed at the hut.

"Yeah."

"Hey, Matt," said Jona, from inside the saddest little home I'd seen in my life. A box spring served as the outside wall and a bedsheet, weighed down by books, as the roof. A piece of cardboard somehow pinned the sheet against the channel wall. Garbage bags bulging with food, clothing, books, toiletries, and trash surrounded the hut, like rusted cars around a mobile home.

"This is where you all live?" I said, stunned.

as creepy as the storm drains. They reminded me of downtown alleys—long,
who or what I might encounter next. The Jets and the Sharks?
at the sun, predicting the Second Coming?

"Yeah," shrugged Bob. "It's kind of temporary. I know it's not much."

"How long have you lived here?"

"About two months."

"I saw some blankets and pillows downstream. Is someone sleeping there?"

"I'm not sure. There was somebody sleeping there a couple nights ago, but I don't think they're there on a regular basis."

I wiped my brow with the sleeve of my shirt, then stepped into the shade of the south wall. Bob continued to adjust the straps of the overalls, which he said he found in a dumpster that morning.

"I waited in the tunnel awhile," I said, "thinking you all might drop by. Two young guys were in there. They were setting up camp."

"Were they tall?" asked Bob.

"Yeah. And one of them was real skinny and had a goatee."

"Dark hair?"

"Yeah. I told them I was waiting for you and Jona, but they didn't seem comfortable with a reporter being around. The skinny one wondered why you had talked to me. He didn't seem too happy about it."

"I think those are a couple guys from Street Teens," said Bob, referring to a daytime shelter near Eastern and Tropicana. "It's OK. I'll talk to them later."

According to the county, more than 2,000 kids live on the streets of Las Vegas. How do so many kids end up on the streets? Parents move to Vegas looking for $40,000-a-year jobs and affordable housing. They often find neither. They do, however, find plenty of slot machines and alcohol and drugs and sex. Some become addicted. They lose their money, their hope, their conscience. They take their frustrations out on their kids, physically and mentally. The kids rebel. Eventually, they're kicked out of the house, they run away, or they're taken away by the county.

Many of these kids end up on the streets of southeast Vegas, near UNLV. Dirty-faced and weighed down with duffel bags, they panhandle and sell drugs and their bodies to survive. They hang out in coffee shops, fast-food restaurants, and parks. They sleep in back lots, abandoned buildings, and on the roofs of businesses. And, as I'd just discovered, some of them even sleep in the storm drains.

"So who all hangs out in that tunnel?" I asked Bob.

"People have been going down there for years," he said, "way before Jona and I discovered it. It's a refuge for an assortment of people. You can see from the artwork on the walls that gangbangers have been down there, kids from Street Teens, some adults. People go down there to get high or to get some peace and quiet. When you're on the street, you don't have privacy like you do when you have your own place. That tunnel's about the most private thing going around here.

"A couple years ago—in fact, not too long after Street Teens opened—a lot of kids started going down to the tunnel. At one point, there was about half a dozen guys sleeping in there. Kids would go there late at night, whooping and hollering and drinking and fighting. The neighbors didn't take too kindly to that, so the police cleared everyone out. Since then, it's been pretty quiet—except for a few people dropping in now and then."

"Why do you and Jona go down there?"

"We go down there to get high, and I suppose it's a refuge of sorts for us. It's just a place where we feel halfway safe and secure about not getting hassled. Plus, it's a lot cooler down there. That's always nice when it's hot outside.

"I used to own a home," continued Bob, looking spiffy in his new overalls. "I'm sure you've heard this story before. I was in real estate sales for a while. I had my own cleaning company. To make a long story short, I was in the wrong place at the wrong time and made a stupid decision. I tried heroin. I had a drinking and drug problem off and on for a long time, but I thought all the horror stories about heroin were overblown. Come to find out they're not. It really does take over your life. You spend all your time just trying to get money to go out and get some more, so you can get high again and keep from getting sick."

"How long have you been on the streets?"

"About five or six years."

"How long have you and Jona been together?"

"Uh, about twenty years?"

"We've been together twenty-one years and married seventeen," said Jona, beneath the sheet.

"Do you all get along with the kids who hang out in the tunnel?"

"Yeah," said Bob. "One of them even kind of adopted us as parents. He started calling us Mom and Pop."

"His name is Matt," said Jona. "He's real tall and skinny. In fact, doesn't he have a goatee, honey?"

"I think he does," said Bob. "He might've been the kid you ran into down there."

"He was real dark and moody," I said, "or maybe he just doesn't like reporters, which I can totally understand."

"Yeah," said Bob. "He's real moody. That sounds like him."

"I think he's bipolar," said Jona.

"We just give him an ear, and a shoulder to cry on," continued Bob. "I guess he appreciates that. A lot of people on the street don't have anybody that's willing to listen to them or have a coherent conversation with them about something that's troubling them. It's all superficial."

I wanted to learn more about the tunnel, the kids who hang out in it, and Bob and Jona—I really did—but the heat was stealing my soul. Even in the shade, it was 100 degrees. The stiff breezes, which threatened to carry away the hut, washed over me like the Devil's bad breath. My head was light. My neck and back were wet with sweat. It was time to move on; it was time to crawl back into the underground. I took a sip from the bottle of water, returned it to the backpack, and glanced upstream. A black rectangle loomed in the distance.

"This channel goes underground at Spencer Street?" I asked Bob.

"Yeah. It goes under Spencer in two tunnels that converge a little ways down. If you keep going, there's a tunnel that takes off in one direction. It's on the right side as you're going down. It goes a long, long way. I walked it one day and never did come to the end. It just seems to keep going and going."

"Is there anything interesting in there?"

"No, not really. Not that I saw. There's a little bit of writing on the walls, just enough to let you know that somebody's been back there."

"Anyway," I said, "I'm glad I found you. I wanted to let you know about the street kids in the tunnel. They seemed kind of pissed."

"Thanks," said Bob. "Good luck down there."

"Bye-bye, Matt," said Jona, beneath the sheet.

Adjusting the cap, I started upstream in the shade of the south wall. A pile of fronds forced me back into the sunlight; the rays stung my eyes and the temperature rose at least 15 degrees. Returning to the shade, I encountered a set of rungs. I climbed the rungs and peeked over the wall, which was smooth and about 10 feet tall, discovering a drab apartment complex just north of Tropicana.

At Spencer, the channel widened and went underground in two six-by-six tunnels. The smell of mildew drifted from the darkness. After stuffing my pant legs into my socks and crossing a patch of gravel—which was as perfectly arranged as a welcome mat—I entered the north tunnel. It swung south and straightened under the street. Cobwebs twirled from the ceiling, trapping moths and leaves. Mosquitoes buzzed in the beam of the flashlight.

About 150 feet up the straightaway, which was crawling with cockroaches, the dividing wall disappeared. I tiptoed into the opposite tunnel, aimed the flashlight downstream, then continued upstream. The dividing wall reappeared and again disappeared, creating an oddly shaped chamber under Trop and Spencer. Graffiti faces stared out from the walls. A poem read, in part:

"THERE NEVER WAS A CHILD

IN YOUR HEAD

NEVER BORN, NEVER DEAD

MAYBE WHEN I'M DONE

I'LL MOURN

NOW I'LL COME WITH FIRE AND SCORN

WITH LUST FOR LIFE

UNDER HOOF AND HORN

BLACK-FLAMED

LAMENT AND FORLORN

BREATHE IN LIFE

I GASP RIVER RED

LOGOS MANIFEST

I AM, I SAID

THERE WAS NEVER A CHILD

IN YOUR HEAD

SELF-BORN, SELF-DEAD

BELIEVE WHAT YOU READ

ONE-THIRD WILL ALL BE BLED."

I reread the poem and tried to make sense of it, but I was much too distracted: Atop a ramp, a five-by-three tunnel arched southward under Spencer; a 10-

by-5 tunnel turned to the west, straightening into perfect darkness; and lateral pipes and manholes, swells and dips, collaborated with the flashlight to create grotesque shadows. I swept the beam over the floor, which was littered with matches, matchbooks, and cigarette butts. Spinning in circles, discovering a pair of jeans tucked in a crevice and editorial cartoons pasted to the walls, I assumed the chamber was another hangout for druggies and street kids.

Curious about what else was in the drain, I ducked into the 10-by-5 tunnel. A newspaper headline on the wall read "X-Men Sighted in City" and graffiti lettering explained, "I Went Under to Get Over." Why did *I* go under, I wondered as I lunged upstream? The ceiling clawed at my cap, ripping the threads. Pools of water broke my stride. Breathing heavily, I cleared cobwebs from a manhole shaft and stood upright. Tropicana rattled and hissed overhead.

Catching my breath, I ducked out of the manhole and continued upstream. The floor dried—my boots slipping on dust—then again went black. The water was three inches deep in areas. I played the beam over the ceiling and walls, attempting and failing to find its source. The graffiti, poetry, and cartoons had vanished. All that remained were the hard concrete and liquid darkness, which washed over me like a wave.

About a quarter-mile into the tunnel, the beam hit something solid. I assumed it was a dead end—the storm-drain system is random like that—but another ramp emerged from the darkness. I pulled up in front of the ramp and took refuge in a manhole. Knees aching, I slipped out of the backpack and reached for the bottle of water. I considered turning around, but quickly banished the notion. If Bob—a hopeless junkie—had walked "a long, long way" in this tunnel, I could certainly find the inlet. Of course, Bob was five-foot-six and 130 pounds. He had plenty of wriggle room in this rectangular tomb. I, on the other hand, felt like I was crawling around in one of hell's heating ducts.

Beyond the ramp, the tunnel narrowed and the floor dried. A fair tradeoff, I decided as I lengthened my stride. Knees bent, back straight, and flashlight arm extended, I surged upstream. My pant legs brushed together, creating a rhythmic swooshing sound. The contents of the backpack clanged loudly, echoing in the depths of the drain.

But soon my back bent, my head dropped, and my eyes fixed on the floor— black pools of water, orange islands of dust, and cockroaches. Disoriented, I looked up. A spider web stretched across my face. I reversed, ducked under the web, then continued into the darkness. Exhausted, I fell to a knee. Again, I considered turning around—but a flickering light lured me deeper into the tunnel.

Another manhole, it turned out, was the source of the light. A dust-filled beam angled through the finger hole of the cover, illuminating a small and clean chamber. I stood upright in the shaft, rolled my neck, steadied my breathing. Cars rattled the cover, blacking out the beam. Exhaust fumes tinged the air. Nauseous and soaked in sweat—the tunnel was as humid as a New Orleans summer—I sat on a ledge and removed the bottle of water from the backpack. It was almost empty. This, I realized, could be a problem. I was three-fourths of a mile into the tunnel and sweating out more water than I could put in my body.

Sipping from the bottle, I surveyed the chamber. A seven-by-five tunnel shot southward. Another seven-by-five tunnel continued to the west, a light flickering in the distance. Returning the bottle to the backpack, I started toward the light. The beam of the flashlight was fading and unsteady. The backpack scraped against the ceiling, producing a faint burning smell. Unconsciously, I lifted my head. The ceiling smacked it down, removing my cap. I stopped, set the flashlight aside, and frisked the floor. The wave broke and the darkness crashed down on me.

Finding the cap, I began to crawl toward the light. My chest tightened. My hands and knees were raw. Chills rattled my bones. I wondered if Floyd Collins experienced these same feelings as he crawled around blindly in Sand Cave.

Collins was a cave explorer, guide, and good old boy from central Kentucky. His family owned Crystal Cave, which he'd discovered in 1917 and was in the same general area as popular Mammoth Cave. While stunning, Crystal Cave attracted few tourists because of its remote location. Collins—sometimes called "The Greatest Cave Explorer Ever Known"—hoped to find a link to Mammoth, which would make his family's cave more accessible and profitable.

For three weeks in January 1925, Collins explored and expanded a hole between Mammoth and Crystal caves that would later be known as Sand Cave. On the 30th of that month, after a few hours of exploration, he entered a large chamber and discovered that his lantern was dying. He had to get out of the cave—and quickly. While crawling in a narrow passageway, the mouth only 150 feet away, Collins knocked over the lamp. The flame went out and the darkness crashed down on him. In a panic, he dislodged a rock from the ceiling. It pinned his leg, trapping him in the cold and wet cave.

Eventually, friends and family realized Collins was missing. They searched his new haunt and found him in the passageway, weary but conscious. They ran a light bulb into the cave to provide light and heat. They brought him food and water. A rescue effort ensued, capturing the interest of the nation. Radio, a relatively new medium in the 1920s, aired daily updates. The *Louisville Courier-Journal* published first-person accounts, courtesy of cub reporter William "Skeets" Miller, which were picked up by newspapers across the country. It was the "Baby Jessica" story of the early 20th century.

But unfortunately for Floyd, this story didn't have a happy ending. After two weeks underground and several rescue attempts, Collins died of exposure and starvation. He was eulogized in folk songs, including the straightforwardly titled "The Death of Floyd Collins":

"THE RESCUE PARTY LABORED.
THEY WORKED BOTH NIGHT AND DAY,
TO MOVE THE MIGHTY BARRIER
THAT STOOD WITHIN THEIR WAY.
TO RESCUE FLOYD COLLINS
THIS WAS THEIR BATTLE CRY,
'WE'LL NEVER, NO WE'LL NEVER,
LET FLOYD COLLINS DIE!'
BUT ON THAT FATEFUL MORNING,
THE SUN ROSE IN THE SKY.

THE WORKERS STILL WERE BUSY:
'WE'LL SAVE HIM BY AND BY!'
BUT OH! HOW SAD THE ENDING,
HIS LIFE COULD NOT BE SAVED.
HIS BODY THEN WAS SLEEPING
IN THE LONELY SANDSTONE CAVE.
YOUNG PEOPLE, ALL TAKE WARNING
FROM FLOYD COLLINS' FATE,
AND GET RIGHT WITH YOUR MAKER
BEFORE IT IS TOO LATE.
IT MAY NOT BE A SAND CAVE
IN WHICH WE FIND OUR TOMB.
BUT ON THAT DAY OF JUDGMENT,
WE TOO MUST MEET OUR DOOM."

Experienced cavers have pointed out that Collins made three mistakes when he entered Sand Cave: He went in alone; he didn't have at least three light sources; and he didn't tell anyone where he was going. I made the same three mistakes when I entered this drain. Are the batteries of my flashlight about to die, I wondered as I crawled toward the light? Is there a loose piece of concrete in the ceiling with my name on it? Would I suffer the same fate as Floyd Collins?

Reaching another manhole, I stood and clutched the rungs. My stomach turned, forcing air—not vomit, as I feared—up my throat. A sharp pain wracked my lower back. My head was light. I felt like a boxer hanging onto the ropes. Letting go of the rungs, I reached for the bottle of water. What in the hell are you doing down here, I wondered as I swallowed the last sip? There's nothing worth writing about in this drain. Hell, Bob told you that. It's a treadmill, a deathtrap, a Roach Motel for bored and stupid human beings. You check in—but you don't check out!

Returning the empty bottle to the backpack, I began to question the whole book project. You took a summer sabbatical from work for this? You're a fool, a sucker, a failure. There's no story in these storm drains. You should've taken a cut of the advance and let Josh crawl around in the gutters. He's the brilliant one, after all. Maybe he could've made some sense of the tunnels, madmen, and myth. Maybe he could've put it all in perspective.

If I could've quit the book project then and there, I certainly would've. I would've ripped off the knit cap, shaken out of the backpack, and smashed the tape recorder against the floor with a therapeutic scream. I would've unsheathed the baton and balanced it on a rung, like a knight laying down his sword, where it would one day confuse a county worker or urban explorer. I would've side-armed the flashlight downstream, listening with pleasure as it clanged and scraped against the hard concrete.

But, of course, I couldn't quit the book project then and there. I was a mile into a mean drain, out of water, and sweating like Shaquille O'Neal. My options were limited. I considered climbing the rungs and trying to pop the manhole cover—but I didn't want to get decapitated by a stripper in a Benz or a cabbie streaking toward the Strip. I thought about calling 911—but my cell phone wasn't getting service and the situation wasn't quite *that* desperate. Really, I had two options: turn around or keep going.

Hoping—*praying*—the nearest exit was upstream, I continued into the darkness. The tunnel transitioned from a seven-by-five box to a six-feet-in-diameter pipe. As far as I could tell, the transition didn't serve any flood-control purpose—it was just more proof of the system's patchwork nature—but it sure as hell made life easier for me. What a difference a foot makes, I marveled as I straightened my knees and back! I relaxed my arms, which were as tight as guitar strings. As I surged upstream, the sweat on my face cooled and began to dry.

The tunnel, however, soon returned to its rectangular shape. Figuring that it was too late to turn around, I staggered deeper and deeper into the darkness. The inside of my thighs were raw. My clothes were soaked with sweat—so soaked that I assumed the recording equipment was ruined. My mouth was dry. When I was 10 years old, I ran Atlanta's six-mile-plus Peachtree Road Race on a humid midsummer morning. In high school, I sprinted and hopped stadium steps for hours in the midday heat. I faced "Forty Minutes of Hell," courtesy of the number-one-seed Arkansas Razorbacks, in the 1991 NCAA men's basketball tournament.

But this was, by far, the most physically and mentally exhausting experience of my life. This was an "Hour and Fifteen Minutes of Hell."

Finally, about a mile and a half into the tunnel, the beam of the flashlight found something solid. Another ramp? A concrete wall? A cruel illusion? Confused and exhausted, I fell to the floor and began to crawl. How humiliating! How tragic! Look at what's become of "The Greatest Storm Drain Explorer Ever Known" (ha, ha, ha). If the two street kids could see me now, I thought, they'd be laughing their asses off. They'd be snorting and farting and having a good old time at my expense.

Reaching out with my free hand, I realized that a piece of plywood was blocking the tunnel. I couldn't tell if it had wedged there during a flood or if it was placed there when the tunnel was built (plywood often marks future extensions and lateral tunnels)—and I didn't really give a damn. All I wanted to know was what was *behind* it. Setting the flashlight on the floor, I pulled on the bottom of the plywood. It popped and splintered, exposing a rusted brace and a second piece of wood (which were obviously placed there during construction). I bent down and squinted through an opening in the wood, hoping to see the bright light of the inlet. It was pitch-dark. I angled the beam through the opening, illuminating a concrete wall—a dust-filled dead end that simply broke my heart.

D iscovering the dead end under Tropicana Avenue, I collapsed against the pieces of plywood. They gave, embracing me like open arms and filling the tunnel with dust. Cutting off the flashlight and closing my eyes, I tried to relax. I reminded myself that it was a clear day, that it probably wouldn't rain for weeks—maybe months; I had plenty of time to grind my way out of the tunnel. There's no need to panic, I told myself. Remember, that's what got Floyd Collins into trouble. Remember, the only thing you have to fear is *yourself*.

After resting in the womb of the tunnel, a spider web tickling my ears and neck, I began the long journey back to the outlet. My pace was steady, my movement economical. There was no wasted motion—not even to scratch a mosquito bite on my flashlight hand. I drifted downstream—ah, yes, *downstream*—in the six-feet-in-diameter pipe. I lunged from manhole to manhole in the seven-by-five tunnel, stretching and resting for two-minute intervals. When I couldn't find a shaft, I calmly took a knee and steadied my breathing in the dark. It felt good to have a destination. It felt good to know that each long stride carried me a little closer to the light (and the convenience store at Tropicana and Spencer Street).

An hour after breaking free of the plywood's intimate embrace, I staggered into the chamber under Trop and Spencer. It no longer struck me as mysterious and creepy. On the contrary, it had a familiarity and ease that almost reminded me of home. I smiled at one of the graffiti ghosts, then started down the cockroach-infested straightaway. The tunnel swung to the east. The walls went gray. Then unlike Collins and the pollos and all the other people who have wandered into their own graves, I stepped out into the sunlight.

Of course, my escape from the tunnel under Tropicana was anything but triumphant. It was draining, humiliating, demoralizing. It made me wonder if the whole damn summer had been a waste of time and money. I also started to feel self-conscious about exploring the drains. I was, after all, a grown-up with a college degree and some graduate credits. Nestled in the plywood and cobwebs, snot dribbling down my face, I couldn't help feeling a little—well—*old* for this *Goonies*-type shit. Shouldn't I be covering City Hall, county government, or at least North Las Vegas, I remember thinking? William "Skeets" Miller won the Pulitzer Prize for crawling into Sand Cave and interviewing Collins. As I groped another manhole, I figured I'd be lucky to place in the annual Nevada Press Association awards (which were once held in a bingo parlor in Pahrump).

Nonetheless, about two weeks after emerging from the tunnel, I found myself standing in front of a storm drain beyond the west walls of the Fremont Street Experience. My body had recovered—the scrapes, bruises, and soreness fading like a bad memory. My confidence, sparked by a better-than-expected rough draft of Chapter Five, had been revived. Lessons had been learned: In my backpack, I carried an extra Mag-Lite (three flashlights total, including the Mini)—and an extra bottle of water; my friend Chip followed me to the intersection of Sandhill Road and

Washington Avenue, where this channel empties into the Las Vegas Wash, then drove me to the inlet (so he knew where I was entering the system and where I planned to exit); and though I'd never explored this drain, I knew a little bit about its background, surroundings, and—damn right—size.

On the night of November 30, 2002, a group of street people were camped out in this drain. Thunderclouds crept over the mountains and dumped more than a half-inch of rain in areas. A wall of water woke the street people. Apparently, a few of them fought upstream to the rungs of an open-air channel. At least two of them, however, were washed away. Firefighters rescued one of them from a manhole near Sandhill and Washington, more than three miles downstream. The body of another—Randy John Northrup—was discovered a few days later, half-buried in the Las Vegas Wash.

Six months before the storm, Josh and freelance photographer Joel Lucas explored the drain. This, you may recall, was Josh's first experience in the system—and it was not a pleasant one. The channel was dark, wet, and long. (It, however, wasn't low.) And it was eerily empty, except for the oversized minnows and crawfish. Before leaving my apartment and driving to meet Chip, I reread what Josh wrote in *CityLife*:

"It was pitch-black before Joel and I had gone thirty feet in the tunnel. But I'd brought a Mag-Lite, the kind of heavy black flashlight favored by cops. It functions as both a powerful light source and a bludgeon, and will keep working even after you smack some poor bastard over the head with it. My eighteen-inch kukri knife was stuck through my belt. We had no idea who or what might be lurking down there, and I really didn't want to be mugged by any random crackheads we might come across … or killed for food by some deranged mutant, hideously scarred by nuclear testing in the 1950s and hiding in the dark ever since, emerging only to drag small animals and children into its terrible lair.

"The chances of finding such a creature were unlikely, maybe … but this *is* Las Vegas. The normal rules of reality end at the city limits."

Indeed, Las Vegas is a freak show—a circus of corrupt politicians, corporate mobsters, and spellbound tourists. The Strip, of course, is the main ring. It features the bright lights, the high-flying stunts, the smiling clowns (literally and figuratively at Circus Circus). The Fremont Street Experience is the sideshow, a collection of second-rate acts desperate for attention. This drain is just outside the tent, so to speak, where the lights begin to fade and the harsh realities of life set back in (out of view of those still enjoying the sights and sounds). It's in a no-man's land crisscrossed with railroad tracks and highway overpasses, where the American dream goes to crawl into a dark hole and die.

Like Josh and Joel, I had no idea who or what lurked in the drain. However, since it was big (two nine-by-eight tunnels) and dry and in an area frequented by the homeless, I expected to have company—and probably plenty of it. I felt the sheath to make sure the baton was in place, then squinted into the west tunnel. It appeared to be empty—but don't they all? A cardboard box and plastic bucket sat along the shade line of the east tunnel, which I entered cautiously. The cardboard box was empty. Shit stains covered the bucket, which obviously served as a toilet.

A breeze blew pigeon feathers as thick as a showgirl's headdress downstream. I followed them into the darkness, discovering canned goods and a purple purse. I picked up the purse, which I assumed had been stolen from a tourist, and unzipped it. It contained a moldy sandwich and red reflector—a combination that I simply could not explain.

About 300 feet downstream, the tunnels merged and formed a 14-by-8 tunnel. I

Did the street people find refuge from the storm in this shaft, I wondered? Could they even see the rungs in the swirling darkness? Did they ever wake? Or did wondered if the ill-fated camp was located in this area of the storm drain: spacious, semi-dark, and marked with soot. Like an archaeologist exploring a cave, I aimed the beam into a wall crack in hopes of illuminating the past. I discovered black tar and white spider eggs, not personal papers and artifacts.

In the early 1960s, archaeologist Yigael Yadin found a cache of letters in a cave high above the Dead Sea. (The cave is now known as the Cave of Letters.) Yadin's discovery shed light on Jewish life in the second century A.D.—which, much like Jewish life in the mid-20th century, was brutal and repressive—and is considered among the most important finds ever in Israel. I, however, was having no such luck in this drain. All I found were stiff napkins, hypodermic needles, and meaningless graffiti scrawls, which led deeper and deeper into the concrete cavern.

At a manhole, the tunnel trended to the east. I stopped beneath the shaft and played the beam up and down the rungs, which were tangled with cobwebs. Did the street people find refuge from the storm in this shaft, I wondered? Did they reach for the rungs as the floodwater swept them away? Could they even see the rungs in the swirling darkness? Did they ever wake? Or did the whole scene play out like a vivid nightmare, a drug hallucination that was all too real?

Water dribbled from a lateral pipe, creating a black ribbon that wound downstream. I followed the ribbon into the darkness, past a crumpled bed sheet and a newspaper pillow. The backlight faded. Water crystals shaped like ghosts floated on the ceiling.

While exploring the storm-drain system, I met several people who swore that the tunnels were haunted. They told me they had heard strange noises late at night—stranger than usual—and had seen apparitions, some of which melted into the concrete walls. Inevitably, they went on to say that someone had died in the drain—overdosed on drugs, murdered by a rival, drowned in a flood—and the noises and apparitions, they grimly concluded, were the spirits of the dead.

I, of course, was skeptical of such stories. More precisely, I thought they were *utter bullshit*. I'd explored many miles of drains—sometimes at three or four in the morning, usually alone, and always on edge. I was an ideal candidate for a haunting, a *Blair Witch Project*-like experience that would've kept my nosy journalistic ass out of the drains for decades—maybe forever. It never happened.

But, I had to admit, there was something strange about *this* storm drain. I couldn't shake the feeling that someone or something else was lurking in the shadows, just beyond the range of the flashlight.

At another pipe, the floor went black. The tunnel twisted and turned like a stripper with the rent due. I rounded the bends hesitantly, half-expecting to hear rattling chains and see the ghost of Randy John Northrup. (I wished that Josh were with me; this would've been the perfect time to yell, "Boo!") Instead, I heard the soft rush of water and saw a faint light. The walls went gray. Then they broke, revealing the drainage ditch near First Street and Bonanza Road where T.J. Weber entered the system.

Crashing through a curtain of mosquitoes, I exited the tunnel. A parallel tunnel—the one I explored at the beginning of summer when tracing Weber's trail—dumped water into the ditch, creating a steady stream. I turned and stared into the tunnel, the stream pressing against my boots. Two and a half months ago, in this same spot, I wondered what Weber experienced in the storm-drain system. How, apparently without a light source, he'd splashed more than three miles upstream. If clues of his escape route remained.

I also wondered what lurked beneath Las Vegas. What secrets the storm drains kept. What discoveries waited in the dark. Shifting my feet in the stream, I felt that I'd answered many of these questions. But each drain—like each cave—has its own history, its own secrets, its own stories to tell. The artifacts and writing on the walls piece together a puzzle jumbled by the hands of time.

Breaking free of my thoughts, I started downstream in the ditch. Another double-barrel storm drain loomed in the distance and the barbwire fence glistened atop the embankments. Skating on the algae, I approached a set of rungs in the south bank. These were the same rungs I used to enter the ditch at the beginning of summer and the ones Josh and I used to exit the ditch in the summer of 2002.

•   •   •

The no-man's land beyond the west walls of the Fremont Street Experience stretches south to the Clark County Government Center, home of the Regional Flood Control District, and north to U.S. Highway 95. Interstate 15 and the Union Pacific railroad form its west and east borders respectively. It's a dusty wasteland filled with trash and rubble. Impeded only by a barbwire fence and the shell of a building-to-be, tumbleweeds roll across it with Old West freedom.

Emerging from the shade of the highway overpass, which sheltered pigeons and men, Josh and I approached the barbwire fence. Plastic bags and newspaper pages pressed against the chain links, as if seeking admittance into an exclusive club. A train rocked gently on the rails and an artificial breeze swept across the Big Nothing, blurring the landscape and dusting our eyes.

Josh and I circled the fence. Its bottom jags touched or nearly touched the ground and the barbwire was taut. Finally, we found a gash in the chain links. We slipped through the gash, which opened like a curtain, and stood on a landing that overlooked a fork in the flood-control system. To the northwest, 15 feet below us, was the drain Josh and Joel had explored. The drain Weber had exited lay to the northeast, Main Street Station looming in the background.

Using a set of rungs, Josh and I descended into the marshy offshoot. We started upstream in one of the three 15-by-10 tunnels that burrow under the sand hill, then turned around and sloshed toward the drain Weber had exited. Josh was quiet and contemplative. He later explained that he didn't really have an urge to feel mud squishing in his boots for miles upon miles. I, however, left him no choice. I was *determined* to explore the drain. After all, one of the reasons we decided to explore the system was to find out what Weber experienced—blinding darkness, shin-deep skank, and all.

But Josh and I did agree on one thing: We both wished that crazy bastard Weber had found a dry drain in which to play *The Fugitive*.

Entering the drain, Josh and I immediately realized it was one of the creepiest we'd explored. The air reeked of decay and we could hear the constant churning of water somewhere in the distance. The walls and ceiling were covered with cobwebs, two-feet deep in areas. We, wrote Josh, felt like Frodo and Sam working our way through Shelob's lair. We half-expected to find a corpse tangled in the webs, the remains of some poor bastard who'd stumbled down here by accident and been ambushed by whatever creature created this tableau.

For the first time all summer, Josh and I *really* began to freak out. We scuttled through the darkness, reversing Weber's trail, assuming there was no one to interview. Besides Weber and the cops who pursued him, it appeared that no one had set foot in this drain since its construction. We approached a four-foot-in-diameter lateral pipe, which puked water into the tunnel. Josh held out the kukri. He wasn't sure what might've been in the pipe, he later explained, but he wasn't taking any chances.

Finally, the floor became corrugated and the tunnel began to roll downhill. Josh and I eased down the slippery washboard surface toward the light. Splashing into the drainage ditch, we exhaled and knocked the cobwebs off our clothes. Like Frodo and Sam, we were happy to have made it out of the lair—but we weren't out of danger. After briefly exploring the downstream drain, we climbed the rungs

The woman was perched like a crow on a pile of rotting wood between the barbwire fence and
Josh and I could only assume the name was a cruel joke played on the residents, as none
It looked more like a place where cheap house paint goes to die, wrote Josh,

to the top of the south bank … and that's where we encountered the madwoman.

"When you got seven and all of a sudden it's twenty to seven, that means fourteen not thirteen," she said cryptically.

The woman was perched like a crow on a pile of rotting wood between the barbwire fence and a rickety shed, which sat behind a house in a subdivision called the Biltmore Bungalows. Josh and I could only assume the name was a cruel joke played on the residents, as none of the homes even earned bungalow status and this sure as hell wasn't the Biltmore Estate. It looked more like a place where cheap house paint goes to die, wrote Josh, a place where middle-aged lunatics dance wildly on piles of rotting lumber.

"Yeah, yeah, yeah!" said the madwoman, flailing against the fence and pulling on her filthy Caesars Palace T-shirt. "Render unto Caesar that which is Caesar's."

"And render unto God that which is God's," Josh finished.

The madwoman stared fearfully at Josh, then continued to sway and mutter. Josh and I stared back at the woman. She was scrawny, red-faced, and sweating like a track star. Her hair was long and greasy. We couldn't tell if she was a schizophrenic, another Vegas meth freak, or both. We tried to ask her about the storm drains below, but she wasn't the ideal source. Her rolling eyes and broken narrative only added to the creepiness of the situation.

"ITT Technical Institute," she said, apropos of nothing. "It's an electrical dilemma. A root, a fruit, a gay man." She glared at Josh. "Let me see the back of your shirt. I'll hold out my hand and see if I can read it."

Josh turned around. The madwoman stared at his Dr. Martens tee.

"Oh my God!" she said. "That's what I thought!" The woman clasped her hands together and stared at the horizon. She fell silent, as if expecting someone or something to swoop down from the heavens and carry her away.

"Do you know anything about the tunnels down there?" I asked the woman.

a rickety shed, which sat behind a house in a subdivision called the Biltmore Bungalows.
of the homes even earned bungalow status and this sure as hell wasn't the Biltmore Estate.
a place where middle-aged lunatics dance wildly on piles of rotting lumber.

Her eyes rolled toward me. "A lot of crap has been going on down there the past few days. You might want to look in there. I feel really jumpy, the road gets bumpy."

"Thanks," I said, feeling like someone who has lingered too long at the scene of a car accident. "Take it easy."

Josh and I backed away from the fence and turned around, eyeing an unlocked gate on the other side of the ditch. To get to the gate, we had to tightrope-walk the top of the south bank and use the fence for balance. I started out onto the ledge. Josh followed. Rabid dogs—the security systems of the crumbling bungalows—crashed against the chain links, nipping at our heels. The madwoman continued to sway and mutter atop the pile of rotting wood.

"Ask Don Henley," she said, as Josh and I balanced high above the ditch. "This is the end of the innocence."

· · ·

Passing the rungs, I squinted toward the top of the drainage ditch. I half-expected to see the madwoman behind the fence, still swaying and muttering to the rhythm of the urban runoff. But she was gone—dead, in prison, or straitjacketed in an insane asylum in the remote Mojave Desert. The dogs remained. They stuck their snouts though the chain links and barked rabidly, as if remembering my scent.

A concrete curb forced the stream into the south tunnel of the storm drain. I stepped over the curb—which is designed to keep runoff out of the north tunnel, protecting its structural integrity and reducing maintenance—then checked the sky for clouds. It was blue, horizon to horizon. Leaving a trail of wet footprints, I entered the 12-by-8 tunnel. A man materialized in the half-light.

"Hey," I said, shocked by his sudden presence.

"What's happening, man?" he said in a hoarse voice.

"Not much."

My eyes adjusted to the semidarkness. Through the haze, I made out a six-foot-tall man with an Afro and medium complexion. He was wearing a white T-shirt, plaid boxer shorts, and headphones.

"I'm just exploring the tunnels," I said. "I entered a drain behind Main Street Station and came out of that tunnel back there." I turned around and pointed into the sunlight. "I was going to walk this tunnel, if you don't mind me cutting through."

"Go ahead," said the man, lowering the volume of a Walkman radio clipped to his boxers. "Go right ahead."

"So how you doing?" I asked the man, stepping into the shadows and trying to start a conversation.

"I'm all right," he said. "I guess I'm all right."

"I think we've met before," I said. "I walked a short way in this tunnel two years ago with a guy named Josh. We talked to a man who was camped out in here. I'll never forget what he said. He told us that he came down here when things got too crazy aboveground. He came down here to get his head right, then he would go back out into the real world. Was that you?"

"It could've been," said the man. "Yeah, it could've been."

"Hanging in there, huh?" I looked around the tunnel. The walls were grainy and graffiti-free. A blanket was spread across the middle of the floor and a plastic bag stuffed with clothes served as a pillow. A jar of Vaseline, jug of water, and flashlight sat on newspaper pages at the foot of the makeshift bed.

"Yeah, I'm hanging in there." The man removed the headphones, which left a shallow impression on his Afro.

"I've been exploring the storm drains all summer," I continued. "I'm working

on a book about them. Did you know there are more than two hundred people living in the drains? That may not sound like a lot, but when you think about what these things are—you know, *flood-control channels*—it's kind of surprising."

"Right. That damn water can take you away."

"At least you have that curb to help keep you dry."

"Yeah, it helps a little bit. Yeah, a little bit," the man said in his trademark echo style.

"How often does the water come over the curb?"

"Shit, we in the monsoon season right now, dog. We in the monsoon season. That water's liable to come over it at any motherfucking moment. You just got to watch out. Somebody drowned on the other end not too long ago."

"Yeah, I know."

"I knew they was going to drown, too. There was hella motherfuckers down there. I was like: 'Damn, somebody's fixing to go.' I could tell by the way the water comes through here. I knew someone was fixing to go. About four or five months later, two motherfuckers got washed away. I guess they was all fucked up and the water came and got them. That was it, man. It took them away."

"It carried them all the way to the Las Vegas Wash," I added.

"Yeah. This thing goes a long way, man."

"What's down there?" I peered into the gloom.

"Just various tunnels," he said. "Some of them pan out to like twice this size and then turn back into something about like this."

"It goes all the way to the wash," I said. "It's about three miles from here, mostly under Washington Avenue."

"I took a walk down there myself one day," said the man, shuffling his bare feet and staring into the gloom with me. "I haven't actually made it to the end, but I've taken a walk down there. I walked for a hell of a long time. It must be three miles—at least."

"Were you around when those guys got washed away?"

"Yeah. I was staying in here, but I get out when the water comes. I got my radio right here." He patted the Walkman proudly. "I get the weather reports. I listen to the weather reports every day. I know when it's going to rain. Other than that, I just watch the weather outside. It doesn't take a whole lot to keep up with it."

"What were those guys doing down there? Crashing for the night or did they have a camp?"

"They were *living* down there. There were hella many of them living down there. There was like twenty of them—twenty of them in a row, up and down both those tunnels. They were mostly older men, you know, transients or whatever. And you could just tell they were out of it. You could just tell they were so out of it that when the water came somebody wasn't going to get out. Next thing I know …

"I thought I'd seen somebody floating in that damn ditch, too," continued the man, turning toward the light. "Channel Three came out here and shit, and the water was pretty high. It was really coming through here. Right before the ambulance came, I thought I'd seen someone floating right out there, getting battered up against that [north] bank. It sure looked like somebody. And then the news people came and I said: 'That probably was someone I'd seen.' He was bleached-out like a motherfucker. The water was coming through so fast. I just saw what looked like a head bobbing up and down. And then I heard that somebody drowned and I said: 'Well, maybe I did see somebody.'"

"Where were you when you saw all this?"

"I was up there on the fence, looking down at the water."

"How high was the water?"

"Ah, it was about up to here." The man placed his hand on the wall, waist high. "When that water gets up to your knees, it's going too fast to get out. When it's that high, you ain't *getting* out. It's right up on you."

"Have you had any close calls yourself?"

"I've had a few close calls," he said, shaking his head. "Yeah, I've had a few of them. I'll be sleeping and stuff—and then, you know, I'm all wet and jumping up out of this motherfucker. I just get up and run."

"This way?" I asked, pointing toward the light.

"Damn right!" The man turned downstream. "You don't want to go that way. They got [manhole] ladders and stuff down there, but it's so dark you can't see shit. When that water comes through here, you ain't seeing nothing. And you won't be able to grab onto nothing, either, unless you see light coming through a manhole or something.

"But nah, that water hasn't gotten me yet. I'll keep my fingers crossed." The

" "

There was like twenty of them—twenty of them in a row, up and
down both those tunnels. They were mostly older men, you know,
transients or whatever. And you could just tell they were out of it.
You could just tell they were so out of it that when the water came
somebody wasn't going to get out. Next thing I know ... ~ Harold

man crossed his fingers.

"How long have you lived down here?" I slipped out of the backpack and set
it on the floor.

"Shit," said the man, arms folded, "I've been down here off and on for a couple
years. Yeah, I'm just kicking it. I got a partner that stays down here, too. I thought
you was him at first."

"The two of you share this camp?"

"Yeah. Two, sometimes three. We try to keep the congregating down, though.
The neighbors don't like that shit. But yeah, we dwell in the subterranean world,
man. We dwell in the subterranean world."

"I'm Matt," I said, extending my hand.

The man shook my hand, paused, then said: "You can call me Harold."

"How'd you end up down here, Harold?"

"It's economical for me. It's just what's economically feasible for me at the
moment. Matter of fact, I'm actually able to save some money staying down here.
I mean, I hope to get out of here soon. I hope to be out of here in six to seven
months. But this is going to enable me to save a little bit and get a place and get
a ride and things like that."

"How will you be able to afford all that?"

"I just got to get my license back and start driving trucks again. Once I get my license back, I'll be good. I'll be back to my old self."

"Do you miss that everyday lifestyle?"

"Well, it's actually kind of an easy life for me right now," he said, laughing. "It's kind of easy. I work when I want to work, then I come down here and just chill out. It don't get no easier than that."

"How do you make money?"

"Oh, I go to work. Yeah, I work."

"What do you do?"

"Lately, I've been working for a fencing company—you know, putting up chain-link fences and shit. Yeah, that's what I've been doing."

"Is it steady work?"

"Yeah, as steady as I want it to be. I tend to go in about four days a week, sometimes five."

"How'd you discover this drain?"

"Just looking around. You know, you walk by and look around and then come on down. You know, you come on down and see if it's all right. And if it is, you stay."

"You weren't scared?"

"Nah. There's nothing to be scared of, man. I'm just taking it day by day. That's what I'm doing, day by day. I'm just doing what I got to do to survive, man. Shit, that's how I look at it. I ain't had no problems down here."

"No ghosts or anything?"

"Nah, man. It's peaceful down here. It's surprisingly peaceful down here, man. You can just chill out. I keep it cool, so I don't have no traffic and no people down here. A lot of times I leave in the evening, so people don't know I'm down here. Yeah, that's how I do it."

"It's strange," I said, shaking my head. "A lot of people live in the drains around

the Strip—but downtown, where most the homeless people are, the tunnels are pretty much empty."

"There's nobody over there?" asked Harold, pointing toward the upstream drain.

"No," I said. "I walked the right [north] tunnel in the summer of 2002 and earlier this summer. It's really wet and creepy. And I just came out of the left one. It's dry on the other end—it's protected by a curb, too—but I didn't see any camps. Just a toilet and some canned goods."

"After that dude drowned, the city put up barbwire fences—well, at least they put up the 'No Trespassing' signs. The barbwire fences may have been up already. I can't remember. Then the police went down there and cleared everybody out. They knew they was piled up down there. You could see them. For their own protection, they put them out. That's good. I'm glad they did. That's less trouble for me."

"Yeah," I said, "the downtown drains seem much more secure. And most of them have water running through them, anyway. This is one of the few dry drains down here."

"Yeah, that's true," said Harold. "That's definitely true."

"Well, Harold," I said, scooping the backpack from the floor, "I should probably keep on moving. I got a long walk ahead of me."

"OK, man," he said. "I got some bags and stuff hanging up down there. Yeah, a few bags and shit."

The headphones hanging from his neck, Harold bent down and picked up his flashlight. He then started downstream. I slipped the backpack over my shoulders, cut on my flashlight, and followed him into the darkness.

"This drain doesn't get low, does it?" I asked him, still not over the Tropicana tunnel.

"You mean low like this here?" he said, pointing the flashlight at the ceiling.

"Nah. This is cool, but some of the ceilings drop down to six feet and even lower."

"Is that right? I ain't never seen a tunnel that low. I wouldn't even want to be in one like that."

"You don't even know," I said, sparing him the whole sad story.

About 300 feet into the tunnel, Harold stopped beneath a manhole. He swept the beam of his flashlight over the floor, illuminating a Coleman camp stove and an assortment of pots and pans. I ran the beam of my flashlight up and down the rungs, which supported four-by-fours—crude shelves that contained oils, spices, and other condiments.

"Anything you want to eat right now, I can fix it for you," said Harold proudly. "I got it all down here, man. I got ham, spaghetti, everything."

I played the beam over the shelves. The lowest one was three feet from the floor, just above the watermark. The highest one hovered beneath the shaft, more than seven feet from the floor. They were lined with canned goods, bottles of hot sauce, bottles of cooking oil, and pots and pans. There were salt shakers and pepper shakers, bags of sugar and bear-shaped bottles of honey—all tightly sealed in zip-lock bags to keep the roaches and ants away.

"How often do you cook?" I asked Harold, amazed by the arsenal.

"I cook all my food down here, man," he said, as if insulted by the question. "I cook every day. Shoot."

"How many meals a day?"

"Two, sometimes three. Yeah, I got everything down here, man." He trained the beam on a canned good that balanced on one of the shelves. "I even got meatballs to go with my spaghetti."

"You boil the water on the stove?" I asked stupidly.

"Yeah," he said. "We can fire that sucker up right now."

Bending over, Harold turned the gas knob. The stove hissed loudly. He retrieved a lighter from one of the shelves, flicked it, and held it to the grill. A blue flame poofed to life.

"I've lost a couple of these stoves," he said mournfully, as he adjusted the flame. "I used to have three of them down here. Two of them got washed away. I got to get me a couple more. That way I can *really* cook like I want to."

"Where do you get the water?" I asked him.

"At a school right up here. They got a spigot. I carry the water on my bike. I got my water bag right over here."

Harold walked deeper into the tunnel and angled over to the opposite wall, stopping at a duffel bag that hung from a nail. He unzipped the bag. Empty plastic containers spilled to the floor.

"I fill ten two-liter bottles at a time," he explained, "but I'm out of water right now. I got to go to that school tonight and fill the bottles up, but I'm fixing to go get me some ice. I'm fixing to go get me some beer. I'm fixing to go get me some wine. I got to stock up on my provisions. I was just fixing to go when you showed up."

Stock up on my provisions? Was he being serious? Or did he say that for effect? Hell, his manhole-pantry seemed pretty well-stocked to me. In fact, he had more food in his tunnel than I had in my ghetto palace. It was quite embarrassing, really.

"OK, man," I said. "Thanks for the tour."

"All right, man," said Harold, starting back toward the light. "All right."

I aimed the flashlight at a wall and focused the beam. Then I started downstream in the tunnel, glancing over my shoulder. The stove, pots and pans, and shelves were silhouetted by the sunlight. I shook my head and smiled. Activists and social workers don't have to worry about Harold going hungry, I thought. He's a one-man soup kitchen. He's the Emeril Lagasse of the Las Vegas storm drains.

The tunnel turned to the west and faded to black. The wind died a quick death and the air became heavy and still. Three-inch cracks, which I attributed to subsidence or heavy flooding, separated the concrete boxes. I stepped over them cautiously, not wanting to break my mother's—or my own—back.

Surveying the ceiling, I noticed a manhole that appeared to be plugged with concrete. Intrigued, I stepped onto the bottom rung of the ladder and touched the seal—which gave, causing me to lose my balance. Regaining my balance, I climbed another rung and pushed on the seal. A piece of Styrofoam, it opened and exposed a barrel-shaped shaft lined with garbage bags.

"Hello?" I said, wondering if someone lived in the shaft.

Creeped out and curious, I climbed higher and stuck my head in the shaft. The bags hung from the rungs, handles stretched and frayed. More bags sat on a partially obscured landing. I touched one of them, immediately realizing it contained aluminum cans. I touched another. It contained shoes. And yet another was stuffed with what felt like winter clothes. Assuming the shaft served as an attic for Harold or a cellar for an aboveground camp, I lowered the piece of Styrofoam back into place and reversed down the rungs.

Farther downstream, the tunnel swung to the east. The cracks between the boxes became bigger and each box was higher or lower than its predecessor. Jumping from box to box, I felt like Mario trying to make his way through a secret and nearly impossible level of Donkey Kong. My biggest fear was that I would somehow fall through one of the cracks, into the mysterious black void below, never to be seen or heard from again.

Unsure of the structural integrity of the boxes—so much for that concrete curb, huh?—I tiptoed around the bend. A lateral pipe puked water onto the floor, coloring it dark brown. Cockroaches played King of the Mountain on scattered heaps of debris. The smell of mildew and decay forced me to bury my nose in my shirt sleeve, until the tunnel straightened and was ventilated by a drop inlet.

Starting down the straightaway, I was greeted by what sounded like a distant waterfall. The floor became corrugated and the tunnel began to roll downhill. I turned sideways, as if negotiating a rain-slicked San Francisco street. My boots slipped into the grooves, ankles twisting violently. My free hand felt for the wall. I assumed I was under the hilly section of Washington Avenue at Las Vegas Boulevard—but it seemed like I was descending into hell. The wind, which had been resurrected with renewed vigor, washed over me like screaming demons. The roar of the water grew louder. Again, I thought about the street people who were washed away. I tried to imagine what it must've felt like to be swept down this long, steep, and corrugated hill. Was it like some twisted Wet 'n Wild ride? Like being in a washing machine during the spin cycle? Like going over Niagara Falls on a moonless night?

About 500 feet down the hill, the roar of the water faded, the floor smoothed out, and the tunnel straightened. A faint light flickered in the distance. As I started toward the light, my thoughts returned to the secret manhole shaft. I wondered if I'd walked under, over, or past other hidden nooks or crannies. If my flashlight had washed over concealed entrances and exits. If—like the Shanghai Tunnels of Portland, Oregon—there was an underworld within this underworld.

It would all start in a bar-bordello along the Portland waterfront. A logger, sailor, or drifter looking for whiskey, women, and trouble (and not necessarily in that order) would swagger onto the wrong section of the hopelessly stained floor. Suddenly, he'd

The cracks between the boxes became bigger and each box was higher trying to make his way through a secret and nearly impossible fall through one of the cracks, into the mysterious lose his balance. The ceiling would start to spin. Everything would go black. He'd finally wake, battered and bruised, on a ship at sea.

From about 1850 to 1940, tunnels beneath Portland's Willamette riverfront supported a ruthless slave trade. Patrons of saloons, brothels, gambling parlors, and opium dens were drugged or physically knocked out and spirited away to the underground. Some unfortunate souls were introduced to it by trapdoors (or "deadfalls"). The men were smuggled through the tunnels to the river, sold to sea captains in need of a crew, and forced into service on ships, many of which were bound for the busy port of Shanghai, China.

This trade, known as "crimping" or "Shanghaiing," thrived in the late 1800s and early 1900s, earning Portland the nickname the "Unheavenly City." It began to fade around 1920, when stricter laws were passed to protect seamen and when steam power—which required a skilled crew rather than brutish grunts—became popular. It finally died at the outbreak of World War II.

According to legend, thousands of men disappeared from the Portland waterfront during those rough-and-tumble times. Most of them were never seen or heard from again. A few returned to the riverfront—several voyages and years later—and shared their stories with friends, family, and any old sailor or soldier or prostitute who'd listen. These stories live on in guided tours of the Shanghai Tunnels, which feature a trapdoor, holding cells, and other artifacts of this half-buried trade. There's even a "Ghost Tour" for locals and tourists who are into that kind of thing.

The sound of mariachi music pulled me from my thoughts. I froze, then tilted my head. Yes, mariachi music—trumpets, guitars, and Spanish lyrics that I could

r lower than its predecessor. Jumping from box to box, I felt like Mario
evel of Donkey Kong. My biggest fear was that I would somehow
lack void below, never to be seen or heard from again.

only assume lamented a lost love or praised a revolutionary hero. What in the hell is going on down here, I wondered? Is the music drifting into the drain through a drop inlet? Is there a camp downstream with a boombox tuned to a Spanish station? Or am I really to believe that a trio of musicians dressed in sombreros, embroidered jackets, and galoshes is splashing about the tunnels playing for tips? I shuddered at the thought. After all, Harold had hit me up for my last two singles.

As I approached the light, the music got louder. The south wall broke, exposing the parallel tunnel and a 15-by-12 ceiling grate. Cobwebs hung from the grate, swaying in the wind. Mosquitoes buzzed in the light. Swatting them away, I splashed into the tunnel and stood beneath the grate. The music poured into the drain, as if from a speaker.

"Hello?" I said, looking up at power lines and a blue sky.

There was no response.

"Can someone *please* turn the music down?" I said. "I can't get any sleep."

Still, no response.

Assuming the music was coming from a car on Washington Avenue, I returned to the north tunnel and continued downstream. One side of the floor cradled a two-inch-deep stream partially dammed by leaves, cigarette butts, and fast-food wrappers. A dusty path ran down the other side of the floor, narrowing and widening. Walking along the path, I lowered the flashlight. A black wall formed in front of me. But the wall was soon breached by another faint light in the distance, which gradually grew brighter and brighter.

Nearing the light, which turned out to be almost a mile away, the stream emptied into a shallow pool. Another break in the wall and ceiling grate shimmered on the water's surface. Bubbles warped the reflection. Bending down, I noticed thousands of mosquito fish—which are planted in the washes to help control the insect

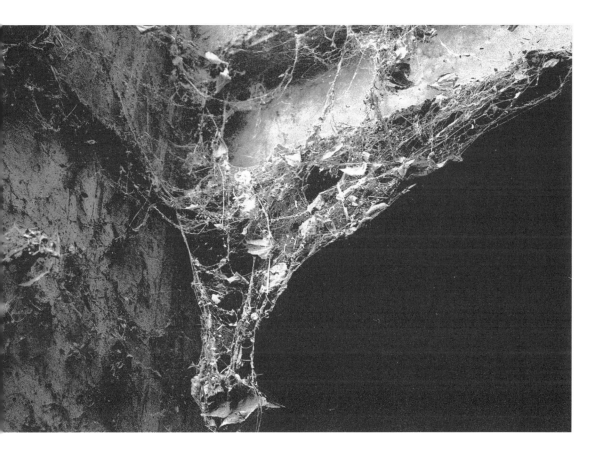

population—spawning in the urban drool. They darted in all directions, seemingly scared or blind or lost.

Three tunnels loomed beyond the grate. Plastic bags and fronds were wrapped around the dividers. Ducking under a cloud of mosquitoes—so much for those fish, huh?—I splashed into the middle tunnel. The stream deepened, swallowing my ankles. Starting down another straightaway, my mind drifted. I wondered how many people had passed through this area of the drain, which was dark and wet and more than a mile and a half from the nearest proper exit. If more people had passed through it on their backs, fighting to stay above the floodwater, than on their feet. How many of them died.

I thought about the ephemeral nature of Las Vegas: old bungalows being bulldozed; friends who appear, then disappear; the Dunes, Sands, and Desert Inn collapsing in clouds of dust. This city eats its children, I thought. Everything here is as disposable as a razor blade—except for the storm drains. They'll be here when the remaining 1950s-era apartment complexes are razed and replaced with high-rise condos. They'll be here after you and I move to Portland or Seattle or the Bay Area. They'll be here when the Bellagio, Venetian, and Wynn are imploded. When Las Vegas is just another Old West ghost town—boom and then bust!—these reinforced concrete boxes will be buried beneath the desert. They're our preservation areas. Our art galleries. Our museums. Our time capsules.

They're also our homeless shelters.

Throughout the long, hot, and lonely summer, I'd struggled with the idea of people living in the drains. It seemed so prehistoric, so cruel, so dangerous. *No one* should be allowed to live like that, I thought. Metro should sweep the drains. The city and county should make outreach workers available to help the displaced. Then they should be placed in hospitals, rehab centers, temporary or permanent housing, whatever's appropriate.

But things are never that simple in Las Vegas. Metro barely has the staff to investigate murder cases thoroughly, so sweeping the storm drains isn't a priority. The city and county don't have enough outreach workers to handle the aboveground homeless—much less the additional 200 to 300 people in the drains. And there's a shortage of hospital, rehab center, and shelter beds. Affordable housing? Maybe five years ago … in Pahrump, Mesquite, or Laughlin.

There's no simple solution to the problem, I admitted. Metro, the city, and the county can't help all these people—and all these people don't want or *need* to be helped. They don't want to deal with the bureaucracy and bullshit that comes with public assistance. Most of them have played that game—and lost. They also realize that aboveground Vegas—with its heat, traffic, and hate—is more dangerous than the underground. If it wasn't, they would live on a vacant lot or in an abandoned building or at a homeless shelter. And let's be honest: A shelter, with its rules and hours of operation, would only cramp someone like Harold's style.

Passing under another grate, I continued downstream in the middle tunnel. White formless masses emerged from the dark. They looked like the crooked bottom teeth of a jaw, but eventually took shape as slabs of concrete. I scanned the floor, walls, and ceiling. They were intact, indicating that the concrete had washed into the drain. Wiping the sweat from my brow, I stood there in awe. The slabs looked like the ruins of an ancient Greek civilization and were, I thought, another testament to the awesome power of floodwater.

The slabs dammed the stream, causing it to deepen. Glass, rocks, and aluminum cans rippled beneath the surface. I weaved around a grocery cart that was turned on its side and half-sunken, like a memorial battleship. Climbing a sandbar, my head nearly hit the ceiling.

Along a half-mile stretch of darkness, the stream went cold. My feet were numb, but I could still feel the glass, rocks, and cans beneath my boots. My ankles were sore. My thighs and back began to cramp. I felt like Memmius, the heathen in Hawthorne's *The Marble Faun*, who was doomed to spend eternity in the catacombs of Rome.

But then the beam of the flashlight hit a wall. The tunnel swung to the north, straightened for 30 or 40 feet, then again swung northward. The west wall went gray and a column of rungs jutted from the east wall. Are these the rungs the homeless man grabbed onto, I wondered? Is this the manhole firefighters pulled him from, bloody and clothes shredded? Is this where he squirmed and screamed, among spiders and cockroaches, until he was heard by some boys playing football in the street?

I continued toward the light, head rising and falling with each step. The tunnel turned to the east. The light grew brighter. What's beyond the bend, I wondered? Another ceiling grate? A drop inlet? The outlet?

Rounding the bend, I noticed a plastic bag on a sandbar. I knelt and aimed the flashlight into the bag, which contained a porno mag and bottle of lotion. 'Nuff said. The tunnel continued to turn to the east. The light grew brighter. The graffiti came to life. Then the walls opened up, revealing a patch of bulrush grass and a sandy embankment.

Exhaling, I staggered out of the tunnel and into the sunlight. Dragonflies buzzed above the bulrush. Doves, startled by my presence, flew from the bank. My eyes adjusted. Through the haze, I could see that the stream spilled over some rocks and trickled into the Las Vegas Wash. Spray-paint cans and plastic cups bobbed in the water. A car tire broke the surface at an angle. Smiling—who knew that someone could be *so* damn happy to be standing in a marsh?—I rinsed my boots in the runoff, then climbed the near bank.

Atop the bank, I removed my cap and looked down at the wash, focusing on the opposite bank. There, a few days after the November 2002 rainstorm, a 12-year-old boy walking home from school discovered Northrup's body. The boy hurried home and told his mom, who called 911. Paramedics responded and Northrup was pronounced dead at the scene. He was 47 years old.

Fully adjusted, my eyes followed the wash downstream. The colors popped—the green-brown water, the cocaine-white sand, the perfect-blue sky. Sunrise and Frenchman mountains, which looked like Hollywood props when I entered the system west of the Fremont Street Experience, rippled like muscles and were unmistakably real. The wash rolled between a trailer park and a stucco housing complex. Destined for Lake Mead, it disappeared amid a swirl of sand and sun.

Placing the cap and flashlight in the backpack, I walked across a deserted lot to Sandhill Road. My hair was matted and wet with sweat. My clothes were streaked with mud, cobwebs, and runoff. My body sagged. I looked like a Confederate soldier limping back to the South. As I approached my car, a man watering his lawn at the corner of Sandhill and Proclamation Place eyed me suspiciously. I sensed that I was a threat to his property value. Another freak who jerks off in the shadows of a storm drain. Another body that will one day be discovered in the Las Vegas Wash.

Fishing my keys from the backpack, I opened the trunk. I took off my boots, which were covered in grass and sand, then turned them upside down. Runoff spilled onto the street. I hoped that a crawfish or mosquito fish had fallen to the asphalt, along with the water, flopping around madly. That would've been a nice touch, I thought as I dried my feet with a towel. That would've really freaked out the neighbors. But by the time I'd put on fresh socks and sneakers, broken down the recording equipment, and closed the trunk, the water had dried and the street was barren.

The inside of the car, which had been sitting in the sun for more than four hours, was as hot as an incinerator. It felt like I'd climbed into a microwave, closed the door, and someone had set it to "nuke." Grumbling, I flipped the ignition switch and cranked the AC. The engine coughed. I put the gear in neutral and revved it. *Vroom! Vroom!* The man glared at me from beneath his visor. I smiled and gripped the steering wheel, which blistered my hands. Then I jammed the gear into drive and sped off with a stylish screech.

Thunderclouds swelled above the mountains. Blue and white, they swept into the valley and dropped a curtain of streamers that teased the terrain. More clouds rolled in, like reinforcements, and a gray veil formed over the Strip, smothering the sun. The Mirage, with its shimmering gold glass, was the brightest thing in sight. Lightning flashed. Thunder volleyed. Finally, a drop of rain fell on the Flamingo Wash.

The cattail and high grass stood at attention. Doves and pigeons took refuge in the girders of the Flamingo Road overpass. At Industrial Road, the wash went underground in a six-tunnel storm drain; the ceiling grates went dark and the inhabitants stirred. Like the doves and pigeons, they could sense the rain in the air. They wedged cardboard mats into the wall cracks. They balanced chairs, mattresses, and milk crates on makeshift tables. Destined for underpasses, convenience stores, street corners, libraries, and hotel-casinos, they placed valued possessions in duffel bags and slumped toward the inlet.

Blown by the wind, the rain fell at an angle. Lateral pipes and tunnels dumped runoff into the wash and pools formed in the ruts. Releasing downstream, the water took the path of least resistance—around rocks, between rows of wildflowers, and under rusted grocery carts that tottered in the sand.

Eventually, a shallow stream ran down the middle of the wash. It snaked under Flamingo, swung to the east beneath a Union Pacific railroad culvert, then fell off a five-foot-high ledge. A sandbar covered with cattail split the stream, forcing it into the outer tunnels of the drain. The water entered in sheets, painting the floor black.

Raindrops dive-bombed the stream. The railroad tracks glistened. I scurried up and down the embankments, like a crazed desert rat, trying to document all the action. "Timber!" I yelled into the mike, as the current toppled one of the carts. I sprinted downstream, chasing a pillow that was moving 15 miles per hour. I was like CNN's Anderson Cooper during Hurricane Katrina—except I wasn't being followed by a camera crew. I was all alone on this assignment. Anyone watching me from the overpass or the Rio hotel-casino must've assumed I was a madman considering suicide, another bad-luck gambler who was folding his hand. Why else would I be standing on a railroad culvert in the rain, constantly looking up and down, and muttering to myself?

There was a low rumble in the distance. I assumed that a train was coming—but the tracks were clear. Suddenly, a two-foot-tall wall of water came careening down the wash. The doves and pigeons flew from the girders. I held onto the railing of the culvert, in case the supports were somehow washed away. The floodwater surged underneath me and crashed over the ledge, which was 100 feet wide, creating a perfect curtain. The sandbar disappeared and the cattail struggled to keep its furry spikes above the surface. Moving more than 20 miles per hour, the water slammed into the drain's dividers and poured evenly into the tunnels.

Hopelessly dusty and dry an hour ago, the wash raged. The floodwater, as gray and chunky as wet concrete, fell off the ledge with the force of a thousand jackhammers. Standing on the bank, I could feel the earth shake. Bedrolls and fronds were caught in the undertow. They seemed to be reaching out of the mist, in hopes of being saved. Not today! Plastic bottles, aluminum cans, tennis balls, tennis shoes, couch cushions, and even a couch (unoccupied) bobbed in the current. Oil, gas, antifreeze, urine, pesticide, paint thinner, and lawn chemicals skimmed the surface.

It was the nastiest brew this side of the county's central sewage plant.

Sirens wailed on the overpass, Industrial, and I-15. When it rains in Las Vegas, I observed, people drive with all the skill and defensiveness of a drunk suicide bomber. It's similar to when a snowstorm hits the South. People lose their minds. And they *think* they know how to drive in such conditions, but they really don't. Their tires spin like slot reels, their steering wheels lock up, panic sets in. Before long, the cops and paramedics—who also don't know how to drive in such conditions—are responding to calls all over town, causing more accidents. It's a big automotive orgy—and one that I sensed was going on all around me.

There was movement upstream, men in blue crawling along the north bank like agitated ants. I trudged up the south bank, crossed the wash at a shallow, and discovered a group of firefighters in life jackets and helmets. Holding onto a rope, two of the firefighters edged into the wash; the water slammed against their shins and TV cameras rolled, as if the whole scene was being orchestrated by a news executive in a Strip-view suite. The firefighters disappeared into a four-tunnel drain, then reappeared on each side of a middle-aged man in a golf shirt and khaki shorts. They escorted the man across a concrete shelf that jutted from the drain. The footing was level and sure. No one was in any real danger here—at least from my perspective—but I assumed the cameras told a different story.

When the firefighters reached the bank, they were greeted by smiles and handshakes and hugs. The cameras continued to roll and the firefighters preened. It was as if they'd rescued someone from the top of Mount Everest in the dead of winter. Stripping out of a life jacket and helmet, the man was less festive. He reluctantly gave a few TV interviews, then slinked off to the side and untied his sneakers.

"You OK?" I asked the man, sitting next to him on the bank.

"Yeah," he said dismissively. "I never was in any danger, but they thought I was. I kept saying, 'What are you'll worried about me for? You'll never worry about me any other time I need help.' I'd already withstood the worst of it. When I saw them coming, I said: 'Come on, guys. Why are you all making such a big deal out of this?' But you know how they are. They said, 'We came all the way in here to get you, so you got to go.' They left me no choice."

"They *made* you come with them?"

"Yeah. They put a life preserver and helmet on me, and then they guided me through the mudholes and got my shit all wet." He took off his sneakers and turned them upside down. "These were all nice and fucking dry. I was just fine where I was, but they were thinking that the water was going to get higher."

"Did you know it was going to rain?"

"I knew it was coming," said the man, who told me he'd lived in the drain off and on for six months, "but I wanted to see how my bed would hold up. I wanted to see if it was going to wash away or not. I was getting a little bit nervous for a minute, but I was never in any danger. It ain't the first rainstorm I've been through in there."

"Is it the worst one you've been through?"

"Hell, nah. Everything has gone through there, man. One time in the winter when it was really cold, the water was over my knees."

"What were you doing when the wall of water hit?"

"I was sleeping. It woke me up. I guess the people who live in the apartments on the other side of the tunnel got worried and butted their noses into other people's business. I guess they called 911 or something. I know a few people who live over there. They probably thought I was going to get washed away."

"What are you going to do now?"

"Just wait until the water goes down and then go back home. I can still sleep in there. It's fine. I just got to wait until everybody leaves."

"How long does it take for the water to go down?"

"It goes down pretty fast," said the man, turning toward the wash. "Look, it's already going down."

The gray veil had drifted to the northwest and the sun was out, making up for lost time. The stream had slackened. In the sunlight, it was muddy brown and looked like raw sewage—and it didn't smell a whole lot better. Traffic helicopters buzzed above the interstate, reporting the bad news. Airplanes, once again, took off from McCarran. And the Rio's sign provided a neon rainbow.

Shaking the man's hand, I started downstream. It, I realized, was time for *me* to get wet. It was time for *me* to disappear into a storm drain. It was time for *me* to see a drain in action—to see it do the one and only thing it was designed to do. I crossed the wash at the shallow, climbed over the railroad tracks, then continued along the south bank. The water fell off the ledge, but the curtain was no longer perfect. It had a few narrow splits, which exposed a rock-and-wire base. The sandbar was submerged, but the cattail had resurfaced. It leaned downstream at an angle. I pulled up next to the drain and looked down at the water. It poured into the six tunnels, lapping against the graffiti-scarred walls.

In Australia, there's a group of urban explorers known as the Cave Clan. The Clan, founded by three Melbourne teens in the mid-1980s, is one of the oldest and most respected urban-exploration groups in the world. Its members started out exploring caves and mines. They moved on to storm drains, train tunnels, utility tunnels, old sewer lines, and other natural and manmade burrows beneath the Land Down Under. The group has chapters in Canada, France, and the United States. It even has its own newsletter (*Il Draino*) and annual awards (the Cave Clan Annual Clannie Awards or "The Clannies"), which include Best Drain and Best First-Year Explorer.

In more than 20 years of underground exploration, a Cave Clan member has never suffered a serious injury or death. One reason for the group's clean safety record, its members maintain, is its golden rule: No drains when it rains! Generally, I think this is a fine rule and should be followed by all *urban explorers* from Melbourne to Stockholm. However, as a *journalist*, I felt obligated to see the drains when it rains. In fact, I thought the summer would be incomplete without the experience (though I don't recommend trying it at home).

Turning sideways and bending my knees, I started down the bank. My right hand dragged over the rocks and wires and my left hand floated in the air, as if reaching for an invisible rope. Crickets, Styrofoam cups, and spray-paint cans swirled in pools below. My boots broke the surface of the stream, then dropped down … and down … and down. Finally, they found the bed of the wash. The water was surprisingly cold and rose well above my knees, threatening the tape recorder hanging from my hip.

I wasn't really ready to start downstream—I figured I'd stand along the bank for a bit and get used to the water—but the current left me little choice. It leaned on my legs with considerable force, buckling my knees and pushing me toward the drain. My right hand kept contact with the rocks and wires. My left hand floated, still reaching for that invisible rope. I climbed out of a rut, the bed leveled off, and my knees—unsteady as a newborn foal's—emerged from the water. Reaching the drain, I let go of the bank reluctantly and stumbled into the 10-by-8 south tunnel.

The drain exhaled hot and humid air, as if alive and breathing. It churned and growled and roared, like a hungry beast. Are the walls really expanding and contracting, I wondered? Or is that an optical illusion created by the backlight, floodwater, and my own profound fears? Feeling like Jonah, I staggered into the shadows. The water, moving 15 miles per hour, was gray-brown and foamed along the walls. It was shin-high in areas, thigh-high in others. Rocks rolled down the floor, like bowling balls down a lane. Gravel, sand, and glass formed foot-high reefs. Each step was an epic adventure.

The air, thick and smoky, was the same color as the water. Visibility was low—10 feet tops. All I could see were two concrete catwalks, each about a foot and a half from the floor, which ran down the walls and provided additional structural support. I slipped out of the backpack, removed the Mag-Lite, and cut it on. It didn't respond. No problem. Remember, I had an extra flashlight. It, too, was dead. "Goddammit!" I said into the mike, assuming the rain or humidity had short-circuited the flashlights. Regardless, I thought, they could *not* have picked a worse time to freak out on me. I was 50 feet into a drain, trying to document a flood, and ... wait! What's that? Another low rumble was building in the distance. I spun around and braced myself, expecting a wall of water to crash into the drain. Instead, in the stream's reflection, I saw a train flash by on the railroad tracks. Exhaling, I fished the Mini Mag-Lite from my pocket and twisted its head. A feeble beam fluttered to life. I focused the beam on a wall—which it barely reached—then continued into the belly of the beast.

The floor arched, providing the sensation of walking on a whale that was skimming the surface of the ocean. On the near side of the arch, the water was knee-deep and moving 10 miles per hour. On the far side, it dropped to my shins and picked up speed. It must've been moving at least 20 miles per hour. A twin-sized mattress and two wooden pallets stood on one of the catwalks, leaning against the wall. Steel poles, sports-betting sheets, and an Asian-language newspaper sat on the other catwalk.

•   •   •

The sky was a thousand shades of blue and the street a slick black. Raindrops bounced off the windshield of the white-boy Camry, which was headed west on Desert Inn Road. The wipers screeched loudly. Josh sat quietly in the passenger seat, adjusting the strap of his headlamp, dressed in a long-sleeve black T-shirt, black jeans, and black work boots. Fiddling with the radio tuner, I was wearing a long-sleeve black tee, Army-green cargo pants, and combat boots. "A Hard Rain's A-Gonna Fall"—or something equally appropriate—broke the silence:

> "And what did you hear, my blue-eyed son?
> And what did you hear, my darling young one?
> I heard the sound of a thunder, it roared out a warning,
> Heard the roar of a wave that could drown the whole world."

Josh and I crossed Paradise Road, then cut under the Strip at 50 miles per hour. The radio went dead … and came back to life. An assortment of gear shifted around in the back seat. At Valley View Boulevard, I flipped a bitch and found my way onto Industrial. Warehouses, strip malls, and adult bookstores blurred by the windows. I pulled into the parking lot of a business complex north of the Flamingo Road overpass.

The air reeked of rain. Though I'd parked more than 200 feet from the wash, in an attempt to be discreet, Josh and I could hear and feel its rumble. Josh gathered his gear from the back seat, then disappeared into the dusk. He returned shortly with a demented smile.

"Oh shit, man," he said. "The wash is flooded."

"How bad is it?" I asked, fitting the hard hat onto my head.

"Pretty bad."

I scooped the flashlight and golf club from the back seat, then jogged to the bank. Rivulets ran down the near side of the wash and the far side cradled a chocolate-milk-colored stream, which tumbled toward the drain. I glanced at the sky. It was a medley of thunderclouds, smoke from wildfires to the west, and looming darkness. Before I could protest, Josh angled into the wash and started for one of the middle tunnels.

"Let's go in the south tunnel," I said. "That's where the Asian guy was."

During our virgin exploration of the drain, on a dry and hellish Fourth of July, Josh and I stumbled on an Asian man about 300 feet into the tunnel. He lay motionless on wooden pallets, which were supported by steel poles that stretched across the tunnel and rested on the catwalks. Initially, I thought the man was dead—a victim of heat exhaustion, a heart attack, or a suicide-drug overdose. His skin was pale and he didn't respond to a series of questions. But he finally opened his eyes, as if waking from a 20-year sleep, and stared up at us blindly.

"Are you OK?" I asked the man.

He answered in a language I assumed was Chinese.

"Is there anything I can do for you?"

The man mumbled another response I couldn't interpret. Assuming that he didn't speak English and he wasn't in danger, Josh and I continued on our way. But now, as we watched the floodwater pour into the south tunnel, we were *seriously* concerned about his well-being.

Josh and I waded warily into the tunnel. The water was knee-deep and moving 15 miles per hour. "This is fucking frightening!" I said into the tape recorder dangling from my neck. "I can't believe we're doing this!" We climbed onto one of the catwalks, which was littered with matchbooks and cigarette butts. We stepped over plastic bags filled with trash. Then we reached the man's makeshift bed, which stretched over the water like a bridge over the Amazon. It was empty.

Unsure if the man had found refuge from the storm or been washed away, Josh and I continued into the drain. Our boots thrashed through the water, creating the sound of a herd of horses crossing a shallow river.

· · ·

As I stood in the middle of the camp, the Mini Mag-Lite fixed on the Asian-language paper, questions flashed through my mind. Who is this man? Where's he from? How'd he end up in America? In Las Vegas? In this storm drain? I also wondered how the man, who apparently didn't speak English, had survived for at least two years in the drain. Is he a panhandler? A credit hustler? Or am I really to believe, as the line sheets suggest, that he's randomly betting on sports teams he doesn't even know how to pronounce?

It would've been nice to hang around and consider these questions, maybe sit on one of the catwalks and strike "The Thinker" pose, but the floodwater was leaning heavily on my legs and the flashlight was fading. The conditions didn't really lend themselves to deep thinking. They did, however, spawn plenty of fear and paranoia. Don't just stand around, I told myself! Get moving! The daylight's dying and these batteries don't have much juice. And please—*please*—be on the lookout for another wall of water. It's coming. I can sense it in the ground, water, and air. Where in the hell are the nearest manhole rungs? They're your only hope!

Downstream from the camp, the tunnel swung to the east. The floodwater slammed into the far wall, turned over, and sped toward a faint light in the distance. The roar intensified. It sounded like a subway train that never passed. Nonetheless,

I could still hear strange rumblings in the depths of the drain—the rush and groan of the interstate, I assumed.

A lateral tunnel dumped runoff into the tunnel, complicating the current. The water swallowed my shins, and rocks and bottles and cans cluttered the floor. I tiptoed downstream, arms extended, like a tightrope walker. If you fall, I told myself, keep the flashlight *above* the water. Don't worry about the baton, the recorder, or your pretty-ass hair. Just *don't* let the flashlight get wet. A pack of cigarettes floated between my legs. I stepped over a half-sunken mountain bike. The water rippled in the light of a ceiling grate, then disappeared into the darkness.

A graffiti face—wide-eyed and tight-lipped—glanced downstream, as if it knew something I didn't. What's it warning me about, I wondered? A madman lurking in the shadows? A dead body wrapped around a divider? A whirlpool that sucked milk crates, mattresses, and homeless men into its indiscriminate vacuum? A lateral pipe dumped more runoff into the tunnel. The water, brown and choppy, rose above my knees and drowned the graffiti. Kicking through the crosscurrent, I waded into a rectangular chamber that was crowned with a 15-by-10 grate. All six of the tunnels emptied into the chamber, which was at least 60 feet wide and 25 feet long. The water was escorted out by two wide tunnels that barreled beneath the Strip.

• • •

Reaching the rectangular chamber, spellbound and scared, Josh and I turned into one of the middle tunnels and started back toward the Inlet. We wanted to check on Gary. We'd discovered Gary's camp—a stool, cooler, and cardboard hut—during our first exploration of the drain and we talked to him a few days later. He told us he'd moved from Seattle to Las Vegas about 20 years ago to kick a cocaine habit—making him, as far as Josh and I could tell, the only person to come to Vegas to get *away* from cocaine. While leaving the coke behind, said Gary, he found plenty of methamphetamine in Vegas. (Doesn't everybody?) Laziness and a meth addiction have kept him on the streets, he said. He'd lived in the drain for about a year.

Walking upstream in floodwater, Josh and I discovered, was much more difficult than walking downstream. The water went after our legs like a linebacker in the final year of his contract. Pine cones, spray-paint cans, and four-by-fours slammed against our shins, and our feet felt as heavy as cinderblocks. With difficulty, we climbed a sandbar. As we splashed into a knee-deep pool, a beam of light shot from the darkness.

"Gary?" I said, shielding my eyes with my free hand. "It's Matt and Josh."

"Hey, guys," said Gary dejectedly, taking the beam off us and sweeping it over his camp. The stool stood in three inches of water, the cooler threatened to float away, and the bottom of the hut was wet and collapsing.

"We came down here to check on you," said Josh. "Are you all right?"

"Yeah," said Gary, who was wearing cutoff shorts and sneakers. A T-shirt was tucked in the small of his back. "I was in the Stardust's sports book. I came back down here to see if anything had washed away."

"Is everything still here?" I asked, surveying the camp. It looked more like scattered debris—the random dregs of a flood—than somebody's home.

"Yeah. I think so."

"What are you going to do?" asked Josh.

"I don't know," said Gary, scratching his bald head. He was tan, clean-shaven, and shiny. He looked a little like Mr. Clean ... with a 30-year meth addiction. "I used to have a few friends who lived in a house not too far from here, but they moved out. I used to stay with them when it rained. But now I don't know what I'm going to do."

"You should get a motel room," I said, reaching into my back pocket. "It's raining now and it looks like more's on the way. Don't even risk it, man."

I gave Gary all the money I had on me, which was only $12. (I'd taken it into the drain for bargaining purposes, in case things got *real* ugly.) Josh gave him seven or eight bucks.

"That's all I have on me," said Josh, shrugging. "Hopefully it will help you get a motel room. You don't want to stay down here tonight, man. It's way too dangerous."

Gary thanked us for the money, then stuffed it into his pocket. Josh and I turned around and started downstream.

"Hey," I said over my shoulder. "Do you know if the Asian guy's OK?"

"No," said Gary. "I haven't seen him in a while. The last time I saw him was when the cops came down here. That was right after the whole T.J. Weber thing. They took us outside and questioned us. The Asian guy had an outstanding warrant, so they arrested him. He had a big wad of money on him, too. I have no idea how he got it."

"Does he speak any English?"

"I don't think so. I really don't know much about the guy."

"OK, man," I said. "Take care."

"OK," said Gary. "You, too."

Josh and I splashed through the pool and climbed the sandbar. Using the golf club as a plumb, we waded through the rectangular chamber and pulled up at the mouth of the south tunnel—30 feet wide, eight feet high, and roaring like a jet engine at takeoff. We realized that if we were going to turn around, this was the place to do it. Underneath the Strip, the drain didn't have any manholes or lateral tunnels or even a proper niche. If a wall of water crept up behind us, our only hope would be to somehow ride the wave and grab onto something—*anything* ... a rung, a column, the leg of an unsuspecting tourist—on the other side of the Strip.

Josh and I looked at each other, smiled, then splashed into the tunnel.

The floodwater climbed halfway up the club and visibility was a cruel and lame joke. The air was so dark and heavy and still that I could barely see Josh, who was walking beside me. Initially, the floor was rocky and slick. But it soon smoothed out and footing became a secondary concern. Our main concern was the wires that sprung from junction boxes on the ceiling and coiled into the water like electric snakes.

Josh and I had neither the time nor inclination to try to explain what we were seeing—light fixtures, power outlets, and water pipes that ran along the ceiling. We were simply trying to survive. We ducked under a rainbow of runoff that poured from a lateral pipe and we weaved around columns, half-expecting to find the Asian man's body tangled among the debris. The walls seemed to be shaking. Are we in a storm drain, I wondered, or an automated carwash stuck on the most expensive and violent setting? I kept waiting for one of those furry rotating brushes to come rolling out of the dark.

Suddenly, the recorder jumped off the snap hook and splashed into the stream. It went under, recording lights blazing like the eyes of a piranha.

"Goddammit!" I screamed. "I just lost the tape recorder."

"You're shitting me," said Josh, who'd been studying the water pipes.

"It had all my notes on it—not that I'll ever forget what I've seen and heard tonight."

"Did it have any other interviews on it?"

"No. But it was a Sony, man. The fucking thing cost sixty bucks."

If Josh and I'd found the recorder nestled in a pile of debris, lights blazing, it would've made one hell of a Sony commercial. But the endorsement contracts were not to be. We splashed under Caesars Palace, the Strip, and the Imperial Palace without being jumped by a wall of water … without discovering the Asian man's body … and without finding the recorder. We then exited the drain at the most bizarre outlet in the flood-control system.

•   •   •

Standing under the grate, in the scattered remains of the day, I cut off the Mini Mag-Lite to preserve its batteries and surveyed the rectangular chamber. Two dividers helped support the eight-foot-high ceiling. In the shadows, the 30-by-8 south tunnel looked like the jaws of a whale—and seemed to be swallowing an ocean. I took two steps downstream, squinted into the abyss, and tilted my head. I then promptly turned around. There was no way in hell I was going anywhere near that tunnel without a backup flashlight, scuba gear, and the poet Virgil as my guide. Wild horses couldn't have dragged me in there under the circumstances.

Cutting on the flashlight, I turned into one of the middle tunnels and started back toward the inlet. I wanted to see if Gary was still around. In the light of a grate, about 200 feet upstream, I made out a camp. Its back border—a banner that stretched wall-to-wall on a metal rod—flapped in the wind, and T-shirts and cutoff shorts hung from the rod. The water rushed under the banner like a bull through a matador's cape.

"Gary?" I said, approaching the camp.

There was no response.

"Gary?"

Still, no response.

Feeling like the fool in a horror flick, I pulled back the banner. A mattress, folding chair, and roll of carpet balanced on a makeshift table—a wooden spool turned on its end—two feet above the water. The spool was three feet wide and three feet high. It looked like it could coil enough cable to run from Las Vegas to Los Angeles. Couch cushions tottered on one of the edges, a milk crate containing cleaning supplies on another. There was even room for a broom.

I cut through the camp and ducked under the front border—a patchwork of cloth, cardboard, and plywood supported by a wooden beam. Coat hangers swung from the bars of the grate, clanking like wind chimes. An office chair was framed by the light. Looking down at the chair, which was wrapped in debris and pinned against the border, it finally hit me: I was the *only* person in the drain. There was no one to interview, no one to rescue, and no one to rescue me. I *was* the fool in a horror flick. Let's get the hell out of here, I told myself, before another wall of water comes careening down the wash. Before that glorified candle in your left hand blows out. Before those "studs" from the fire department have to put on an encore performance. Let's get the hell out of here … and come back in the morning.

• • •

The following morning, the wash was as still as an O'Keeffe painting and eerily quiet. I hardly recognized it. Where's all the water, I wondered as I walked along the bank? Where are the plastic bottles, aluminum cans, tennis balls, tennis shoes, couch cushions, and couch (probably occupied)? What happened to that writhing, roaring beast? Am I at the same place? Was the flood real? Or was it just a vivid dream?

As I angled into the wash, it became obvious the flood *was* real. The rock-and-wire bank was ripped and crumbling. Tangled with newspaper, plastic bags, and clothing, the cattail leaned downstream like a Mohawk and the ruts cradled yellow-green pools bubbling with mosquito fish; if it doesn't rain in the next three days, I realized, they'll all be dead. Weaving through the cattail, which was as dense as the jungles of Vietnam, I passed a waterlogged TV and window-unit air conditioner. Bees and dragonflies buzzed above the stalks.

Approaching the south tunnel of the storm drain, I shook out of the backpack and carried it by its top loop. Ankle-deep water pooled at the inlet. I splashed through the water, stepped into the shadows, and removed the Mag-Lite (which was dry and equipped with fresh batteries). The backlight burned brightly. I couldn't see anything—but I could feel the mud, three inches deep, squishing beneath my boots. A cobweb tickled my face. I swatted it away, then wallowed deeper into the mire.

The Asian man's camp was as I'd left it the day before: The mattress and pallets stood on one of the catwalks, leaning against the wall; the poles, sports-betting sheets, and newspaper sat on the other catwalk. Assuming the man had spent the night at an aboveground campsite or a motel, I cut through the camp and rounded the bend. The watermark was three feet from the floor and cockroaches crawled on the walls and ceiling, apparently not realizing the flood had subsided. I passed the lateral tunnel. I stepped over the mountain bike, which was ribboned with debris. As I approached the rectangular chamber, graffiti appeared on the walls. With each step, it became more intense and dramatic.

The walls of the chamber, shrouded in darkness the day before, were tattoo sleeves of color in this black-and-gray world: blue, green, yellow, orange, purple, pink, and red. Interlocking letters stretched from the floor to the ceiling. Arrows zipped and sparkles danced, like tourists thousands of miles away from their hometowns—and their inhibitions. *Anime* girls with big eyes, small noses, and pixie haircuts crouched in the shadows, as beautiful as angels.

When Josh and I discovered this art gallery, a different exhibit was on display. A giant wasp, wings up and stinger down, floated on an off-white plane. "Diagram for Self-Destruction" was scrawled in the background and the wasp's anatomy was labeled in block letters: "Just Know/That We/Must Learn/to Use/Things and/Love People/Not Love/Things and/Use People." Next to the diagram was a portrait of a man with a stone face and Caesar haircut. Its legend read, "Embrace Truth in a World of Lies."

The gallery was the most beautiful thing Josh and I'd seen in Las Vegas, maybe the *only* beautiful thing. Vegas loves the spectacle—the flashing lights,

the 10-stories-tall signs, the mainstream themes—but there's little in the city that displays any real taste or depth. It's a neon river bordered by stucco boxes, cinderblock walls, and a scrub desert, only sufferable at night. In the daytime, it's ass-ugly—chain stores, tattoo parlors, and strip joints … strip malls and gravel and sand. As Springsteen said, there's just devils and dust.

After admiring the latest exhibit, which was more interesting than anything I'd seen in the high-priced galleries overhead, I turned into the second tunnel from the south and started back toward the inlet. The graffiti—bubble letters, creepy silhouettes, and leery faces—burned into the darkness. My boots disappeared in wet gravel. Bending down, I scooped up a handful of gravel and let it sift through my fingers. Pebbles and shards of glass fell to the floor, leaving a penny in the palm of my hand. I cleaned the penny with the bottom of my shirt, then put it in my pocket. What the hell, I thought? You can always use a little luck in Las Vegas—especially in the storm drains.

I exited the drain, then looped into the third tunnel. Sunlight reflected off the standing water, blinding me temporarily. Shielding my eyes with my hand, I stumbled downstream. Wet carpet, blankets, and rebar were strewn across the floor. Around the bend, a beam of light angled through a grate and shattered the darkness. Graffiti lined the walls, flowing all the way down to the art gallery.

Turning into the fourth tunnel, chased by shadows, I heard a sweeping sound. I stepped over a gravel dam and waded through a reservoir of water. The sweeping sound grew louder.

"Gary?" I called out, approaching the back of the camp.

The sweeping sound stopped. "Yeah. Who is it?"

"Matt," I said, pulling back the banner. Through a gap in the front border of the camp, I saw a bald and tan man standing beneath the grate, wearing cutoff shorts and sneakers. Leaning on a broom and pushing metal-frame glasses up the bridge of his nose, he glistened with sweat. "I met you a couple years ago," I continued, "when I was exploring this drain with a guy named Josh."

"Hey, man," said Gary. "How's it going?"

"All right," I said, cutting through the camp. "I'm working on a book about the drains. You got a minute?"

"Yeah," he said, propping the broom against a wall. He ducked into the camp, disappeared behind the border, then reappeared with two couch cushions. He dropped them on a dry patch of floor.

"So you survived the flood?" I said, sitting on one of the cushions and leaning against the wall.

"Yeah," said Gary, sitting next to me on the other cushion. "I'd been expecting it to rain for three days, so I had all my stuff—my mattress, my carpet, and everything—off the floor. I was sleeping in my chair beneath my skylight [the grate] when I felt raindrops hitting me. As soon as I felt the rain, it was time to get out of here—or else be stuck in here all day and night. So I left. As soon as I got out of the tunnel, the main barrage came down. I got soaked running up to the Flamingo overpass. I hid from the rain under there."

"For how long?"

"Until it stopped. Then I went to the tunnels under Valley View to see how my friends made out."

"They OK?"

"Yeah. They actually built a dike to direct the water away from their tunnel."

"When did you come back down here?"

"Late last night. The water was still flowing through here. I had to go further down the tunnel and dig up some of that gravel, so the water wouldn't back up. I had to dig a trench to let the water flow all the way through. Otherwise, it just stays here."

"How'd you sleep with all the water going through?"

"I didn't sleep. A friend of mine got me high and that motivated me to go out and make more money, so I could stay high.

"I usually go somewhere else when it rains," continued Gary in a low voice. "I hang out in a casino or something like that. I don't like being stuck down here. It's too noisy. The water rushes through here, echoing off the walls and pounding your brain. It's too much."

"What do you do after it rains?"

"I come back down here as soon as I can. There's usually gravel all over the floor. The first thing I do is shovel and sweep all that away. Then the debris—the twigs and garbage and everything else—is stuck right there." He pointed at the office chair and front of the camp. "I got to haul all that stuff further down the tunnel. As you can see, I haven't gotten around to doing that yet. Then I just wait for all the water to evaporate off the floor, so I can put my mattress and carpet back down and set everything up again … until the next time it rains."

"You're from Seattle, right?" I asked Gary, recalling our prior conversations.

"Yeah," he said. "I moved here about twenty-two years ago."

"What brought you to Vegas?"

"I was trying to escape a cocaine addiction."

"You thought you wouldn't be able to find coke in *Vegas*?"

"No. It wasn't that. I just wanted to go someplace where I didn't know how I could get cocaine. Coke is easier to get than a bottle of beer most places you go, but you still have to know somebody. As long as I didn't know anybody here, I hoped I'd stay off it."

"Do you regret moving here?"

"Yeah. This city sucks. It's Sodom and Gomorrah all over again. I think it's going to be blown off the map."

"How?"

"Terrorists probably. I don't know. I just want to be around to see the big bang when it happens. I like big bangs."

I laughed uncomfortably. "What don't you like about Vegas?"

"It's a police state. It's the most jail-happy city I've ever been to. They arrest you for anything: defacing a hamburger, interfering with the flight of a pigeon, conspiracy to commit jaywalking. I've gone to jail just because I nodded off in the keno lounge at the El Cortez.

"The police and politicians here suck," he continued. "They suck big-time. This is Sin City. Everything here's based on money and sex and gambling. It's all screwed up. Everyone treats you like shit. They treat you like garbage. If you don't have money, you're nobody to them."

"How'd you end up on the streets?"

"I procrastinate," said Gary, who told me he was 47. "I'm the king of procrastinators. Why look for a job today when I can look for one tomorrow? Then tomorrow becomes the next day, and so on, and so on. Drugs are to blame, too. I got a speed [meth] habit."

"How long you been addicted?"

"About thirty years. But for a long time, I couldn't find any. In Seattle, it completely disappeared. When I came to Las Vegas, I found it again. To supply my habit, I was going out and stealing ephedrine to make the speed. But you can't find ephedrine on drugstore shelves anymore. It's all behind the counter. Since that happened, I basically have to hustle the casinos for money to buy it. And I'm getting real tired of doing that."

"You make the drug yourself? Down here in the drain?"

"Yeah. Me and a friend made it down here a couple times last summer. I can make it if I get all the right equipment."

"What do you need?"

"Ephedrine, red phosphorus, iodine crystal—those are the three main ingredients. You also need a glass coffee pot. You put the ingredients in the pot, weighing out each one. Everything's based on how much ephedrine you have. Then you put heat on the pot and it starts a reaction."

"What do you use for the heat?"

"A propane torch works. You just let the coffee pot heat until the ingredients reach a certain color. Then you filter out the red phosphorus and add some lye. You pour some water in there. And then you boil out the water, and what's left is dope.

"It's about a four-hour process. The reason it takes so long is you got to separate the ephedrine from the pills. The pills are just sinus tablets. You got to remove all the buffer and wax and everything else. Otherwise, it would take about an hour."

"How do you do the drug?"

"I just slam [inject] it."

"Getting high in here must be real trippy," I said, scanning the walls.

"At first," said Gary, "it was real strange. But now it's just like home. It's just like being in an apartment or a house. Plus, I've always been the type who likes to go ghost-hunting. I've always liked to get high on a stormy day and go into an abandoned house and listen to all the creaky noises."

"What's the creepiest thing you've done down here?"

Gary dropped his head. "Just being stuck down here when it's raining and there's three feet of water coming through and not being able to get out," he said, noting that his six-foot-two and 200-pound frame is too big to squeeze through the grate. "At first, it's real scary. But I've been stuck down here four or five different times now. The last time was Christmas night.

"After a while, when you've been stuck down here for hours and hours and hours, and you don't have a cigarette or anything, it gets *so* boring. You can't move. You just got to wait for the water to go down. It's *so* cramped. You start aching in every bone of your body, because you're stuck in one position."

"What position's that?"

"I sit on that big cable spool. It gets real cramped, especially when you got as much of your stuff as you can salvage up there with you. You don't want to move and

> It's just so dark down here sometimes. I mean, every night it's pitch black. You can't see anything—but you swear to God that you see things reaching out from the walls and trying to grab you. Or you think you see something running across the tunnel or jumping in front of you and trying to hide or get out of your way. ~ Gary

knock something off. You're just stuck up there."

"Do you worry about the water pushing the spool over?"

"I'm dying anyway," said Gary, explaining that he has colon cancer. "It really doesn't matter to me whether I die today or six months from now. Matter of fact, I'm thinking about getting a whole lot of heroin and just getting it over with. So no, I'm not worried about getting wet or drowning. I just don't want to get too cold up there on that spool. I just don't want to touch that freezing water, because it's colder than shit during the winter. I just don't want to get wet and be stuck up there shivering." He crossed his arms, pulled his legs to his chest, and shook violently.

"What other scary experiences have you had down here?"

"It's just so dark down here sometimes. I mean, every night it's pitch black. You can't see anything—but you swear to God that you see things reaching out from the walls and trying to grab you. Or you think you see something running across the tunnel or jumping in front of you and trying to hide or get out of your way. That happened a lot when I first moved in here, but now I don't even pay attention to it. If there's something down here, any apparitions or spirits or whatever, I just try talking to them and telling them to sit down and keep me company or let me keep them company."

"How do you explain the things you've seen?"

"It's like a sensory-deprivation chamber in here, where they put you in water with so much Epsom salt that you automatically float. It cuts off all your senses. You can be in here for a half-hour in the dark, and you're totally hallucinating and seeing all kinds of weird shit. Your brain doesn't know how to react to the pitch dark."

"Any other scary experiences?"

Gary glanced at the grate and smiled, revealing a gap in his bottom teeth. "About three weeks ago, around five o'clock in the morning, some teenagers were spray-painting up on the interstate. They were looking for an escape route, and one of them decided to climb down into the tunnel through the skylight. He was squeezing down through the bars when I walked over and grabbed his leg. He started screaming his ass off. It really freaked him out."

"Hell, yeah," I laughed. "Can you imagine?"

"It was funny, because he could barely squeeze down through there. And when I grabbed his leg, he tried to pull himself back up—but he was stuck. He couldn't move. He was just screaming. It was funny as hell.

"Finally, he got out. When he looked down through the skylight and saw me, he asked if they could come down through here. I told him, 'Yeah,' and they climbed through the bars and took off that way." He pointed toward the inlet.

A breeze fell through the grate, rustling the front of the camp and stirring up dust. I closed my eyes. As the breeze slowly died, I reopened them and turned toward Gary. "How'd you discover this drain?" I asked him.

"I was taking a break from walking around and hunting credits in casinos," he said. "I spotted this one when I was walking from the Rio, and I came down here to check it out. I was working with a lot of [meth] cooks at the time, hunting credits and stealing ephedrine. I started coming in here as a place to get away from the cooks. They were constantly hounding me about going out and stealing more and more ephedrine. I couldn't take a break, so I would come down here and hide out for a couple days. At the time, I wasn't worried about a place to live, because they were all giving me places. They were buying my food, cigarettes, dope, everything. But I just needed to take a break from it all.

"One day, I came down further into the tunnel and noticed the skylight. I decided it would be better to hang out down here than up there [near the inlet], because this allows me more light during the day. I've been hanging out down here ever since."

"How long's it been?"

Gary hesitated. "I've been living down here for about three years," he said, "but I've been hanging out down here for five or six. See, I got lots of privacy down here. On a hot summer day, I can sit around naked. It's a lot cooler that way. Almost nobody comes down here. And the few people who do are my friends.

"But it's so black at night that nobody comes down here, except for the artists who spray-paint the walls. They know I like my privacy and they don't bother me. I see them, but they never come up and talk to me."

"What do you think about the art gallery?"

"Well, I'm an artist myself," said Gary, explaining that he draws pencil portraits of women out of nudie magazines, "so I'm pretty much intrigued with it. I think it's good, but I think they're wasting their talent by doing their work way down here where nobody sees it. Of course, anywhere else they do it the city or the county comes along and paints right over it.

"The first time I walked all the way down there, about five or six years ago, the gallery wasn't even there. The tunnel was still being constructed. You walked down there and you could look up and see Flamingo Road. There weren't any walls or ceiling."

"Who does the artwork down there?"

"When I first started seeing them, they were teenagers. Now they're twenty to twenty-five years old. They're the only ones I've ever seen down there."

"Local graffiti crews?"

"Yeah. I think they're all from around here."

"How often do you hear people down there?"

"It's been over a month since I've heard anybody down there, but sometimes they come so often it's irritating. My bathroom's further down the tunnel, and I can't use it when somebody's in there. Sometimes they're down there often enough that it's irritating, because I have to find someplace else to use the bathroom.

"But voices," he continued solemnly, "you hear them down here all the time—and there's nobody there. I've even seen what I'll call an apparition."

Gary shifted on the cushion and stared into the darkness. Finally, he turned back toward me. "When I first moved into the tunnel, I saw a black guy dressed in dark-brown slacks, a cream-colored shirt, and a light-brown sweater vest. He caught me pleasuring myself. I looked up and saw him, and the first thing I thought was: How in the hell did this guy walk so far into the tunnel without making any noise? Then he just melted into the wall."

"Were you high at the time?" I had to ask. "Could you have been hallucinating?"

"I have hallucinated," said Gary. "I've been so high and rushing so hard on speed that I have thought that I've seen things. But that time I wasn't high or anything."

"So how do you explain what you saw?"

"I don't know. I do believe in the afterlife. And I believe that there are people who don't realize they're dead and they're just stuck here on Earth. But the voices are real, because I'm not the only one who hears them. Everybody who comes down here to visit me hears them, too, but you can never quite figure out what they're saying. You can almost make it out, but you just can't grasp it."

"Some of the voices may be drifting in through the grates," I suggested.

"Basically, I've figured out what a lot of it is. It's the echoes from the cars overhead. The interstate is directly above us, and the echoes go back and forth off the walls. It's like turning on an air conditioner and thinking that you're hearing voices."

"And, of course," I said, "other people live in the drain."

"At the beginning of summer," said Gary, "all the tunnels had somebody living in them. I had Charles Manson living at the front of mine. This guy was a real nutcase. He was crazy-eyed. He looked just like Manson. I think he got picked up by the police and put in some type of mental institution or something."

"Was he a problem for you, trying to come and go from your camp?"

"No, not really. It was just a little strange. As I walked by him, I would just make sure that he wasn't going to try to sneak up behind me. But it didn't stop me from doing anything."

"Have you seen the Asian guy lately?"

"No. He doesn't associate with anybody in the tunnels. I don't think he's around that much. I think he's a credit hustler. I don't know. He won't even attempt to talk to anybody."

"What happened to all the other people who lived in here at the beginning of summer?"

"The first time it rained, they all got scared off. There are more permanent camps in the tunnels under Valley View, where my friends live."

I shifted on the cushion and stretched my legs across the floor. "How you holding up health-wise?" I asked Gary. "You going to be all right?"

"I don't know," he said, pushing the glasses up the bridge of his nose. "All I know is that I haven't shit a hard turd in over a year."

"How long have you had cancer?"

"I don't know. But I know it's untreatable, because I waited too long to find out about it."

"Do you worry about dying down here and nobody knowing about it?"

"I don't really care if I die down here or on a street corner in front of a hundred people. It doesn't make any difference to me. I've told my family all along that when I die they should just take me behind a supermarket and throw me in the dumpster—take my ID and don't let anybody know who I am. That way, the state will take care of my funeral expenses. It won't make any difference to me. I'll be dead.

"I don't want to die in some hospital, stuffed full of tubes and shitting all over myself. That's why I'm seriously considering getting some heroin and just going to sleep permanently. That's all it is. Just going to sleep.

"The last few months, I've seen three different people overdose on heroin. I've gotten a lot of experience helping them out and keeping them alive until the paramedics arrived. Anyway, I know that ODing is no big deal. All you do is go to sleep. It seems like a nice peaceful way to go. I don't want to wait until I'm so weak that I can't get out of here and I end up dying of starvation or thirst."

"You're in touch with your family?"

"About eight or nine years ago, my sister put out a missing-person's report on me. I found out about it when I went to jail, so I ended up getting in touch with her. My mom's dead. My dad's probably dead; I haven't seen him in thirty years. My sister, last I heard, was doing time in Alaska for heroin distribution.

"But they don't know I'm down here in this tunnel. If I don't talk to them before I die, I'll see them in some other life. It doesn't make any difference to me. Life goes on after death." Using the wall for support, Gary stood. He then leaned over and

"

> There are so many theories out there about what happens when you die that I don't know which one to believe. But maybe it's just a matter of trading in your old body for a new-and-improved model. Or better yet, maybe we travel to the astral planes—far, far away from physical reality—and do everything at the speed of thought. Or something like that. I just don't know. ~ Gary

picked up the couch cushion. "There are so many theories out there about what happens when you die that I don't know which one to believe. But maybe it's just a matter of trading in your old body for a new-and-improved model. Or better yet, maybe we travel to the astral planes—far, far away from physical reality—and do everything at the speed of thought. Or something like that. I just don't know."

Carrying the couch cushion, Gary disappeared into the camp. I stood, picked up the other cushion, and followed him into the shadows. Gary and I stacked the cushions on top of the spool, then he reached into a canvas bag and removed his sketchbook. He flipped through the pages: A young woman with soft lips, oval eyes, and flowing hair fondled herself; another woman's legs were spread as wide as the Khyber Pass; and the shirt of yet another was falling off her shoulders, exposing her big breasts. The portraits were shaded and finely detailed. Gary definitely had a talent for drawing lips, eyes, and noses (among other features of the female form). I bought one of the portraits for $20—a souvenir of my summer in the storm drains—then continued toward the inlet.

A warm breeze followed me into the fifth tunnel. Around the bend, I noticed movement downstream. I froze and cut off the flashlight. Is it Gary, I wondered? Shadows? An *apparition*? In the faint light of the art gallery, I made out what appeared to be two men in an all-terrain vehicle. One of the men lifted a flashlight above his shoulder and aimed it at me. In response, I cut on my flashlight. The vehicle sped off, disappearing into the darkness.

Spooked and curious—are kids today so bored that they've taken to riding ATVs through the storm drains and harassing the homeless?—I jogged down to the gallery. Shadows darted about like demons. They seemed to be trying to hide or get out of my way. After five or six years in the drain, said Gary, he was used to them. He tried to talk to them and tell them to keep him company or let him keep them company. I figured I'd give it a try, too.

"You guys still around?" I said.

"You guys still around? You guys still around? You guys still around?"

Eventually, I found tire tracks leading into the north tunnel under the Strip. I followed the tracks into the shadows, rubbing the penny in my pocket and then— more practically—tickling the baton. Mountains of gravel rose from the floor. Climbing them, I ducked under electrical tubing and light fixtures bolted to the ceiling. The lights, former Caesars Palace employees told me, were installed when the drain was built in the late 1970s and were designed to make it easier to clear out debris following a flood. But apparently, they'd done more harm than good. They'd long ago been shorted out by floodwater, busted out by teenagers, or stolen and scrapped by street people. As far as I could tell, the only thing the tubing and fixtures had done in the past 25 years was obstruct the water.

The dividing wall, which was made of cinderblocks (a sure sign that the drain was old), gave way to a row of concrete columns. I weaved through the columns and entered the south tunnel. A junction box stuffed with wires hung from the ceiling. Apparently, the wires once powered two halogen lamps—or, literally, *floodlights*— that were now busted out and covered with graffiti. The cord of a power outlet

looped over the tubing, reminding me that electrocution is the number-two flood killer behind drowning, and water pipes obscured the top of the far wall. Obviously, the drain doubled as a utility tunnel. Too bad I didn't pack my wire cutters, I thought. Maybe I could've made the whole Strip go dark, like Sammy Davis Jr.'s character did in the original *Ocean's 11*.

Returning to the north tunnel, I followed the tubing into the darkness. The dividing wall re-formed and wild-style graffiti covered every inch of it, creating one seemingly never-ending scroll of words. Since I was under Caesars Palace, I was tempted to compare the drain to the catacombs of Rome. These catacombs—dug beginning in the second century A.D. and stretching for more than 60 miles—served as houses of worship for Jews and Christians, who were persecuted aboveground, and as a necropolis for their martyrs and saints. To this day, funerary art adorns the walls. Faded paintings, friezes, and mosaics pay homage to Christian icons, symbols, and practices. Sculptures and altars lurk in the shadows.

But actually, the drain—which was anything but sacred—reminded me more of the quarries of Paris than the catacombs of Rome. (By the way, the Paris hotel-casino is just 500 feet south of this storm drain.)

The digging of the Paris quarries began around the 12th century A.D. The limestone, gypsum, and clay provided the raw materials needed to build the city, including Notre Dame, the Louvre, and the Bastille. (The limestone was used to make buildings, the gypsum to make plaster, and the clay to make bricks and tiles.) But after six centuries of digging, the bedrock was full of holes. Worried about the stability of the city, the council of King Louis XVI commissioned a study on the condition of the quarries. The findings were so alarming the council created an agency to map out and stabilize the underground. The agency was divided into two groups: one dug inspection galleries, which allowed workers to explore the earth and search for quarries; the other mapped and stabilized them.

Over the past four centuries, a stunning collection of art has accumulated in the quarries and inspection galleries beneath Paris. The earliest known marking is dated 1609; the most recent was made yesterday. The art was created over a period of time that includes the storming of the Bastille (1789), the Great Terror of the revolution (1794), the Prussian siege of 1870, the German occupation of 1940, and the liberation. It was left by an array of people: engineers, quarrymen, Prussian and German soldiers, artists, tourists, and street people.

Over the past four centuries, a stunning collection of art has

The earliest known marking is dated 1609;

Some of the art's official, some of it's illicit. It includes inscriptions (e.g., the date on which a quarry was stabilized), directional signs, graffiti, sculptures, mosaics, and installations. The subject matter is ridiculous (politics) and sublime (soft porn). Concerts and festivals have been held in the quarries, subversive films shown on the walls. There's even a tombstone down there, which marks the spot where Philibert Aspairt was found and buried. Aspairt, the doorkeeper of the Val-de-Grace hospital, made a secret solo descent into the underground in 1793 (apparently in search of wine stored in the cellars). He never emerged. In the turbulent times of the revolution, his disappearance caused little—if any—concern. But in 1804, a group of surveyors found a leather belt and rat-gnawed bones beneath the Val-de-Grace. A set of keys helped identify the remains as the hospital's former doorkeeper, who'd disappeared so many years ago.

Reality and myth merge in the quarries—and like the light and dark, it's tough to tell where one ends and the other begins. Rumor has it Marat found refuge in the underground during the revolution. Apparently, Charles X threw parties in the catacombs before the revolution of 1830. And Balzac is said to have escaped his creditors by using the mazelike 180 miles of tunnels.

But unfortunately, they resisted the urge to write their names on the walls.

While trying to read the names on the walls of the drain—Wayne Newton? Steve Wynn? Tony "The Ant" Spilotro?—I was nearly decapitated by a water pipe that ran across the ceiling. The pipe was a foot in diameter, rusted, and tangled with cobwebs. It didn't appear to be a sprinkler-system line. In fact, it looked more like a water main that connected two of Caesars Palace's many towers.

Beyond a fleet of triangular columns, the tunnel went dark and deadly silent.

ccumulated in the quarries and inspection galleries beneath Paris.
he most recent was made yesterday.

There were hundreds of thousands of people somewhere overhead—but the only sound I could hear was the chirping of crickets. The lettering on the walls finally broke, deteriorating into artless scrawls: "Holly, Will You Marry Me?" (how romantic!) and "Johnny Will Die!" and "Kill Jew Faggots." Declarations of love and hate, goodwill and vengeance, intelligence and ignorance—the madness and desperation that paint every inch of the Las Vegas canvas.

About a half-mile from the art gallery, a row of dividers created four smaller tunnels. I entered the south tunnel, which emptied into a 125-foot-wide chamber supported by columns. Fluorescent lights flickered on the ceiling. At the far end of the chamber, natural light burned behind a sectioned wall.

When Josh and I discovered this chamber, we were utterly confused. We'd expected the drain to tunnel all the way under the Strip, then empty into a wash. We couldn't make sense of what we were seeing—columns, a low ceiling, lights. It looked like an underground parking garage.

"Where *are* we?" asked Josh.

"Somewhere we're not supposed to be," I answered.

Even now, more than two years and 50 storm drains later, it didn't make any sense. I still could *not* believe what I was seeing: The storm drain opens in the middle of the Imperial Palace's property and its *driveway* doubles as a flood channel. This zoning variance was approved by the County Commission in the 1970s—another juice job, as far as I could tell from my research. This is exactly the kind of thing that qualifies as smart growth in Las Vegas.

Avoiding a floor grate that protected a water pump, I slalomed through the columns. The ceiling rose and the natural light grew brighter. Tire tracks crisscrossed the floor. (Obviously, whoever or whatever I'd seen in the art gallery was real; it wasn't a shadow, a hallucination, or an apparition.) A section of the wall was held open by

chains, exposing the Imperial Palace's driveway and an approaching forklift.

"Hey," said the driver, as I stepped out of the shadows drenched in runoff and sweat. "How's it going?" He was wearing an Imperial Palace work uniform and galoshes. His name tag read "Matt from Arkansas."

"Matt from Arkansas," I said, breathing heavily. "I'm Matt from Georgia. I'm a journalist. I'm working on a book about the drains. I was exploring the other end of this drain and I thought I saw two guys in some kind of ATV. I'm trying to figure out who they are and what they were doing in there."

"On the other side of the wash?"

"Yeah."

"Ah," drawled Matt from Arkansas, smiling and shaking his head. "They told me about that. They said they saw someone in there with a flashlight. They said you scared the shit out of them. They thought you were a crazy bum or something."

"That's funny," I said. "They scared the shit out of me, too. When they took off, it kind of confused me. I figured they weren't with the county or the casinos. I thought they were kids in an ATV."

He laughed.

"Do they work for the IP?" I asked him.

"Yeah."

"What were they doing in there?"

"Riding around in a little golf cart. When the water comes through there real hard, it wraps all the mattresses and everything else the bums have around the pillars. We have to go in there and clear it out, so the water doesn't back up."

"Where are they now?"

"They're around here somewhere," he said, looking up and down the driveway. "I'm not exactly sure where they are right now, but they should be back soon. We got to clear everything out today."

"OK," I said, slipping out of the backpack. "Tell them I'll be waiting for them in the dark."

Matt from Arkansas laughed. "All right, man. Take care." He then sputtered into the chamber, a steel bin balanced on the forklift.

A breeze swept down the driveway. I turned to face it, took off the cap, and closed my eyes. Fall was on the way. I could feel it in the air, which was no longer nuclear and actually dried the sweat on my face. I'd survived another Mojave summer—and a damn-crazy one at that. I followed the footsteps of a psycho killer. I two-stepped under the MGM Grand at three in the morning. I partied with naked crackheads in a drain behind a Budget Suites. I chased the ghosts of Benny Binion, Bugsy Siegel, Elvis, Frank Sinatra, and Howard Hughes.

I was blinded by darkness in the brightest city on Earth. I saw men who fought for their country dying of AIDS, cancer, malnutrition, and loneliness, without any attention (medical or otherwise). I found hypodermic needles, busted bottles, and broken dreams beneath the hippest hotel-casino in town.

I discovered that a manhole can feel a lot like heaven. That there are no pots of gold under the neon rainbow. That in some ways, I prefer underground Las Vegas to aboveground Vegas: It's cooler, quieter, slower, and there's a hell of a lot less traffic.

I learned how to make meth. That art is most beautiful where it's least expected. That maybe the afterlife is just a matter of trading in your body for a new-and-improved model. Or better yet, maybe we travel to the astral planes—far, far away from physical reality—and do everything at the speed of thought. Or something like that. Hell, Gary, I don't know either. But it sure sounds good to me. See you there.

Opening my eyes, I placed the cap and Mag-Lite in the backpack's main pouch. The Mini Mag-Lite, expandable baton, and sheath soon followed. Then I put the tape recorder, wire mike, and holster in the secondary pouch, being careful not to wrinkle Gary's portrait. Stealing a sip from the bottle of water, I started up the driveway.

Reaching the Strip, the air smelling like cotton candy, I turned south on a sidewalk. A herd of tourists stampeded me, carrying cell phones and shopping bags, camcorders perched on their shoulders like rocket launchers. I angled over to the edge of the sidewalk, where a sunburned man in a hat and headphones handed me a flier: "One Girl for $35, Two Girls for $80, or Three Girls for $99." Well, I thought fleetingly, it *had* been a long summer.

The front doors of O'Sheas were thrown open. Passing the casino, I could feel the cool air and smell the cigarette smoke and taste the watered-down drinks. I squinted into the shadows, which were as deep as any in the drains, and saw the Big Six wheel spinning and the silhouette of a blackjack dealer pitching cards around a table. Players slumped in their chairs, heads down and still, as if attending a funeral for their money. A roar erupted in the crap pit, drowning out the whirring slot reels and chirping poker chips.

I crossed the street and continued south on the sidewalk. The promotions—"Take a break from the heat of Las Vegas Boulevard and grab an ice-cold domestic draft for only a dollar!"—faded out and the squealing brakes of taxis, rental cars, and charter buses faded in. Arms jutted from passenger-side windows, aiming cameras and cell phones at the hotel-casinos. The sun setting between two of its towers, Caesars Palace seemed as big and glorious as the Roman Empire in its heyday. I stopped in front of a fountain. Tourists posed prettily at the water's edge and fliers skimmed the surface. The storm drain—the Asian man's camp, the art gallery, the slabs of cardboard, the light fixtures, and Gary—was somewhere below. I dug the penny out of my pocket, closed my eyes, and flipped it high in the sky.

Mike, the Vietnam vet with the razor-blade scar and sharp sense of humor, died in a ditch along the railroad tracks on September 21, 2005. He was 55 years old. According to the coroner's report, the cause of death was a gastrointestinal hemorrhage. I guess he never had that hernia surgery. No insurance, no hospital bed.

After 11 years of floods, black widows, and loneliness, Ernie moved out of his pipe. Imagine my surprise when I went to visit him—and discovered the crack-smoking older man from the Valley View Drain in the three-feet-in-diameter burrow. Well, at least he was clothed. Dentures gleaming, the man told me that he hadn't seen the younger woman he was smoking with "in a good while" and that Ernie was living behind a gas station up the street. I guess he never hit that royal flush. I guess he never found that pot of gold under the Las Vegas Strip.

The last time I saw Gary, about four months ago, he was emptying a makeshift toilet in the art gallery. (Watch your step!) He told me that his camp had been washed away in a flood and he'd built a new one in a different area of the drain. He was in good health, he said; the cancer must be in remission. He was also doing well financially, thanks to a friend he'd made in front of the Rio. The man, who was playing in the World Series of Poker, took a liking to Gary—or perhaps thought Gary might bring him some luck—and hung out with him and gave him money. He even offered to pay to have Gary's teeth replaced and to fly him home to Seattle. Gary told me he was considering the offer—but since he didn't have a mailbox, he couldn't correspond with the man. I gave Gary my business card and told him the man could mail letters to me, and I'd bring them into the drain. He took the card, but I never received any letters.

Harold the Chef is living in his "winter home," the south and mostly dry tunnel of the Weber Drain. He says the tunnel, for some reason, is warmer than the downstream drain's north tunnel, which is his "summer home." He'll move his Coleman camp stove, condiments, and pots and pans into the downstream drain around May, he says—if he's still living in the drains. He hopes to be out of there in six to seven months. He hopes to be back to his old self soon.

When I returned to the Cappadocia Drain to ask Jim a few follow-up questions, the only response I got was his steel staff scraping against the concrete. I took that as a "No comment" and scurried back to the light. I haven't returned to the depths of the drain since—and probably never will. Let it be known: "Here There Be Dragons" … and ghosts, madmen, and maybe even a troll.

Last I checked, Phillip and about five of his friends were living in the Valley View Drain. Tyrone wasn't among them. He moved into a pallet shack along the railroad tracks, then disappeared from the area. I haven't seen or talked to his mother, Gwen, since I met her on that blast-furnace day in the summer of 2004.

Lawrence still sleeps (on his elevated bed) with the crawfishes. Timmy "T.J."

Weber is still on death row at Nevada's Ely State Prison. Josh moved to San Francisco … and then moved back to Las Vegas a month later, battered and broke. (And he thought the storm drains were rough.) He can be found on the patio of the UNLV Coffee Bean & Tea Leaf, crouched menacingly over his laptop, sipping ice-blended mochas, and chain-smoking Marlboro Ultra Lights. He can also be found at www.zenarchery.com.

The words at the outlet of the Street Kids Drain have been painted over. Obviously, the county didn't find them as raw and touching as I did. I haven't seen the two young men since our awkward encounter—but knowing a little bit about the local social-service system, I assume they're still on the streets (and maybe still in the drains). Bob and Jona's sad little hut no longer leans against the wall of the open-air channel.

There was more death in the Death Drain. On December 17, 2006, a homeless man discovered the bodies of Kendra Krummel and James Belanger about 800 feet into the drain. Initially, the police thought Krummel and Belanger had drowned; their bodies were found facedown and rainwater had washed over them. But once the scene was processed and the bodies were moved—in something straight out of *CSI*—it was obvious they'd been beaten and stabbed to death. Police speculated that Krummel, 43, and Belanger, 57, lived in the drain with a few other people and an argument broke out. The argument escalated, police said, leading to the deaths. No arrests have been made—and probably never will be.

David, Eddie, Cary, and the Asian man have all disappeared, proving that the only thing creepier than discovering a camp in a drain is discovering that a camp is *not* in a drain. Questions flood the basin of the mind—and never release: Did the camp and inhabitant get washed away? Did they move to another tunnel or drain? Did they ever really exist? Or were those outlines only shadows? Those voices only echoes? Those hands, eyes, and teeth only graffiti?

No matter how many tunnels I explore, no matter how much library research I do, there will *always* be questions about the storm drains that can't be answered.

After my summer sabbatical, I returned to *CityLife* in the fall of 2004. Nonetheless, I continued to explore the drains. In late 2004, while taking follow-up notes on the Midnight Drain, I discovered a burned-out car in a culvert under Decatur Boulevard south of Russell Road. (Apparently, the car had been abandoned in the desert and had washed into the culvert.) In the summer of 2005, on the hottest day of the year, I entered a virgin drain near Craig Road and Martin Luther King Boulevard. Two miles into the drain, the ceiling dropped to five feet. (Oh shit!) Finally, more than five miles in, the drain dead-ended into a trash rack. (You've got to be kidding me!) I was ready to call 911—but my girlfriend, who was waiting to pick me up, saved the day. She helped me pop a manhole cover, then dead-lifted me from the darkness. I guess it was true love after all. In the summer of 2006, I explored a drain near Flamingo Road and Swenson Street that formed the foundation of an under-construction high-rise condominium. I was only somewhat surprised to discover that people had moved into the drain before anyone had moved into the condo.

The final draft is set. The book is in production. Still, I keep the boots and backpack in the trunk of my car and occasionally return to the drains. I check on Harold and Gary. I bring the inhabitants food on Thanksgiving and Christmas. I escort friends, family, and journalists to the art gallery. Much like the inhabitants, I keep swearing off the drains … and they keep pulling me back.

Matthew O'Brien
December 31, 2006

Books

Alden, Peter and Friederici, Peter. *National Audubon Society Field Guide to the Southwestern States.* New York: Alfred A. Knopf, 1999.

Archer, Caroline and Parré, Alexandre. *Paris Underground.* West New York: Mark Batty Publisher, 2005.

Dante (translation by Robert Pinsky). *The Inferno of Dante.* New York: Farrar, Straus and Giroux, 1994.

Grynberg, Michal (editor). *Words to Outlive Us: Eyewitness Accounts from the Warsaw Ghetto.* New York: Picador, 2002.

Hickey, Maeve (photos) and Taylor, Lawrence J. (text). *Tunnel Kids.* Tucson: The University of Arizona Press, 2001.

Kazik (Simha Rotem). *Memoirs of a Warsaw Ghetto Fighter.* New Haven and London: Yale University Press, 1994.

Klemp, Klaus and Sack, Manfred (text) and Seidel, Peter (photos). *Underworld: Sites of Concealment.* Santa Monica: Hennessey + Ingalls, 1997.

Hugo, Victor. *Les Misérables.* London: Penguin Books, 1982.

Mangold, Tom and Penycate, John. *The Tunnels of Cu Chi.* New York: Berkley Books, 1986.

Marshall, Robert. *In the Sewers of Lvov: A Heroic Story of Survival from the Holocaust.* New York: Charles Scribner's Sons, 1990.

Moehring, Eugene P. *Resort City in the Sunbelt: Las Vegas 1930-2000.* Las Vegas and Reno: University of Nevada Press, 1995.

Morton, Margaret. *The Tunnel: The Underground Homeless of New York City.* New Haven and London: Yale University Press, 1995.

Poe, Edgar Allan. *The Fall of the House of Usher and Other Tales.* New York: New American Library, 1998.

Portella, Ivana Della (text) and Smith, Mark E. (photos). *Subterranean Rome.* Könemann, 2000.

Reid, Donald. *Paris Sewers and Sewermen: Realities and Representations.* Cambridge, Mass. and London, England: Harvard University Press, 1991.

Toth, Jennifer. *The Mole People: Life in the Tunnels Beneath New York City.* Chicago: Chicago Review Press, 1993.

Verne, Jules. *A Journey to the Center of the Earth*. New York: New American Library, 2003.

Geologic Tours in the Las Vegas Area. Reno: Nevada Bureau of Mines and Geology, 2001.

History of Flooding, Clark County, Nevada, 1905-1975. Reno: U.S. Department of Agriculture Soil Conservation Service, 1977.

Insight Guides: Turkey. Singapore: Apa Publications, 2003.

Articles

Ellis, Joshua and O'Brien, Matt. "Notes from Underground" and "Belly of the Beast." *Las Vegas CityLife*: June 27, 2002 and August 8, 2002.

Frazier, Joseph B. "Portland's Tunnels Led Unlucky Sailors to Shanghai." *The Seattle Times*: April 29, 2001.

Taylor, Peter Lane. "Off the Face of the Earth." *National Geographic Adventure*: June/July, 2004.

Documentaries

Dark Days. Palm Pictures, 2000.

In Search of History: Catacombs of Rome. A&E Television Networks, 1997.

Modern Marvels: Tunnels of Vietnam. A&E Television Networks, 2006.

Newspapers

Las Vegas CityLife
Las Vegas Review-Journal
Las Vegas Sun

Web sites

http://members.tripod.com/cgs-mthood/shanghai_tunnels.htm
www.google.com
www.wikipedia.org

MATTHEW O'BRIEN was born in Washington, D.C., and raised in the Atlanta area. He has lived in Las Vegas since 1997. His fiction has been published in *Red Rock Review*, *In the Shadow of the Strip* (a collection of short stories published by the University of Nevada Press), and other literary journals. His nonfiction has been published in several magazines and newspapers, including *High Country News*, the *Las Vegas Review-Journal*, the *Tucson Weekly*, the *Reno News & Review*, and *Las Vegas CityLife*. He's currently news editor of *CityLife*. For more information on Matt and this book, visit www.beneaththeneon.com.

DANNY MOLLOHAN moved to Las Vegas in 2000 to pursue his dream of becoming a professional photographer. With $300 in his pocket and a Lieca M3 in hand, he made his mark working for several weekly newspapers, showing in local galleries, moonlighting in nightclubs, and roaming the countryside. He's from a small town in South Carolina and has recently relocated to the Bedford-Stuyvesant neighborhood of Brooklyn, New York. Danny can be reached at killerbeard@priest.com (don't ask).